THE ONCE AND
FUTURE WORKER

THE ONCE AND FUTURE WORKER

A VISION FOR THE RENEWAL OF WORK IN AMERICA

OREN CASS

BOOKS

New York • London

The following chapters include extended excerpts from the author's prior essays, used with permission from the original publishers:

Chapter 2:   "The Inequality Cycle," *National Review*, October 2015

Chapter 4:   "Is Technology Destroying the Labor Market?," *City Journal*, Spring 2018

Chapter 5:   "Reform the Clean Air Act," *National Review*, March 2015
             "The New Central Planners," *National Affairs*, Spring 2016
             "Modern Management for the Administrative State," in *Unleashing Opportunity: Policy Reforms for an Accountable Administrative State*, ed. Yuval Levin and Emily MacLean (Washington, D.C.: National Affairs, 2017)

Chapter 6:   "Teaching to the Rest," *National Review*, July 2017

Chapter 7:   "Fight the Dragon," *National Review*, June 2014

Chapter 8:   "More Perfect Unions," special issue, *City Journal*, 2017

Chapter 10: "The Height of the Net," *National Review*, October 2013
             "Send Spending Power Back to the States," *City Journal*, Winter 2016
             "Our Medicaid Mess," *National Review*, August 2016

Chapter 11: "The End of Work," *National Review*, June 2016
             "The UBI's Parent Trap," *City Journal*, March 2017
             "Policy-Based Evidence Making," *National Affairs*, Summer 2017

First American edition published in 2018 by Encounter Books, an activity of Encounter for Culture and Education, Inc., a nonprofit, tax exempt corporation.
Encounter Books website address: www.encounterbooks.com

Manufactured in the United States and printed on acid-free paper. The paper used in this publication meets the minimum requirements of ANSI/NISO Z39.48-1992 (R 1997) (*Permanence of Paper*).

FIRST AMERICAN EDITION

LIBRARY OF CONGRESS CATALOGING-IN-PUBLICATION DATA
Names: Cass, Oren, 1983– author.
Title: The once and future worker : a vision for the renewal of work in America / by Oren Cass.
Description: New York : Encounter Books, [2018] |
Includes bibliographical references and index.
Identifiers: LCCN 2018014245 (print) | LCCN 2018021379 (ebook) |
ISBN 9781641770156 (ebook) | ISBN 9781641770149 (hardcover : alk. paper)
Subjects: LCSH: Political planning—United States. | United States—Economic policy. | United States—Social policy. | Wages—United States. | Foreign workers—United States. | Labor market—United States.
Classification: LCC JK468.P64 (ebook) | LCC JK468.P64 C377 2018 (print) |
DDC 331.10973—dc23
LC record available at https://lccn.loc.gov/2018014245

Interior page design and composition: BooksByBruce.com

In memory of Irv
who always liked a good argument

CONTENTS

THE WORKING HYPOTHESIS

American public policy has lost its way. Since the middle of the last century, it has chased national economic growth, expecting that the benefits would be widely shared. Yet while gross domestic product (GDP) tripled from 1975 to 2015, the median worker's wages have barely budged. Half of Americans born in 1980 were earning less at age thirty than their parents had made at that age. Millions of people have dropped out of the labor force entirely.

The primary response to the failure of rising GDP to lift all boats has been a dramatic increase in economic redistribution. Since 1975, total spending on the safety net has quadrupled. Yet the average poverty rate in the 2010s was higher than it was in the 1990s, which in turn had a higher rate than the 1970s. Analysts debate whether upward mobility has merely stalled or sharply fallen, but no one claims that it has improved. Meanwhile, families and even entire communities have collapsed; addiction has surged; life expectancy is now falling.

Rather than reversing course, policy makers wait expectantly for rescue to arrive from an education system that can transform those left behind into those getting ahead. If this were readily available, it would indeed help ease the growing crisis—and, for that matter, solve any number of society's problems—but no such miracle appears imminent. Despite the nation doubling per-pupil spending and attempting countless education reforms, test scores look no better than they did forty years ago. Most young Americans still do not achieve even a community college degree.

With good reason, then, confidence in national institutions has eroded. Most Americans have felt the country is on the wrong track since even before the late-2000s financial crisis struck. Most Americans expect that the next generation will be worse off than themselves. Outsider candidates across the political spectrum, most notably, of course, Bernie Sanders and Donald Trump, have gained huge followings that would have seemed inconceivable only a few years earlier, simply by observing that we are in fact lost—no matter that their own road maps are flawed in important ways. Even residents of the most prosperous and cloistered enclaves are discovering that, in a democracy, a miserable majority is everyone's problem.

This book explains where we went off-track and how we might turn around. Its argument, at its most basic, is that work matters. More specifically, it offers what I will call the *Working Hypothesis*: that a labor market in which workers can support strong families and communities is the central determinant of long-term prosperity and should be the central focus of public policy.

Alongside stable political institutions that protect basic freedoms, family and community provide the social structures necessary to a thriving society and a growing economy. Those institutions in turn rely on a foundation of productive work through which people find purpose and satisfaction in providing for themselves and helping others. The durable growth that produces long-term prosperity is the emergent property of a virtuous cycle in which people who are able to support their families and communities improve their own productivity and raise a subsequent generation able to accomplish even more. Conversely, without access to work that can support them, families struggle to remain intact or to form in the first place, and communities cannot help but dissolve; without stable families and communities, economic opportunity vanishes.

Economic growth and rising material living standards are laudable goals, but they by no means guarantee the health of a labor market that will meet society's long-term needs. If we pursue growth in ways that erode the labor market's health, and then redistribute income from the winners to the losers, we can produce impressive-looking economic statistics—for a while. But we will not generate the genuine and sustainable prosperity that we want. Growth that consumes its own prerequisites leads inevitably to stagnation.

Regrettably, neither political party has genuinely concerned itself with work for decades. Politicians on all sides talk incessantly about "good jobs," but the policies they pursue speak louder. What a coincidence that cutting taxes and shrinking government, expanding health care entitlements and fighting climate change, all were jobs programs as well.

Republicans have generally trusted that free markets will benefit all participants, prized the higher output associated with an "efficient" outcome, and expressed skepticism that political actors could identify and pursue better outcomes, even if any existed. Their labor-market policy could best be described as one of benign neglect.

Democrats, by contrast, can sound committed to a more worker-centric model of growth, but rather than trusting the market too much, they trample it. The party's actual agenda centers on the interests advanced by its coalition of labor unions, environmentalists, and identity groups. Its policies rely on an expectation that government mandates and programs will deliver what the market does not.[1] This agenda inserts countless regulatory wedges that aim to improve the conditions of employment but in the process raise its cost, driving apart the players that the market is attempting to connect. Better market outcomes require better market conditions; government cannot command that workers be more valuable or employment relationships be more attractive, but by trying, it can bring about the reverse.

The economic landscape is pocked with the resulting craters. Starting in the 1960s and 1970s, payroll taxes and workplace rules directly and substantially raised the cost of employing lower-wage workers. Aggressive environmental regulation reduced investment in industrial activity and thus the demand for workers whose advantage lay in relatively more physical work, while the education system's obsession with college for all left many students ill prepared to join the labor force at all. A system of organized labor that once helped broaden prosperity began instead to hoard it for a dwindling membership, at everyone else's expense. Our immigration system increased the supply of low-wage workers available to employers by millions, while free trade increased the supply by billions—to the advantage of those seeking to use such labor, but not those seeking to provide it. All the while, an ever-expanding safety net provided more benefits to a rising share of the population, reducing work's economic and social value.

The problem is not so much that public policy has failed as that it has succeeded at the wrong things. America is like the classic romantic-comedy heroine who, as the trailer intones, "had it all, or so she thought." She has the prestigious job and the elegant apartment, yet she is not happy. She has pursued the wrong goals, she discovers, and to reach them, she sacrificed the things that mattered most.

We got exactly what we thought we wanted: strong overall economic growth and a large GDP, rising material living standards, a generous safety net, rapid improvements in environmental quality, extraordinarily affordable flat-screen televisions and landscaping services. Yet we gave up something we took for granted: a labor market in which the nation's diverse array of families and communities could support themselves. This was, I will argue, the wrong trade-off, based on incorrect judgments about policies' true costs and benefits and a poor understanding of what we were undermining. What we have been left with is a society teetering atop eroded foundations, lacking structural integrity, and heading toward collapse.

* * *

If the Working Hypothesis is correct, neglect and mismanagement of the labor market have been the central failures of American public policy for a generation. This is infuriating, insofar as it reminds us that our problems are of our own making. But a happy corollary of the hypothesis is that, if bad policy choices rather than irresistible forces or unintended consequences are responsible for the nation's predicament, then better policy choices might help.

The economists, policy makers, and commentators who led and cheered America into the wilderness are understandably reluctant to accept responsibility. They often prefer to blame phenomena like "automation" for our troubles. But that is no explanation. Technological innovation and automation have always been integral to our economic progress, and in a well-functioning labor market, they should produce gains for all types of workers. The economic data these days all point to declining productivity growth, suggesting that progress is "destroying jobs" more slowly than ever. Others continue to insist either that *their* policies would have worked but for the confounding influence of the other side—if only government had been smaller, with lower taxes and spending, less regulation, and thus more room for economic dynamism— or else if only government had been bigger, with more infrastructure investment, more checks on the market, a more generous safety net, and thus a prosperity more widely shared. Regardless, the prevailing consensus holds that ever more growth paired with ever more redistribution (along with, of course, the ubiquitous boosting of "skills") must be the right solution, indeed, the only solution. Not so.

The alternative is to make trade-offs that instead place the renewal of work and family, sustained by a healthy labor market, at the center of public policy. Rather than taxing low-wage work to cut other tax rates and expand entitlements, we can do the reverse: we can provide a subsidy for low-wage work, funded with higher tax rates and reduced transfer payments. Instead of organized labor piling burdens atop the ones that federal regulators already place on employment relationships, we can repurpose unions to help workers and employers optimize workplace conditions. We can expand the demand for more of the work that more Americans can actually do if we place the concerns of the industrial economy on an equal footing with those of, say, environmentalists. We can prepare Americans to work more productively if we shift some attention and resources from the college track to the other tracks down which most people actually travel. And if we acknowledge that while the influx of foreign persons and products can greatly benefit consumers, it can also harm workers, we can even rethink our embrace of effectively open borders. If we give workers standing, if we make their productive employment an economic imperative instead of an inconvenience, the labor market can reach a healthy equilibrium.

The theme that recurs here, and throughout the book, is one of acknowledging *trade-offs*. Much pessimism about the future of work for the typical American begins from the assumption that we cannot possibly make concessions on any of our other priorities. And yes, if the preferences of the typical urban professional are always the most valid and important, if the maximization of economic efficiency and material consumption is inviolable, if businesses retain the incentive to find the cheapest possible workers anywhere in the world, then the future of the American labor market indeed looks grim. But all this merely begs the question, what *should* our priorities be? In the past, our society was much less affluent, and yet the typical worker could support a family. How could it be that, as we have grown wealthier as a society, we have lost the ability to make that kind of arrangement work? Or do we just not want to?

If work is foundational to our society, then we have a duty to make the changes and trade-offs necessary to support it. Certainly we cannot dismiss the goal as impossible before we even try. Nor can we dismiss it as too expensive, unless we know the alternative's real cost. Departing from the market's default outcome will always appear expensive if the "efficient" default *is defined as the overriding social goal*. But if some other outcome is better for society, then the efficient outcome is actually the more expensive one. The nations that succeed in the global economy will not be those that pledge blindest fealty to the market; they will be those that figure out which other values need to count too.

*   *   *

Part I of this book elaborates on the Working Hypothesis and its implications. Chapter 1 traces the rise of what I will call *economic piety*, the consensus view now held by the Center Left and Center Right that public policy should aim primarily to "grow the economic pie" and then ensure that everyone gets a large enough slice, via redistribution, if necessary. It explains how the flaws in this view have led to the abandonment of too many American workers.

Chapter 2 offers an alternative vision for long-term prosperity, which I will call *productive pluralism*, rooted in the fact that productive pursuits—whether in the market, the community, or the family—give people purpose, enable meaningful and fulfilling lives, and provide the basis for the strong families and communities that foster economic success too. Different people will accomplish this in different ways, so for this prosperity to be inclusive, it will also need to accommodate numerous pathways, even at the expense of some efficiency.

Chapter 3 turns to the nature of the labor market: the process by which the economy aligns the work that society wants people to perform with the work that members of society can perform. It explains why this market provides the foundation for a thriving society and why—unlike with most markets—we should not expect whatever efficient outcome it produces to be sufficient. It then outlines the tools that we have at our disposal to alter the market's conditions in ways that could improve its outcomes.

Chapter 4 considers how broader technological trends have influenced the labor market and how they may intersect with efforts to strengthen it. Automation boosts productivity and should benefit a well-functioning labor market. It has not caused recent struggles, and within a proper policy framework, it need not—robots can be workers' best friends. Likewise, the geographical effects of technological change will in some instances benefit major cities while in others benefiting smaller ones or even rural areas.

The once and future worker is not the same person, nor did workers of the past do the same jobs in the same ways that those in the future will. But the role of the worker in society will remain fundamental, and it is within our power to ensure its vitality. If we create the conditions in which employing American workers productively is the most attractive path to earning profits, our economy can support a thriving, self-sufficient society that enjoys dynamism and growth as well.

Part II discusses those conditions in detail, offering in-depth explorations of the policy areas that most influence the labor market. Each chapter tells a separate story:

- environmental regulation and its effect on what kind of labor our economy demands
- education and its effect on what kind of labor our workers can provide
- trade and immigration and their effect on who produces and consumes in the market
- organized labor and its effect on how agreements are made in the market
- taxes and subsidies and their effect on what jobs are created at what wages

Each of these issues, endlessly debated across the partisan divide, looks different and requires different solutions when viewed through the labor-market lens.

Finally, part III considers some of the factors beyond the labor market that influence work. Chapter 10 discusses the challenge of constructing a safety net that protects those who cannot work while ensuring that those who can, do. Chapter 11 takes up the question of how social norms and culture either devalue work or help reinforce its importance—a topic more amorphous and less amenable to government intervention but no less crucial to a healthy society.

The book concludes by considering what redistribution, or "doing your fair share," should mean if a stronger labor market, not the benevolence of a government check, is what those in need really require. A plan for economic growth that focuses solely on tax cuts promises a free lunch for everyone. A plan for government programs to address every problem assures voters that another, richer person will foot the bill. In practice, both rely heavily on deficits for someone else to repay at a future date. A commitment to work and family, by contrast, acknowledges real trade-offs but also offers a positive vision for durable prosperity.

*   *   *

These arguments are conservative ones. They prize self-sufficiency, assign a central role to family and community, and prefer the private ordering of free markets to the centralized dictates of government. But their endorsement of markets is not unconditional, which is why they depart from the Republican Party orthodoxy that has become synonymous with "conservatism" in American politics, despite hewing much closer philosophically to libertarianism. The Working Hypothesis recognizes the free market as a powerful *mechanism* for fostering choice, promoting competition, and allocating resources. But it does not regard creation of the freest possible market as an end unto itself or the most efficient outcome at any moment as necessarily the best one for the long run. Sometimes the efficient outcome is the wrong one not because of some well-defined "market failure" to be corrected but because the market is only one component of a flourishing human society. The first-order question must be what we want for our society and how we can best channel the free market toward accomplishing those ends.

Conservatives and libertarians have generally found common cause defending free markets against an overbearing government, but whereas conservatives regard markets as a constructive means to the end of a cohesive and vibrant society, libertarians embrace the free market without reservation and presume its outcomes to be good ones. When markets produce outcomes that are plainly undesirable for social cohesion, the two philosophies must part ways.[2] That is precisely what has happened in America, and it helps to explain the disarray within the Republican Party and the view of many pundits that a broader realignment of the nation's politics may be under way.

President Donald Trump exploited this fissure in his stunning run to the White House, ignoring the standard economic debates over bigger versus smaller government in favor of an emphasis on the way markets had failed large segments of society. The Working Hypothesis offers a way to understand why those failures have occurred, and the discussion of public policy to follow outlines a coherent agenda for addressing them. In some places, as with environmental regulation, the proposals here will parallel Trump's, though they go much further. In others, as with trade, immigration, and education, the analysis will support Trump's view that the status quo is untenable but provide a different view of what has gone wrong and thus how we can do better.

Throughout, the goal is to demonstrate the importance of moving beyond the standard choices of trusting or trampling the market toward creating the conditions in which it can produce the best outcomes for society. This is what a genuine commitment to free markets requires.

Consider the patent. The government awards a patent to an inventor, which allows him to exclude others from using his invention for a period of years. Even the fiercest libertarian—often *especially* the fiercest libertarian—will defend this rule as crucial to a well-functioning market. Without patent protection, if people could freely use each other's inventions, what incentive would anyone have to spend the time and money developing something new? Fair enough, though empirical research calls into question whether stronger patent protection necessarily correlates with higher rates of innovation. Companies will often choose to keep their discoveries hidden as trade secrets rather than filing for patent protection at all.[3] Still, stipulating that patents equal innovation, notice what this implies: a rule that obstructs transactions, suppresses output, and raises prices for consumers in the short run can also be the rule that is best for the market and for society over time.

Things become even more complicated when we introduce an international boundary and conflicting legal regimes. We protect patents on new drugs, but what should we do when drugmakers voluntarily sell those patented drugs in Canada at prices far below what they charge in the United States—because the Canadian government requires the lower price? Should someone be allowed to buy the drug in Canada and then resell it in the United States, undercutting a drugmaker's U.S. price? We call this *drug reimportation*, and we prohibit it, again on the basis of bolstering the free market, again with strong support from libertarians. Some politicians will offer a rationale of "safety," as if we can't trust Canadians to monitor their drug supply as well as we do. The actual rationale is that we wish to insulate what we consider to be our freer market in drugs from contamination by the more controlled Canadian market.

Canada is hardly the archetypal case of market distortion. China, for instance, disregards intellectual property law entirely and floods its producers with subsidies too. So if reimported drugs from Canada are a problem, why not artificially cheap Chinese products? What if the Chinese government reimburses its producers for the cost of licensing patented technology so that those companies can behave as if there are no patents at all—should products made that way be allowed into the United States? The point is not that these questions are easy but that they are hard. They represent policy choices necessary to the management of a free market, but they are not ones where a particular choice moves obviously closer to a free-market ideal or where such an ideal would necessarily achieve the best outcome.

Such examples abound and are often complicated by the introduction of nonmarket values. Where should we zone a neighborhood as residential, even though a commercial developer might pay more for the land? What taxes should we collect from whom, to provide what benefits to whom, especially if both the taxes and the benefits discourage productive activity? In what circumstances should we allow a factory to emit air pollutants, demand it install scrubbers on its smokestacks, or shut it down altogether? How many immigrant workers should we allow into the country each year? When should workers be allowed to bargain collectively with employers, and over what? Which skills should we expect public schools to instill in prospective workers, and which are the responsibility of employers?

Viewing questions like these from the perspective of labor-market health offers new answers and new ways to understand the implications of our choices for society. Like sudden shifts in tectonic plates, the earthquake of a political realignment shoves new ideas and coalitions into contact. Ideas stranded in the desert by a prior divide can land suddenly on fertile ground. And policy makers, lost for decades, can begin to find their way back.

PART I

WHAT WORK IS WORTH

CHAPTER 1

AS AMERICAN AS ECONOMIC PIE

The abandonment of the American worker began in the middle of the last century. No particular date marks the moment—the process unfolded gradually, pushed along by evolving economic theories and the misguided public policies based on them. But it would be a mistake to call the abandonment accidental. The approach to economic policy that emerged after the Great Depression and the Second World War discounted the interests of the typical worker and the stability of his social environment in favor of faster overall national growth and greater consumption, including by redistributing money to those left behind. Policy makers understood the implications of the ideas they embraced and the actions they took, and they largely accomplished their goals. Even today, mainstream politicians struggle to comprehend the popular disgruntlement about what they perceive as clear achievements.

The worker's dilemma can be linked with two major developments in postwar economic thinking, which combined to produce the central metaphor of modern American politics: the *economic pie*. The first was the overwhelming importance assigned to measurement of the economy's total size. This had been critical to the federal government's Keynesian response to the Great Depression, which relied on public spending to boost demand and thus production. Such management of the economy required accurate knowledge of production levels and trends, so the U.S.

Department of Commerce developed the system of national accounting that became the GDP, a Herculean effort whose leader, Simon Kuznets, would win the Nobel Prize in Economic Sciences for his work on economic growth.[1] When the Depression gave way to a global military conflict, the outcome of which would turn on the industrial capacity of the Allied and Axis economies, GDP became an existential concern.

As the economy regained its peacetime footing, national accounts recorded fewer M4 Sherman tanks headed to the front and more Chevrolet Bel Air convertibles destined for the suburbs. Notwithstanding Kuznets's warning to Congress that "the welfare of a nation can . . . scarcely be inferred from a measurement of national income,"[2] GDP transitioned smoothly into the primary measure of prosperity, and GDP growth became the primary goal of economic policy. Long after saturation bombing ended, and even after national economies had revived, cross-country comparisons of GDP remained the means for assessing national power; GDP per capita defined a citizenry's well-being.

The second key mid-century development in economic thinking was the ascent of consumers and the priority given to their interests at the expense of producers. Although this observation conjures a vision of two constituencies vying for the same resources, here the dynamic is more complex. Every individual is both a producer and a consumer, the economy an engine of both production and consumption. If unions drive wages higher and prices rise, households might benefit in their paychecks and suffer in the checkout line simultaneously. If cheap imports drive domestic manufacturers out of business, the reverse might be true. The choice of which identity gets preference has substantial consequences for how we define prosperity; a goal of rising productivity for all workers leads toward a very different policy agenda from one that aims to maximize what each household can consume.

For most of history, drawing a distinction between the roles of consumer and producer would have meant little. While individuals within a family or other close-knit social group have always specialized in certain functions, as a unit, they once relied almost exclusively on their collective output to sustain themselves. Increases in consumption were increases in production, and vice versa. But the story of economic development since at least the start of the Industrial Revolution has been in large part a story of disaggregating these activities. Increased specialization has driven the productivity gains and innovation responsible for the stunning improvement of material living standards around the world.

Households began to specialize in particular outputs and trade within their communities to meet their needs. Trade between communities stitched together national economies that shared a common language, currency, legal system, and physical infrastructure. Topeka supplied wheat; Detroit, cars; Louisville, baseball bats. In the era of globalization, entire nations produce surpluses of certain goods and services that they trade for the surpluses of others.

Meanwhile, the creation of various financial products allowed economic actors, whether individuals or nations, not only to consume different things than they produce but also to do so at different times. When we say that someone is saving money, we mean that she is converting current production into future consumption; a borrower, by contrast, funds consumption now through a promise to produce later. Government influences the roles of producer and consumer too, using its taxing and spending powers to translate the production of some into the consumption of others.

* * *

As the activities of production and consumption drifted further apart, policy makers increasingly adopted the consumption lens. This had long been a tenet of classical liberalism: "consumption is the sole end and purpose of all production; and the interest of the producer ought to be attended to, only so far as it may be necessary for promoting that of the consumer," wrote Adam Smith in *The Wealth of Nations*. "The maxim is so perfectly self-evident, that it would be absurd to attempt to prove it."[3] But only with the enormous influence of Keynesian economics did the principle entrench itself. Although GDP does refer to gross domestic *production*, the initial premise of its measurement was to ensure sufficient demand during the Depression. In the consumer-driven boom of the postwar years, it was only natural to view GDP as a measure of what people were consuming—and the primary goal of society as growth in consumption.[4]

The broader 1960s cultural shift toward individualism and the priority placed on fulfilling desires also moved the consumer toward the economy's center. In modern America, efforts to promote the virtue of production over the vice of consumption are often regarded as archaic curiosities. "There is almost nothing more important we can do for our young than convince them that production is more satisfying than consumption," wrote Republican senator Ben Sasse in his best-selling 2017 book *The Vanishing American Adult*.[5] In its review, *The Atlantic* characterized this view as "stoicism" and "self-denial."[6]

These trends helped bring about a dramatic expansion of the welfare state. Trillions of dollars poured into low-income households as the welfare system sought to guarantee an individual's right to consumption, while doing nothing about (if not actively retarding) his ability to become more productive. Today, a welfare benefit like the Supplemental Nutrition Assistance Program (SNAP, or "food stamps") gets credit for "lifting people out of poverty" merely because the benefit's cash value raises the recipients' income above the poverty threshold, even though it does nothing to help them gain a foothold in the economy and provide for themselves.

That GDP offers a reliable proxy for prosperity and that each individual's satisfaction depends on the share of GDP she can consume are the key components in the concept of the economic pie, which was born in the postwar years as well. When serving a pie, each portion's size depends on both the size of the dish and the share allocated to each slice. Likewise, the thinking went, each person's consumption depends on the size of the overall economy and the share he receives. Fighting over shares is a zero-sum game, but if we concentrate on baking an ever-larger pie, then everyone's slice can grow. And who doesn't like pie?

The tenets of this "economic piety" were quickly embraced and remain widely accepted today. The phrase *economic pie* first appeared in the presidential lexicon in 1952, when Harry Truman quoted from a *Business Week* article that used the term. John F. Kennedy used it when addressing the U.S. Chamber of Commerce. Presidents Lyndon Johnson, Gerald Ford, Ronald Reagan, George H. W. Bush, Bill Clinton, and Barack Obama used it too.[7] The media and think tanks across the political spectrum bandy it about with ease.

Republicans tend to promote free markets that will grow the pie rapidly, while grudgingly accepting a role for government in apportionment. Democrats focus more on the role of government in guaranteeing big enough portions for all but generally recognize that more growth will mean more to go around. On its own terms, this approach has delivered. The overall economy has grown enormously: from 1975 to 2015, the nation's GDP increased threefold.[8] Redistribution has widened the smaller slices: during the same period, spending on programs targeting lower-income households increased fourfold.[9] Federal regulators' budgets expanded faster still,[10] yet the American economy remained the dynamic and innovative envy of the world. For Americans of all socioeconomic strata, material living standards, access to technology, and consumer variety all marched steadily higher.

*   *   *

Tempering these impressive gains, however, were a variety of costs—the other side of the trade-offs made in pursuit of growth. Cheap goods and plentiful transfer payments ensured that nearly all Americans could afford cable television and air conditioning[11] but not that they could build fulfilling lives around productive work, strong families, and healthy communities. To the contrary, cheap goods and plentiful transfer payments tended to undermine those other priorities. Consistently, segments of society that were thriving saw their fortunes improved, while struggling segments faced further distress.

The prevailing policy approach acknowledges the existence of economic losers but holds that any losses are exceeded by the gains to winners, which means that with careful redistribution, everyone can emerge ahead. But what if people's ability to produce matters more than how much they can consume? That ability cannot be redistributed. And what if smaller losses for those at the bottom of the economic ladder are much more consequential to them than the larger gains for those already on top? Under those conditions, rising GDP will not necessarily translate into rising prosperity.

Such considerations have implications as well for society's longer-term trajectory. Even if gains exceed the costs initially, what happens if the losses undermine stable families, decimate entire communities, foster government dependence, and perhaps contribute to skyrocketing substance abuse and suicide rates? What if the next generation, raised in this environment, suffers as well—perhaps reaching adulthood with even lower productive capacity? What if, in the meantime, cheap capital from foreign savings has fueled enormous increases in government and consumer debt, while the industrial policies of foreign governments have left the American economy with fewer opportunities to create well-paying jobs for less-skilled workers? Such costs show up nowhere in GDP—at least initially. Sadly, they appear to have been much more than hypothetical and much costlier than anyone imagined.

While the Great Recession of 2007–9 is often understood as the catalyst for the economic frustration of the next decade, a majority of Americans hasn't told Gallup that they are "in general, satisfied with the way things are going in the United States at this time" since January 2004.[12] In the quarter-century prior to the Great Recession, median weekly earnings for full-time workers rose only 1 percent in real terms—not 1 percent per year, 1 percent total—and that increase was confined to women and to those with college degrees. Among all men, and among all people with less than a bachelor's degree, full-time earnings declined.[13] While in 1979, the typical man with a high school degree could support a family of four at more than twice the poverty line, by 2007, his earnings cleared the threshold by less than 50 percent.[14]

And those are the figures for people who were working. After peaking at 84.5 percent of the population in 1997, the share of prime-age Americans (twenty-five to fifty-four years old) either working or looking for work began an unprecedented decline, falling by 2015 to 80.8 percent. A three- or four-point decline seems small, but it represents more than 4 million people missing from the workforce, which exceeded the total number of unemployed prime-age workers still in the market. Count the "unworking," who are excluded from standard statistics, and the unemployment rate doubled.[15]

Furthermore, these data count *any* work as employment. Social thinker Nicholas Eberstadt has shown that total paid hours increased only 4 percent during 2000–2015, despite an 18 percent rise in population; work per adult civilian fell 12 percent.[16] At the same time, the share of employment in "alternative work arrangements"—temps, independent contractors, and freelancers—climbed from 11 percent in 2005 to 16 percent in 2015. During the decade, such jobs were the source of the nation's entire employment gain across all age groups.[17]

Widening the lens beyond economic metrics reveals an even more devastating collapse of social health. Maladies once thought the province of the very poorest communities have been ravaging the working class for decades and begun making inroads even higher up the socio-economic ladder. Readers often think of *Hillbilly Elegy*, J. D. Vance's memoir of Appalachian dysfunction, as depicting the social circumstances that fed Donald Trump's rise. But Vance was not describing post–financial crisis America; the backdrop for his troubled upbringing was the go-go 1990s.

In *Coming Apart*, a study of demographic and cultural trends during the period from 1960 to 2010, Charles Murray described the fate of the 30 percent of Americans with no more than a high school degree working in a "blue-collar job, mid- or low-level service job, or a low-level white-collar job." To control for any race-related factors, Murray focused specifically on whites.[18] Within that group, he found that the married share of thirty- to forty-nine-year-olds declined from 84 percent in the 1960s and 1970s to 48 percent by 2010. Fully 95 percent of children were living with both biological parents when the mother turned forty in the 1960s, but by the 2000s, the figure was plunging toward 30 percent. Likewise, between the 1970s and the 2000s, the share of thirty- to forty-nine-year-olds not involved in any secular or religious organization tripled to more than 30 percent. By 2010, only 20 percent said that, generally, "people can be trusted"; fewer than half believed that others "try to be fair." Those figures were declining too. In barely half of households was a full-time worker present.[19]

Murray's focus on whites for purposes of analytical clarity does not imply that they are uniquely affected by these trends. To the contrary, his objective was to show that alarming conditions once associated with minority communities in America were now persistent across all races. What's new is not the challenge of social decay but rather the way it has metastasized into once-healthy communities and the downward trajectory that this portends for ever-wider socioeconomic strata. Far from offering an excuse to ignore long-standing urban poverty, the widening crisis should rededicate the nation to addressing the underlying problems wherever and for whomever they are present. But we should also remember, in developing a plan of attack, that we are sending reinforcements into a "War on Poverty" that we have been fighting to little avail for fifty years.

Beginning with Lyndon Johnson's launch of the Great Society in 1965, means-tested government spending increased from $73 billion (2015 dollars) to $332 billion in 1980, $611 billion in 2000, and $1.1 trillion in 2015—by which point the United States was spending more than $20,000 annually for every person in poverty.[20] Yet the average poverty rate for 2000–2015 was no different than it was for 1985–2000, and actually *higher* than it was in 1970–85.[21] Government benefits helped to address many of the immediate material needs of low-income households, but they appeared to provide no upward lift—if anything, their effect has more likely been corrosive. Eberstadt observes that, by 2013, nearly half of all prime-age, nonworking white males received Medicaid; nearly three-fifths received disability benefits.

*   *   *

A social science literature has developed that argues that conditions are much better than the data indicate. Incomes look better or worse, depending on the measure of inflation, it contends.[22] Poverty levels look higher or lower, depending on the accounting for government benefits—for instance, Harvard professor Steven Pinker highlights our progress lifting people above the "consumption poverty line."[23] And so many people have iPhones! Such observations aren't persuasive, though, because neither readjusted data nor celebration of gadgetry does anything to improve the reality of deteriorating individual, family, and community health. Claims that overall growth is robust and wages not so bad don't remedy ongoing social collapse, reverse workforce abandonment, or lessen government dependence—they only underscore the disconnect between conventional economic measures and the quality of life for which those measures are supposed to provide proxies. If policy analysts ask, "Who are you going to believe, me or your lyin' eyes?" Americans will—rightly—choose the latter.

Thus, "despite the sustained cyclical upswing and the country's fundamental strengths," observed former Federal Reserve chairman Ben Bernanke in a 2017 speech titled "When Growth Is Not Enough," "Americans seem exceptionally dissatisfied with the economy, and indeed have been for some time."[24] Since the last recession's end in 2009, during one of the longest economic expansions and periods of uninterrupted job creation on record, the average response to Gallup's question about satisfaction with life in America has been 24 percent satisfied versus 74 percent dissatisfied.

Maybe that is because people increasingly see their children struggling and their neighbors sick or dying. Between 1975 and 2016, the share of men aged twenty-five to thirty-four earning less than $30,000 per year rose from 25 to 41 percent.[25] At the end of 2016, Stanford professor Raj Chetty released a landmark study that used millions of tax records to compare parents' and children's earnings. For children born in 1950, 79 percent had higher earnings by age thirty than their parents had at the same age. But for those born in 1980, only 50 percent could say the same.[26] Looking ahead to the next generation, only 37 percent of Americans expect that "when children today in our country grow up they will be better off financially than their parents."[27] The problem is not one of unequally shared gains. A significant share of the population, perhaps even a majority, has seen no gains at all and may now be going backward.

And then there are the "deaths of despair." Mortality rates have risen since the turn of the century for middle-aged white Americans, driven by higher levels of suicide, liver disease, and drug overdoses for those with only a high school degree.[28] Such an upsurge had no precedent in American history, and nothing similar is occurring in other developed nations.[29] The crisis has spread to younger Americans as well, with the death rate for twenty-five- to forty-four-year-olds rising 8 percent during 2010–15.[30] Life expectancy nationwide fell in 2015, for the first time since 1993, and then again in 2016, marking the first consecutive years of decline since the early 1960s.[31]

The nation's suicide rate climbed 24 percent between 1999 and 2014, with stunning increases of 43 percent and 63 percent for men and women aged forty-five to sixty-four.[32] Of even greater concern is the epidemic of opioid overdoses. Deaths from such overdoses have risen every year since at least 2000,[33] when the mortality rate already exceeded that of prior drug epidemics.[34] But it has only recently burst into the national consciousness; deaths in 2016 rose a staggering 28 percent from 2015, exceeding forty-two thousand.[35] This brings the annual toll close to the peak of the HIV/AIDS crisis, which claimed fifty-one thousand lives in 1995.[36]

The tragic coda to this unraveling is that growth spluttered too. Without the stable foundation of a labor market that allowed for self-sufficiency, social structures buckled, social capital drained away, and the national economy struggled. Broken families and collapsing communities are not, it turns out, effective incubators of a productive workforce. Economic growth during 2000–2016 averaged 1.8 percent, half the rate recorded during 1950–2000. The best growth rate of the past decade, 2.9 percent in 2015, fell below two-thirds of the years in the prior century's second half.[37] Having forsaken the healthy society that makes economic growth possible, Americans now found that they had neither. What they do have is a political system straining at the seams, its unfunded liabilities skyrocketing and its compromises exposed as unsustainable.

By some measures, the economy had achieved a robust recovery by early 2018. The unemployment rate dipped below 4 percent. More than 1 million prime-age workers had returned to the labor force. Numerous stories described companies struggling to find workers and wages surging.[38] While these were all positive developments, none changed the underlying conditions.

Yes, things looked better than in the depths of the recession, but they looked terrible as compared with the peaks of prior business cycles after long periods of economic expansion. Twenty percent of prime-age males were not working full time at the start of 2018. This represented an enormous improvement from the 27 percent in that situation in early 2010, but prior to the Great Recession's start, it would have been the worst figure on record going back to 1986. In 2007, the figure was below 17 percent; in 2000, it was below 15 percent.[39] Median weekly earnings for full-time workers fell between the fourth quarters of 2016 and 2017, and median twelve-month wage growth (which compares individuals' earnings with their own income a year earlier) was lower in December 2017 and January 2018 than at any point in the prior two years and at any point from 1998 to 2008.[40] Productivity growth, the ultimate driver of long-term wage growth, turned in a seventh straight year below 1.5 percent in 2017. Since 1948, the nation had never experienced more than a three-year run so anemic.[41]

By 2016, the typical man with a high school degree did not earn enough for a family of four to clear the poverty threshold by even 40 percent. Lifting his earnings to double the poverty threshold would require twenty years of 2 percent wage growth, girded by real gains in his productivity, after nearly forty years of stagnation. A strong economy is a good start—though no better a start than the stronger economies of the late 1980s, late 1990s, and mid-2000s, all of which proved to be mounds on a downward slope.

A genuine, durable recovery of the nation's fortunes requires an overhaul from its foundations; it will be the work of a generation.

* * *

The 2016 presidential election threw American politics into disarray. The Democratic Party's coronation of former first lady, senator, and secretary of state Hillary Clinton as its nominee for president was interrupted—and nearly derailed—by Senator Bernie Sanders, a self-described socialist from Vermont who long resisted the Democrat label. The Republican Party's crowded field of conservative senators and governors lost to Donald Trump, a socially and fiscally liberal TV host who had made a habit of supporting Democrats himself. In the general election, one in eight Sanders voters backed Trump over Clinton.[42] Less-educated and lower-income voters swung toward the Republican candidate, who assailed bad trade deals and corrupt Wall Street, while better-educated and higher-income voters moved toward the Democrat, who seemed the more natural ally of the multinational corporation.[43]

The economic, social, and political upheaval of 2016 should have triggered a rethinking of priorities and agendas on all sides. Yet rather than embrace that opportunity, or even acknowledge the need to change course, people pleased with the status quo reacted to the ungratefulness of the masses with equal measures of indignation and obstinacy. Some concluded that typical voters must be either too stupid to recognize how good they have it or else too closed-minded to put aside their provincial fears and embrace the wonderful modern world created for them. Others took the dissatisfaction more seriously but attributed it to inadequate implementation of existing approaches.

One prevalent narrative emphasized "globalization" as both the catalyst for disruption and the axis of political realignment. "The new divide in rich countries is not between left and right," asserted *The Economist*, "but between open and closed":

> Debates between tax-cutting conservatives and free-spending social democrats have not gone away. But issues that cross traditional party lines have grown more potent. Welcome immigrants or keep them out? Open up to foreign trade or protect domestic industries? Embrace cultural change or resist it?[44]

Washington Post columnist Fareed Zakaria, among others, endorsed the same open versus closed framing, lauding former British prime minister Tony Blair's "remarkably prescient" view that "the most significant political divide of the future was not between left and right, but between open and closed."[45]

As their framing makes clear, those purveying the open–closed dichotomy regard only one of its sides as valid. They elevate the free flow of goods and people as the nonnegotiable underpinning of both economic and social progress. Anyone with other priorities is condemned to the closed camp—closed-minded, even racist.

Yet how does the open agenda, which has already characterized the past generation of American policy, address the critical challenges facing the nation? It does not. Rather, the standard response is that this openness must be paired with a renewed commitment to helping those left behind, as if only a lack of focus and resources has prevented government programs from transforming people's prospects. Invariably, the suggested solution is education. Zakaria calls his approach "open and armed," because it requires "a far more ambitious set of government programs" to equip Americans with "a bristling armory of tools and training."

The vision is supposed to be an inspiring one, in which people are lifted upward to greater opportunity. Its real implications are less exalted: if the economy no longer works for the average worker, it is he who needs to transform into something it likes better. If government programs could change human capabilities to match whatever the market might compensate highly, public policy would become rather easy. But the insufficiency of this as a response to the nation's challenges recalls the joke about the economist's solution to finding himself shipwrecked among boxes of canned goods: "First, assume a can opener."

By all means, let's keep striving to leave no child behind, turn coal miners into coders, and more. Few things would do more to benefit the nation. But the reality is that we do not know how to do it, let alone on a broad scale. Chapter 6 discusses this issue in depth, but here it will be enough to note that test scores in American high schools have been flat or declining for decades. The question that policy makers must grapple with is this: insofar as government is not successfully transforming individuals, or helping them transform themselves, what then? The answer for now appears to be that society's obligation to the uncompetitive worker ends there—that she should continue to bear the costs of the present economic trajectory and the risk that we will not solve the education challenge.

Without education as a deus ex machina, a commitment to openness turns out to mean little more than merging together and doubling down on existing programs of growth and redistribution, offering a veritable buffet of warmed-over policies—all served with a heaping side of self-righteousness. "I'm for globalization and a strong safety net" seems likely to become for the next generation of insulated but determinedly respectable professionals what "I'm socially liberal and fiscally conservative" was for the last. But this assumes that things are going well or that they would be going well if only the current approach were pursued more wholeheartedly—or that the values underlying openness have such inherent importance as to deserve priority, regardless of results.

This same word, *openness*, is what Allan Bloom in *The Closing of the American Mind* called "the virtue, the only virtue, which all primary education for more than fifty years has dedicated itself to inculcating." Openness, observed Bloom, "pays no attention to natural rights or the historical origins of our regime, which are now thought to have been essentially flawed and regressive. It is progressive and forward-looking....There is no enemy other than the man who is not open to everything. But when there are no shared goals or vision of the public good, is the social contract any longer possible?"[46] The obsession with openness that dominates the politics of the educated is the direct descendant of the one that dominated their education.

Now, some are abandoning even the pretense of solving our problems and of maintaining an inclusive society, instead laying the groundwork for a "universal basic income," in which high-income taxpayers provide every household with an unconditional stipend. Facebook's Mark Zuckerberg presented this idea in his commencement address to Harvard University's Class of 2017.[47] We have reached a point where the rich think paying everyone else to go away represents compassionate thinking.

* * *

The philosophical conflict is not over the value of an "open" society; it is over the quality and stability of the nation's economic and social structures. One side is basically satisfied and wants to maintain current arrangements. The other side sees these structures succumbing to modern stresses and believes that repair and reinforcement—an overhaul, really—must come before pushing ahead.

Building higher atop a crumbling foundation is a mistake. Noting sagely that both trade and automation worsen employment opportunities for less-skilled workers does nothing to improve their opportunities—nor is it accurate. Selling unrelated priorities like fighting climate change as solutions only compounds the problem. Subjecting lower socioeconomic strata to ever-greater pressure without offering more than superficial fixes is a recipe for political and social collapse.

At least, one might say of those demanding a new course, they know that something is wrong. At least they are recognizing the nature and magnitude of the challenge and searching for solutions—and voters will ultimately choose a bad overhaul over none at all. Everyone shares an interest in strengthening society's foundations, even if that means pausing work on the next glamorous expansion. Otherwise, it may all come tumbling down.

CHAPTER 2

PRODUCTIVE PLURALISM

In making GDP growth and rising consumption the central objectives of public policy, the broad view that I have called *economic piety* represents a truncated and ultimately self-undermining concept of prosperity. Workers have no standing, in this view of the economy; neither do their families or communities. Households that see their economic prospects plummet or their livelihoods vanish should ask for a government check and be placated when they get one. Towns that can no longer sustain themselves become places that people should just leave. Politicians will pay lip service to the importance of education and retraining, but they will not hold themselves accountable for such programs actually working. The economic pie's expansion, regardless of what or who gets left behind, is the goal; maintaining a healthy, inclusive society is a hoped-for by-product, not an end in itself.

This isn't to say that economic growth isn't important; of course it is. Growth is a prerequisite to improved living standards, which we should want to achieve. But while growth is necessary to a prosperous society, it is not sufficient. Not all growth is equally beneficial, and the policy choices that yield the most immediate short-term growth don't necessarily prepare the ground for sustained economic and social progress. To the contrary, policies that target growth without concern for the economy's longer-term trajectory, or for the well-being of the society

29

within which that economy operates, will tend to erode the capacity for growth. Politicians who equate GDP growth and rising consumption with prosperity pursue agendas that often bear little resemblance to what their constituents want or need.

A constructive definition of prosperity must look different in two ways. First, within the economic context, it must emphasize the ability to produce rather than the ability to consume. Second, it must attend not only to economic outcomes but also to social foundations. Much modern policy analysis works from the assumption that only quantifiable economic impacts matter, either because economic growth and the accompanying rise in consumption is an end unto itself or because growth and consumption can be trusted to benefit society more broadly. This is wrong: economic policies have dramatic effects on family and community health, and the health of those social institutions in turn influences the economy profoundly.

As an alternative to economic piety and its GDP-based definition of prosperity, I suggest what I call *productive pluralism*: the economic and social conditions in which people of diverse abilities, priorities, and geographies, pursuing varied life paths, can form self-sufficient families and become contributors to their communities. This chapter explains why productive pluralism offers a superior definition of prosperity, why strong families and communities are central to its operation, and why it will also produce more growth in the long run.

* * *

Superficially, consumption seems a sensible focus. In popular culture, consumption is an obvious good. The toil of production, by contrast, is only a necessary means to that end—and if one manages to consume more while producing less, all the better. "The interest of the producer ought to be attended to, only so far as it may be necessary for promoting that of the consumer," as Adam Smith put it. But allowing the consumption tail to wag the production dog distorts our understanding of prosperity. Only through production does the ability to consume exist. Production without consumption creates options; consumption without production creates dependence and debt.

Most of the activities and achievements that give life purpose and meaning are, whether in the economic sphere or not, fundamentally acts of production. Yes, material living standards contribute to prosperity, but accomplishments like fulfilling traditional obligations, building strong personal relationships, succeeding at work, supporting a family, and raising children capable of doing all these things themselves are far more important to life satisfaction. What these things have in common is their productive nature not as boosts to GDP but as ways that people invest effort on behalf of others. Our social norms recognize productive activities as essential to a functioning and prosperous society, and so we award respect, dignity, and gratitude to those who perform them.

Without work—the quintessential productive activity—self-esteem declines and a sense of helplessness increases.[1] People become depressed—unemployed Americans are twice as likely as full-time workers to receive treatment for depression; the long-term unemployed are three times as likely.[2] In empirical "happiness" studies, life satisfaction drops ten times more from unemployment than from a substantial loss of income.[3] And while people return to their previously self-reported levels of happiness several years after marrying, divorcing, becoming widowed, or welcoming a first child into the world, they never get used to joblessness.[4] Such studies of life satisfaction typically focus on paid employment, but in *Coming Apart*, Charles Murray offers an insightful look at whether paid work or productive activity more generally is the true source. The U.S. General Social Survey, he notes, asks the question "On the whole, how satisfied are you with the work you do?" of all respondents, not just of employed workers. It is homemakers, not wage earners, for whom high job satisfaction translates most directly into a high level of happiness.[5]

The choice between the consumption and production emphases also has political consequences. To paraphrase President John F. Kennedy, will people ask what they can do for their country or what their country can do for them? Will they feel that they owe society the best they can produce or that society owes them what they want to consume? An emphasis on consumption offers what looks like a get-out-of-jail-free card: government spending. Connecting people to productive activity is a complex challenge that requires a healthy civil society and labor market. Public policies can support or hinder that process in myriad ways, but if preserving it is a priority, then sacrifices will inevitably be required elsewhere. When the goal is consumption, conversely, those challenges and trade-offs vanish. Like a medieval indulgence, a promise of redistribution cures all. And if replacing lost income with a government benefit solves little or makes a bad problem worse, this merely drives the indulgence's price higher next time around. By emphasizing consumption, policy makers can ignore the actual experience of society's struggling segments and point to statistics that depict an alternate reality.

As the term *productive pluralism* suggests, a critical corollary of a focus on production is a commitment to respecting the diversity among individuals. Measures like GDP create the convenient illusion of a homogenous population benefiting (or suffering) in lockstep. Money being fungible, everyone is presumed to have access to whatever she might choose to buy. Production is not so simple. People have different priorities, excel in different ways, and find meaning in different places, so a production-oriented prosperity that extends across society must offer numerous paths to its achievement. Cities may be more economically productive, for example, but not everyone wants to live in a city. A traditional college degree may correlate with higher earnings, but most people will not attain one. Having two parents work while the children attend daycare may be more efficient, understood in a narrowly economic sense, but a community consisting entirely of such households is one that many families would rather not live in. Growth may be fastest if we channel everyone to wherever his economic output is greatest, but pluralism will improve real prosperity if the options it leaves available more closely match people's abilities and the range of life choices they wish to make.

Pluralism offers a form of genuine opportunity, not "equal opportunity," which has come to stand in American politics for the unachievable objective that every child should have equal life chances of arriving at any destination.[6] That is plainly impossible in a world in which individuals possess different innate characteristics and grow up in different environments. Perhaps it could be reached by replacing unique individuals with generic clones and diverse family environments with state-run children's homes. Most people would agree that this is not desirable.

Pluralism's genuine opportunity, by contrast, means that every person, no matter where she begins, has some agency to set the direction of her life, to pursue accomplishments that give her life meaning, to support a family, and to raise children who will themselves have a wider range of choices than was available to her. There is no guarantee that she *will* achieve those things, or that her children will be insulated from the costs of her mistakes. But pluralism does require that, no matter what, those children will have that baseline level of opportunity to build a life themselves. Unlike today's "equal opportunity," the genuine opportunity of pluralism is a realistic goal, one that still offers the promise of long-term prosperity—a trajectory of improvement on the outcomes that matter most.

*   *   *

Pluralism should not, however, be confused with unconditional wish fulfillment or "having it all." Trade-offs are unavoidable, whether between location and profession, or lifestyle and income, or family and career. A math whiz may not earn within commuting distance of his hometown what he could in Silicon Valley; he may not find use for his math skills at all. But he should be able to achieve vocational success, support a family, and so on. Likewise, someone whose academic talents will not take him beyond high school should be able to make it in New York City if he so chooses, though he may lose many of his old community ties in the process.

In other words, society should maintain a bias in favor of preserving proven options, with the expectation that rising prosperity will open new paths over time. The promise of pluralism lies in maximizing the choices that lead toward productive activity so that they are accessible to as many people as possible. If, historically, small towns and big cities were both able to thrive, economic development that eliminates the former is suspect—boosting overall consumption at the expense of fundamental life choices valued by millions does not raise prosperity. If, historically, two-parent families could support themselves with only one parent working outside the home, then something is wrong with "growth" that imposes a de facto need for two incomes.

Conversely, we should be skeptical of efforts to conduct social engineering in favor of new choices that enjoy no historical precedent. Single parenthood, to choose an obvious example, generally narrows other choices—one may need to live close to a supportive extended family or possess the skills to find work that is both highly compensated and flexible. Cultural and legislative efforts have failed to invent new ways for a single adult to build a healthy and self-sufficient family free of such constraints.

For Democrats especially, the temptation to engineer a preferred outcome, regardless of empirical evidence, can often prove overwhelming. Take the "childcare calculator" created by the liberal Center for American Progress (CAP) to show the purported opportunity cost of staying home to raise children.[7] CAP pretends that its goal is merely to place "financial tradeoffs in the economic framework of opportunity costs," helpfully explaining that "Jane," an elementary school teacher who has her first child at age twenty-six, will lose $707,000 of lifetime income if she leaves the labor force until her child starts kindergarten. But the bias is obvious if the value of staying home is not presented alongside the value of working. Why no opportunity-cost calculator for delegating your child's upbringing? For that matter, why no opportunity-cost calculator for choosing to work at CAP instead of becoming a petroleum engineer?

Lest its motive remain unclear, CAP complements its calculator with a "policy solution": a new government program to pay for childcare, worth up to $14,000 per child. This would be offered in the name of relieving financial "constraints," but that would not be its effect. Even a minimum-wage job will typically cover the cost of childcare, albeit without leaving much income to take home.[8] If someone prefers working to staying home, finances do not constrain that choice; recall, the point of CAP's calculator is to show that *staying home* is expensive.

CAP's policy proposal merely ensures that anyone who does face financial constraints will pursue *its* preferred—and now government-subsidized—decision. Going to work would generate both earned income and taxpayer funds to take care of the kids. Staying home would mean neither. This is a twofer for CAP, advancing the progressive goals of getting women out of the home and into the workforce while also producing more income that can be taxed to fund yet more government programs. The benefit that CAP touts is not satisfied parents, healthier kids, or stronger families and communities; rather, it's "an additional 5 million women in the labor force and $500 billion in increased GDP."

A policy maker committed to productive pluralism, by contrast, would ask how to expand Jane's options so that she can strike the balance between earned income and other productive pursuits that she finds fulfilling. One option might be to encourage sufficient new construction to make housing affordable for one-income families. Another could be allowing Jane to borrow against future earnings during the years that she stays home or works part time, smoothing her consumption despite family-induced income volatility.[9] Yet another might be framing labor regulation in a way that gives employers an incentive to offer a range of different relationships to employees with different priorities—the opposite, it's worth noting, of the current approach, which aims to bar via discrimination law any sign of differential treatment.

A view that always celebrates the triumph of new and more efficient economic configurations over the traditional or obsolete naturally chafes at the idea that preserving or creating choices should be an object of public policy. The answer to this must be "yes, but." Yes, those efficient economic dynamics drive GDP higher, reward innovators, and improve material living standards broadly over time; but we must acknowledge the costs to genuine long-term prosperity as well, and we should not expect the benefits always to be larger.

In other contexts, we have no trouble acknowledging such realities. The premise of environmental regulation, for instance, is that pollution's intangible costs to public health sometimes exceed the value of economic activity. Zoning offers a more direct analogy: even the most valid and widely supported zoning provisions are efforts to preempt forms of economic development that would interfere with people's enjoyment of their communities. If market interventions to preserve those values at the expense of GDP can be prosperity enhancing, why not ones that keep struggling communities alive or career paths open? Yes, some such interventions would be futile, or even counterproductive, but that doesn't mean that all are.

The rural machinist skeptical of the benefits of foreign-trade deals, concerned about illegal immigration's effects on his local schools, and enraged by the Environmental Protection Agency's regulation of local wetlands may voice those positions with less sophistication—but we should recognize their reflection in the arguments, made by Prius-driving, high-income capitalists at their toney suburb's town meeting, against plans to build an affordable-housing high-rise in their neighborhood and a Walmart downtown.

*   *   *

To say that productive pluralism relies on families and communities is true, in part, as a matter of definition: self-sufficient families and communities are integral to prosperity. A strong family is one whose members fulfill their commitments to one another and provide for one another's needs. A strong community is one to which engaged members make productive contributions. But the relationship also goes much deeper, because it is family and community, not material resources, that instill in individuals the capacity to become productive members of society and build strong families and communities of their own.

One of the most stunning and underreported statistics about modern America comes from a 2014 study by the Brookings Institution's Richard Reeves.[10] Reeves used data from more than five thousand Americans born mostly in the 1980s and 1990s to compare the income quintile in which they were born to the income quintile they later reached. So, for instance, of those born into households with income in the bottom 20 percent of all American households, how many found themselves in the bottom 20 percent as adults?

Family structure dictated opportunity. For someone born in the bottom quintile to a never-married mother, the odds of rising to the top quintile (5 percent) were one-tenth those of remaining in the bottom quintile (50 percent). But for someone born in the bottom quintile to a married mother and raised by both parents, the odds of reaching the top quintile were *higher* (19 percent) than remaining in the bottom quintile (17 percent). Indeed, those children faced almost perfectly equal chances of landing anywhere as adults (between 17 percent and 23 percent in each of the five quintiles). The critical implication is not the higher income per se but that children from two-parent families had access to a far wider range of opportunities to become self-sufficient contributors to society. Stanford professor Raj Chetty reached a complementary conclusion from examining economic mobility across regions of the country. A low fraction of children with single parents was the best predictor of upward mobility within a region.[11]

The benefits for children of two-parent families are now well documented across the social sciences and include better physical and mental health, less substance abuse, and better educational outcomes. Children raised by married parents are also less likely to become single parents. And the married couples also benefit themselves: they experience better health and less substance abuse, face less material hardship, and attain higher levels of wealth.[12]

Family characteristics within a community also influence each other. For instance, someone is far more likely to divorce his own spouse if he has a direct social tie to someone else who is divorced.[13] More surprisingly, Chetty's work on economic mobility studies not only the characteristics of individual families but also the aggregate characteristics for the regions in which they live. It finds that being raised by a single parent reduces opportunity, yes, but so does being raised in a community with many *other* single-parent families. This holds even for individuals who are themselves raised in two-parent families.

In addition to preparing the next generation, families and communities also operate as economic units whose capacities dictate in large part the options available to their members. When two individuals commit to building a life together, they dramatically expand their joint horizons. They can support one another in multiple ways—pursuing further education, for instance, or coping with challenges like job loss or illness. They can divide the responsibilities of a household in ways that best match their respective interests and capabilities. Their joint pursuit of productive activities will likely allow them to meet their own needs and those of their children and leave a surplus of effort and resources to dedicate to the community.

Communities create parallel benefits through their dense networks of relationships. The next-door neighbor or the local bank may be far more capable of evaluating a small business owner's creditworthiness than a much larger but more distant financial institution relying on the latest metrics and analytical tools. The safety net offered by friends, family, and church will always be more responsive and tailored than a government bureaucracy—and it is more likely to come with some much-needed moral judgment or a swift kick in the pants. Sending the kids across the street or down to the grandparents' is a far more efficient and cost-effective option for emergency childcare than anything the government or the market might provide.

All this makes obvious the error of emphasizing "income inequality" as the root cause of America's economic challenges and social decay. Looking at things from a consumption-oriented view of prosperity, impoverished households' lack of material resources seems a likely culprit—and greater income redistribution to support greater consumption a reasonable solution. But while social dysfunction now correlates strongly with income, that relationship is historically anomalous. In the 1960s and 1970s, class-based gaps on social indicators from marriage to child-rearing to labor force participation and community health were small to nonexistent.[14] Even today, controlling for family and community, income appears to determine little.

Senator John Edwards inadvertently illustrated this point in his famous "Two Americas" speech at the 2004 Democratic National Convention.[15] Edwards began by acknowledging his parents, both in the audience that night. "You taught me that there's dignity and honor in a hard day's work," he said. "You taught me to always look out for our neighbors, to never look down on anybody, and treat everybody with respect." He told the story of his upbringing in a small town where his mother and father both worked, of his mother's eventually running a small business to help pay his college tuition, and of all the other men and women in town who "worked hard, and [who] tried to put a little money away so that their kids and their grand-kids could have a better life."

Edwards intended this account to outrage his fellow Americans. His town was in the unfortunate of his two Americas. In his telling, he grew up on the wrong side of a divide separating those "who have lived the American dream" and "are set for life" from those "who struggle to make ends meet every single day" and "live paycheck to paycheck." "It doesn't have to be that way," he insisted—meaning that government should step in and make things right.

The argument made little sense, though. Wasn't Edwards, in fact, living the American Dream? The material hardship he assailed looked surmountable, his opportunity substantial, his achievements impressive. And as he emphasized, it was the noneconomic endowments of his youth—a two-parent family instilling strong values, a community filled with hard-working role models committed to the betterment of their children—that made it possible. If there are two Americas, his was, in many ways, firmly ensconced in the fortunate one. It is the other one, with few consistent caregivers, regular exposure to stresses and traumas, extended families and communities bereft of role models, and a broader culture that reinforces destructive norms and values, that should concern us.

* * *

A properly broad definition of prosperity can seem intangible and unquantifiable, but that does not make it less correct. As Friedrich Hayek lamented in 1975, "to an economist today . . . only that is true which can be proved *statistically*, and everything that cannot be demonstrated by statistics can be neglected."[16] GDP might appear a more straightforward and objective measure, but it is every bit as incomplete and reliant on value judgments as other metrics; it merely assigns 100 percent of its value to economic transactions and 0 percent to everything else. As a discrete metric for describing one dimension of economic performance, GDP provides useful information. But as the guidepost for public policy, its self-imposed isolation from factors critical to society's flourishing encourages neglect.

While GDP growth *can* signal rising material living standards and prosperity for a society, it guarantees neither. It might only reflect an increase in people available to work, whether because of immigration, rising fertility rates, or declining savings that force the elderly to postpone their retirements. It might mean that existing workers are clocking more hours because they love their jobs or because they struggle to make ends meet; either way, even once everyone is gainfully employed, reductions in leisure equal increases in GDP. Sometimes growth is an accounting artifact, with work formerly done in the home moving into the market. For example, two mothers who would prefer to take care of their own children would create GDP growth by hiring each other as nannies instead, because unpaid work for one's own family goes uncounted but paid work for someone else's represents new economic activity.

Another limitation of the GDP growth metric is that it treats "bads" and "goods" alike—all that matters is the completion of tasks that have a dollar value attached. Though GDP offers a useful measure of the resources available to each side in a war, the rising GDP associated with mobilization is hardly something to celebrate. In an especially macabre case of double-counting, the subsequent reconstruction after a war appears in the GDP accounts as a boon to growth too. Or consider the unemployed, many of whom can likely spur more growth through drug abuse that requires frequent hospitalization than they would by getting jobs.

Conversely, GDP growth doesn't encompass many of the things we value most. The internet gets credit for growth to the extent it helps us work more efficiently. But free and instant access to most of humanity's knowledge, not to mention FaceTime calls with grandma, appears nowhere in GDP. Neither does friendship, community, or tradition. A high-priced divorce lawyer who returns home to run the struggling family business and care for an ailing parent does his nation an economic disservice, at least if GDP is the measure—analysts would have to declare a Depression if such choices became widespread.

No metric is perfect, and many can be helpful if interpreted properly. But while economists know well its limitations, they have still taken to deploying GDP as the all-purpose arbiter of good policy. Tax cuts, stimulus spending, regulatory reform, infrastructure, trade, immigration, free college, fighting climate change, reforming health care—all are justified as spurs to GDP growth. Overreliance on the easily quantifiable illustrates the distinction between precision and accuracy: a dart thrower who hits the exact same spot three times is precise, but if that spot happens to be halfway across the room from the bull's-eye, then she is also inaccurate. Economic measures may be precise, but we should care more that our policy choices fly at least in the general direction of the dart board.

Measuring genuine prosperity need not even be uniquely difficult. The government undertakes each quarter to estimate the nation's total economic output with a precision that allows detection of fractional-point increases. Every month, it surveys sixty thousand households to develop an estimate of every American's employment status.[17] The Environmental Protection Agency justifies its rules by estimating the dollar value of reducing by 1 percent the risk of asthma attacks from air pollution. If assigned similar importance, comparable measures of family and community health could be developed and tracked too.

For instance, the same household survey that tracks employment could just as easily provide data about marital status and the share of children living with their biological parents. Just as the University of Michigan's Survey of Consumers tracks economic sentiment and expectations, it could provide data about community sentiment and the ability to support a family. Many of these data do in fact exist, but they are collected intermittently, compiled slowly, and released obscurely. What if the first Friday of each month heralded the release of the prior month's employment data and the following Tuesday brought an update to the Social Index?

Measurement could change within the economic realm as well. For instance, although stagnant incomes are a central focus of many policy discussions, 92 percent of Americans say that "financial stability" is more important to them than "moving up the income ladder." That share actually *rose* seven points from 2011 to 2014, during a period of economic recovery.[18] This result should not be surprising in a context where prosperity depends more on self-sufficient families and social health than on consumption. Yet what policies on anyone's agenda aim to increase stability at the expense of income? What measure even indicates whether we are delivering that stability?

One measure that we do have, and it's particularly well tailored to genuine prosperity, is the personal savings rate—the share of personal income *not* spent each month. By definition, it highlights the prevalence of households able to produce more than they consume, reflecting the achievement of self-sufficiency with a margin for reinvestment in themselves or their communities. Not surprisingly, in the context of economic piety's rise, Americans' personal savings rate reached a high above 13 percent in 1971 and then declined precipitously across four decades, falling below 3 percent in 2005. While the savings rate jumped above 7 percent in the Great Recession's aftermath, it had returned to 3 percent by 2017.[19] In the short run, so low a savings rate boosts GDP. In the long run, it is good for no one.

* * *

This brings us to the final advantage of productive pluralism: it offers a formula for *long-term* prosperity. The conditions it describes are crucial not only to society's flourishing at any moment in time but also to providing the foundations for replicating themselves over time. In other words, productive pluralism is *sustainable*.

Sustainability has a technical meaning. The term is flung around casually in politics and, increasingly, in corporate marketing materials. But the canonical definition, provided by the United Nations's World Commission on Environment and Development in 1987, is striking: sustainable development "meets the needs of the present without compromising the ability of future generations to meet their own needs."[20] This provides a practical and moral principle divorced from any particular policy context—a litmus test that can be applied anywhere.

Many things that one might presume to be unsustainable—for instance, consuming the world's known supply of oil at a rapid rate—turn out to present more complex questions. If the supply of oil dwindles, its price will rise, slowing its consumption and forcing users to find either new sources of oil or substitutes. This has happened in practice, as humanity has shown a remarkable capacity to develop new resources faster than it depletes old ones. Fears of "Peak Oil" have given way to world energy markets awash in excess supply. Paul Ehrlich's prediction of imminent mass starvation, made in his 1968 best seller *The Population Bomb*, was already discredited by 1980 when he made his famous wager with economist Julian Simon. Simon predicted that the prices of whatever raw materials Ehrlich might choose would decline that decade—a bet on abundance over scarcity. Ehrlich put his money on rising prices and lost badly.[21]

While sustainability is generally associated with environmentalism, the issues it raises are not only, or even primarily, ones of natural and ecological resources. What matters is the vitality of the endowments that allow society to replicate and expand its prosperity, year after year, generation after generation. If economic growth fails to nourish the endowments on which it relies, it is not sustainable. Farmers want to maximize crop yields, but most know better than to do this at the expense of their soil.

Scarce environmental endowments have proven much harder to deplete, and markets and technology have proven much more adaptable, than most environmentalists predicted. Society's economic endowments of physical and intellectual capital—the infrastructure and machinery and innovation that power the economy—are also quite robust; the capitalist system naturally invests in their upkeep and ensures that economic activity expands rather than depletes their stock. Social endowments are another matter. America's families and communities are responsible for transmitting opportunity, protecting pluralism, shaping minds, and instilling values from one generation to the next. Families are overwhelmingly responsible for socializing children and preparing them for productive lives. Communities play an important role in that process too, and, in addition, their economic profiles and support structures largely dictate the choices available to their members.

Unlike economic endowments, social endowments have proven themselves highly vulnerable to depletion from—among other things—consumption-oriented policies. This does not make GDP growth inherently incompatible with social health and thus unsustainable; to the contrary, the two goods can be mutually reinforcing. But whether the relationship between them is negative or positive depends on the manner in which growth is pursued.[22]

When the approach to growth is one that disregards social prerequisites, we should not be surprised that it fails to foster them. Economic piety trusts GDP growth to produce widely shared prosperity and the thriving society that is our ultimate objective. But this places the cart in front of the horse. It is the healthy society that produces the requisite human and social capital from which true economic prosperity emerges—and toward which policy should orient itself. Conversely, when opportunity declines, a downward spiral is set in motion, in which the next generation, beginning from a worse point, can likely offer even less to the one that follows. When ways of life vanish or towns crumble or industries flee overseas, they are not easily replaced. When self-sufficiency gives way to dependence, cultural norms shatter. Families that fail to form leave both adults and children adrift. It should not be shocking if, under these conditions, growth stalls.

Productive pluralism fosters the opposite dynamic. It prioritizes outcomes that nourish and replenish social endowments, supporting the formation of strong families and the vibrancy of strong communities. That is not a coincidence; it means that people understand prosperity, and measure their own lives, in terms of the contributions they make to continued social health. This virtuous cycle of productive citizens creating even greater opportunity for the next generation of productive citizens is what long-term prosperity looks like.

One might still object that to push material living standards and consumption to the side is perhaps noble but certainly naive. After all, aren't Americans today the beneficiaries of centuries of consumption growth that created their current prosperity and afforded them the luxury to muse about the virtues of productivity and personal fulfillment? Not really. As noted earlier, the shift to a consumption-oriented understanding of prosperity is a recent phenomenon. Neither the low taxes nor large safety-net programs nor high volumes of trade and immigration that economic piety considers the sine qua non of progress display any correlation with America's past success. Imports as a share of GDP were lower in 1970 than in 1929, before tripling between 1970 and 2006.[23] The foreign-born share of the U.S. population fell from 15 percent in 1910 to below 5 percent in 1970, before rising back to 14 percent in 2015.[24]

Material gains are better understood as the *emergent property* of long-term prosperity. Alongside stable political institutions that protect basic freedoms, it is the productive pluralism of strong families and communities that leads to entrepreneurship, innovation, and rising productivity. Beyond equipping individuals for success, families and communities also create the conditions for free markets to function well. Measures of social trust, for instance, are highly correlated with GDP across countries and entrepreneurship across individuals.[25]

At the national level, whereas traditional economic theory suggests that specialization is key to prosperity, MIT professor César Hidalgo and Harvard professor Ricardo Hausmann have shown the opposite to be true. The more diverse is the array of knowledge and capabilities within an economy, the stronger is its long-term health.[26] This would suggest that when economic growth undermines pluralism, it may eventually undermine itself as well. Emphasizing consumption allows productive capacity to atrophy, but that capacity is not something that we can scale down and back up at will. Experience must accumulate; supply chains must develop; productivity must grow percentage point by percentage point, year by year. Where capacity and know-how are lost or not built, it becomes necessary to start over from behind those who moved more steadily forward. Where poor investments—or no investments—are made at one point, negative effects ripple outward for years.

Residential mobility is the issue that best captures policy makers' misunderstanding of prosperity, the social endowments that foster it, and thus what should be their own objectives. The willingness to pack up and move in pursuit of opportunity is part and parcel of the American Dream and a key element of the nation's economic vitality. Yet, as hardship has increased in recent decades, the share of the population that relocates has declined.[27] If things are so terrible, some economists grumble, why won't anyone move? They have built elaborate models to show how much higher GDP would be if only people lived where their productivity would be highest.[28]

This gets things backward. Strong families and communities launch people into the world to seek their fortune. Relocation requires deep stores of social capital. Without the skills and habits to access opportunity, failure is likely. Lacking a strong support base, it can be hard to get started. If someone is already dependent on government benefits and a move places those benefits at risk, staying put can seem the better bet. Geographic mobility can't rescue America from the consequences of its socially unsustainable growth—because lower geographic mobility is one of those consequences.

Certainly genuine pluralism requires the opportunity to relocate. But in most circumstances, it should also include the opportunity to stay, a choice that has always been and remains the norm—and one we should applaud, not lament. Even when mobility was much higher, it rarely amounted to the abandonment of existing communities. The migration of "Okies" from the "Dust Bowl" of the 1930s may be the iconic American image of relocation in search of opportunity, but Oklahoma's population declined only 2 percent during that decade. In Kansas and Nebraska, the declines were less than 5 percent. As technology obliterated agricultural employment, the population of Iowa held steady or increased in every decade from 1880 to 1980.[29]

Relocation tears people away from their communities. If a critical mass relocates, it can decimate the community left behind. The idea that struggling communities should disband themselves is not a return to "how things used to be"; it is an admission of catastrophic failure and a prescription for further disaster. If we want to enjoy the fruits of long-term prosperity, including widespread relocation in pursuit of opportunity, we will need to restore its prerequisites. And that requires, literally, work.

CHAPTER 3

THE LABOR MARKET

And so we arrive at this book's central subject: creating an economy
in which workers of all kinds can sustain strong families and communities. And that requires a policy emphasis on *meaningful* work.
Understood narrowly, any activity can count as work. A five-year-old
assembling Legos is "working." *Reason*, the leading libertarian magazine,
ran a 2017 cover story titled "Young Men Are Playing Video Games
Instead of Getting Jobs. That's OK. (For Now)," in which writer Peter
Suderman argued that modern video games function "less like traditional
entertainment and more like employment simulators" for young men
disconnected from the labor force.[1] "They don't put food on the table,"
Suderman acknowledged. "But they do provide, at least in the short to
medium term, a sense of focus and success, structure and direction, skill
development and accomplishment." This is economic piety's reductio ad
absurdum brought to life: upon discovering the cost of forsaking productive activity, a consumption-obsessed society attempts to package work's
benefits as consumable experiences.

Productive pluralism has a much richer sense of work. Contrary to
the typical commencement address, however, what makes work meaningful doesn't depend on its inspirational nature or on it having a transfor-
mative effect on the world. Work is meaningful because of what it means

to the person performing it, what it allows him to provide to his family, and what role it establishes for him in his community.

In *The Dream and the Nightmare*, Myron Magnet drives home this distinction at the expense of Felix Rohatyn, a prominent New York liberal who lamented the "dead-end lives" of "the man and his wife slogging away in menial jobs that are dead-end jobs, with three kids, trying to deal with an environment that is very depressing."[2] If the man is a short-order cook and his wife cleans hotel rooms, observed Magnet in the early 1990s, their income would support a "threadbare but adequate" lifestyle. (Though note that, based on New York City's median wages for his hypothetical couple's occupations, their income in 2016 would have been 15 to 20 percent lower than when he wrote.[3]) He continued:

> But you do not judge people's lives only from the material point of view. Suppose that these two have brought up their children to respect the parents' hard work, to be curious about the world, to study in school, to take pleasure in family and community life, to consider themselves worthwhile people, to work hard and think about the future, to become skilled tradesmen or even professional as adults, and to bring grandchildren to visit. If this is a dead end rather than a human accomplishment worthy of honor and admiration, then it is hard to know what human life is about.

A job may appear to be a "dead end" on a company's organizational chart, but that's not how it looks to a family. That doesn't describe its value to the community members who benefit from the product or service. Nor does it even begin to capture the role that the job plays in the worker's life.

For the individual, work imposes structure on each day and on life in general. It offers the mundane but essential disciplines of timeliness and reliability and hygiene as well as the more complex socialization of collaboration and paying attention to others. It requires people to interact and forges shared experiences and bonds. It promotes goal setting and long-term planning. True, other pursuits can provide these kinds of benefits—for example, raising children, keeping a home, or volunteering in the community. But sleeping, couch surfing, or, pace *Reason*, playing video games does not. And for out-of-work men in particular, such idle activities tend to fill up their time.[4]

Work (again, especially for men) helps establish and preserve families. Where fewer men work, fewer marriages form.[5] Unemployment doubles the risk of divorce, and male joblessness appears the primary culprit.[6] These outcomes likely result from the damage to both economic prospects and individual well-being associated with being out of work, which strain existing marriages and make men less attractive as marriage partners. The so-called marriageable-men hypothesis associated with sociologist William Julius Wilson, which suggests that a lack of job opportunities contributed to the collapse of two-parent families in the African American community, remains controversial.[7] But that debate is largely about whether lack of economic opportunity was the underlying cause of male idleness. Few would question that such idleness would tend to reduce the likelihood and the stability of marriage.

Current economic conditions do appear to play a role in harming marriage formation. MIT professor David Autor and his colleagues found that U.S. regions facing greater competition from China experience lower rates of marriage and higher shares of children born to single mothers and that this effect appeared only when the economic disruption affected male employment.[8] Johns Hopkins professor Andrew Cherlin and his colleagues sought to study the "relationship between economic inequality and sociodemographic outcomes such as family formation," for which they noted a lack of "satisfactory evidence on the mechanisms by which inequality may have an effect."[9] When they accounted for a region's availability of "middle-skilled jobs," accessible to high school graduates and paying above-poverty wages, they found that the labor market, not the inequality, was influencing family formation. The issue was less who earns how much more than whom and more who has a chance to earn a living at all.

Work is both a nexus of community and a prerequisite for it. Work relationships represent a crucial source of social capital, establishing a base from which people can engage in the broader community—whether it's playing on a softball team, organizing a fund-raising drive, or hosting a field trip for the local preschool. This dimension of employment is especially relevant outside of urban centers. In such settings, the workplace can become a central meeting point. Communities that lack work, by contrast, suffer maladies that degrade social capital and lead to persistent poverty. Crime and addiction increase, their participants in turn becoming ever less employable;[10] investments in housing and communal assets decline; a downward spiral is set in motion.

The role of family and community in transmitting opportunity to the next generation also depends on work. When parents lose their jobs, their children tend to do worse in school, graduate at lower rates, and have less success as adults.[11] Recall that, while productive activity provides direct benefits to workers, its worth also derives from the dignity and respect that society confers on self-reliance and productive contributions. In a community where dependency is widespread, illegality a viable career path, and idleness an acceptable lifestyle, the full-time worker begins to look less admirable—and more like a chump.

This is consistent with what our intuitions tell us. John Edwards described the "dignity and honor in a hard day's work" as among the most important values instilled by his parents.[12] "I still remember vividly the men and women who worked in that mill with [my father]," Edwards observed. "I can see them. Some of them had lint in their hair; some of them had grease on their faces. They worked hard, and they tried to put a little money away so that their kids and their grand-kids could have a better life." No one should be surprised if children raised in households and communities that lack the dignity and honor of work show less inclination or ability to climb onto the economic ladder themselves.

*　*　*

Where does meaningful work come from? In an agrarian economy, most people worked on the land, producing directly the things their families needed. Capitalism has the labor market, which can seem like an abstraction, disconnected from everyday life. In the stock market, people bid on shares, their fluctuating prices scrolling across the electronic ticker. The supermarket overflows with produce bins and cereal boxes, each displaying a price that the potential buyer can take or leave. But finding a job or showing up for work seems different, somehow. After all, what is being bought and sold—a person, or his time, or some set of services? And who is doing the buying and the selling? We speak colloquially of workers needing jobs and of employers providing them, but workers are really the labor market's producers and the employers its customers.

In fact, like any market, the labor market is a tool for connecting people who wish to exchange one thing for another. A "job" is the relationship formed by someone who can perform work and someone who wants that work performed. The labor market's conditions—who can perform what kind of work and who needs what kind of work performed, what wages will be offered and accepted, and which rules govern work relationships—determine how many jobs exist, of what types, located where, and at what pay scale. The result aligns buyers and sellers engaged in mutually beneficial transactions.

It's tempting to conclude, then, that the labor market largely should be left alone to do its thing. Let it find equilibrium, just like other markets, and the result will be an efficient allocation of resources that maximizes the economy's output. If we're unhappy with the distribution of benefits captured by the labor market's winners and losers, then we can equip people to do better next time, or we can redistribute after the fact.

The problem with this conclusion is that, in one critical respect, the labor market is *not* like other markets: people are not products. This is obviously true with respect to the intrinsic worth of human beings. But the observation also has two concrete economic implications.

First, people are not created for the purpose of selling their labor, so the potential supply of prospective workers does not always respond to market signals. Perhaps under conditions of subsistence agriculture, when resources governed population growth, the available supply of labor was directly a function of the work to be done. But one triumph of modern civilization is that this relationship no longer holds. The decision to have children depends little on their economic value, for instance, and the survival of those children throughout their lives depends little on their own productive capacity.

Not only the quantities of available workers but also the characteristics of workers are determined to some degree independent of market demand. This is entirely the case with respect to natural endowments, and it is often true with respect to the familial and social environments in which children grow up. Among those showing a particular set of physical and mental skills, yes, we may have some success in tailoring training—encouraging more computer programmers and fewer accountants among analytically inclined college graduates, say, or more plumbers and fewer carpenters among tradesmen—but as the market's persistent wage differentials make clear, even screamingly loud signals don't automatically induce families to switch their "production lines" from cashiers to chemists. When the labor supply does adjust, it does so gradually—typically over the course of a generation. Job switching is common, but career switching, especially as people get older, is much harder. Retraining has met with limited success. In sum, the nation's population is generally less flexible than the market would optimally desire.

This becomes a problem when it collides with the second economic implication of people not being products: society can't be indifferent to where the price and quantity of work settle. Among a typical market's core functions is to discover the price that brings supply and demand into alignment and to send that information to other potential buyers and sellers. Whether oil costs $50 or $100 per barrel, whether a new car costs $10,000 or $20,000, society wants to know. People may drive more or less and companies invest more or less in searching for new oil fields; consumers may upgrade to the latest model sooner or later and firms expand or contract assembly lines. In each situation, the market translates external conditions and individuals' preferences into an efficient result.

Typical markets can cope with oversupply—but the solutions they reach aren't of the kind that we can tolerate if applied to society's members. When a business finds it has overproduced, it takes a loss. When economy-wide demand for oil declines, producers provide less. A widget will gladly sit on the clearance shelf until it is sold. That's not how people work. An insolvent family can't be acquired and restructured; an oversupply of workers can't be written off like obsolete inventory.

That is what our current policy framework too often does: it writes people off. Labor becomes one economic input among many. If capitalists have the ability and the incentive to make the most productive use of all the resources available to them, in whatever combinations they see fit, they will create the greatest amount of output for consumption. And that output can then be shared (redistributed), even among those who did not participate. If the economically efficient solution is one that sidelines a sizable segment of the population, so be it.

This dynamic—society needing the labor market to absorb the available supply of workers at a sufficiently high wage, even though that supply remains imperfectly responsive to market signals—is at the heart of America's economic challenges. Productive pluralism is not satisfied with an efficient labor-market outcome per se. It requires a *particular* outcome: the provision of sufficient meaningful work to sustain families and communities. If the labor market settles on an efficient outcome in which large segments of the population lack meaningful work, our response can't be to say "thanks, understood" and then to wait for those displaced people suddenly to transform themselves into something else, or simply to give them government aid. Our response must be "that needs to change."

* * *

The path to strengthening the labor market can start with the observation of Harvard professor Edward Glaeser: "Every underemployed American represents a failure of entrepreneurial imagination....Joblessness is not foreordained, because entrepreneurs can always dream up new ways of making labor productive."[13] Yet saying that entrepreneurs *can* always dream up new ways of making labor productive does not mean that they *will*. Only so many entrepreneurs put their time—and investors their capital—into so many businesses each year. If their most attractive opportunities involve the deployment of American workers, they will pursue that course. If investing in continual improvement of each American worker's productivity is critical to their success, they will do that too. But if other workers are more profitable to employ than Americans are, or if business models that rely less on labor present them with lower risks and higher rewards, then those entrepreneurs—and the economy—will respond accordingly.

The answer is not to blame the labor market for acting like a market. Again, a market is a tool that translates underlying conditions into the most efficient outcome. Even when conditions bring a bad outcome, the market mechanism itself remains hugely valuable. It preserves liberty and fosters choice for individuals, creates incentives via competition for innovation and investment, and helps resources flow toward the most productive uses. To observe an inadequate result at the macro level, that is, is not to imply that we know the correct result at the micro level. Productive pluralism says nothing about who should work for whom or at what wage, and trying to outperform a free market in answering such questions would be foolhardy. Instead, public policy should focus on those underlying conditions: why is the market settling where it does, and under what circumstances would it settle somewhere better?

The labor market's conditions dictate its behavior along five dimensions—and it can be improved along all five, depending on the trade-offs that society chooses to make. These are the subjects of the five chapters in part II; here, I provide a brief overview of each.

DEMAND

What work does the economy need done? Consumer preferences and industry economics dictate much of the answer, but, at the margin, the rules that government puts in place can alter the balance. For instance, heavily regulating industrial activity and imposing stringent environmental regulation on physical infrastructure, while leaving the digital economy mostly free from regulation, will tend to constrict the demand for manufacturing workers, while expanding it for software engineers. Targeting taxes at energy-intensive activities, while aggressively subsidizing health care and higher education, will have profound effects on which industries stall and which thrive.

Over time, these kinds of choices can begin to affect consumer preferences and industry economics. Innovation will start to shift to those areas where entrepreneurs anticipate building the most successful businesses—whether that's in manufactured goods or high-end services, housing renovations or artistic performances. And where greater investment accumulates, the efficiencies of scale and expertise and supply chains develop too. A country consistently seen as the second-best location for a new factory will watch as factories get built in other places, and the researchers and suppliers and distributors follow—and soon it won't even be the fifth best location.

SUPPLY

What work are people prepared to do? The employer bears significant responsibility for training workers to meet its needs and improving their productivity over time. But for this investment to make sense, the worker must demonstrate basic capabilities at the outset. The better prepared the prospective workforce, the faster an employer can bring workers on board and the higher their wages will be.

The students to whom the education system tailors its efforts will experience the greatest boost in their work prospects. This emphasis will also influence demand, as entrepreneurs build businesses where they expect to find well-prepared workers. If public schools offer a wide range of programs and lavish attention on those connected to the weakest segments of the labor market, they can push outcomes in a positive direction. If they adopt an attitude of "college or bust," we shouldn't be surprised to find a workforce consisting primarily of college graduates and busts.

BOUNDARIES

Who gets to perform work and who gets to purchase it? When trade and immigration policies expand the pool of employers and consumers demanding various types of work, the workers able to provide it will likely see more opportunities—and higher wages. But when policies dramatically expand the supply of workers able to meet existing demand, domestic workers will suffer. In establishing a labor market's boundaries, balance is therefore crucial.

Unfortunately, in a wealthy country like the United States, balance will rarely be achieved for less-skilled workers if residents of poorer countries can participate without limit in the same labor market. Entrepreneurs gain access to a vastly larger and cheaper supply of labor, while imperatives vanish to build businesses that use the existing domestic labor supply or make investments in improving domestic workers' capabilities. This effect swamps the smaller uptick in demand for less-skilled American labor that those workers might expect to see from the poorer countries' consumers.

TRANSACTIONS

How do workers and employers establish and manage their relationships? The set of negotiable terms and conditions and the rules of negotiation have a significant influence on the nature of transactions in any market. This is triply true in the labor market, where overlapping regimes of contract law, employment law, and labor law govern the efforts of workers and employers to reach mutually beneficial agreements. Any contract they wish to sign must grapple with the myriad rules that government imposes about hours, wages, conditions, benefits, and much more. On top of those rules, the presence of a union may introduce an additional layer of collective bargaining, itself controlled by government rules.

In principle, allowing workers to bargain collectively should give them an opportunity to secure better terms than they might each achieve individually. Furthermore, by placing workers and employers on equal footing, concerns of unequal power and unfair agreements fall by the wayside, reducing the need for government dictates. Why does the Department of Labor need to set the standard for overtime pay when the parties can be reasonably expected to work out this issue for themselves? But done poorly, a system of organized labor can have the opposite effect, creating industry-wide cartels that negotiate agreements in the long-term interest of no one.

TAXES

How do the employer's total cost and the worker's take-home pay differ from the agreed-upon wage? The term *tax* is meant here in the broadest sense. Obviously, the direct taxes imposed on both employers and workers represent a large wedge inserted between the bargain that the parties might like to strike and the costs and benefits that they ultimately experience. But many other factors play a similar role, adding to the cost of becoming a worker or hiring one.

Conversely, government can offer subsidies that offset tax burdens or even raise the transaction's value to one or both parties beyond what the market offers. If society wants more from the labor market, it must consider paying for it. This can take forms ranging from tax credits for the employer or worker to direct subsidies that boost wages to better infrastructure that lowers transportation costs. Such policies are more expensive than other reforms, though.

*   *   *

In each of these areas, America's choices have been misguided. We over-tax and underinvest in less-skilled workers, make them costly and risky to employers, and discourage investment in the industries where they could work most productively. At the same time, we free employers from the constraints of using the existing domestic workforce, offering them instead an option of using much cheaper foreign workers overseas or bringing the cheaper workers here. The immediate effects of these policy choices have often appeared beneficial, even to the workers who now find themselves disadvantaged. But those policies have, over time, reshaped the economy's contours in ways that have left too many people out.

CHAPTER 4

A FUTURE FOR WORK

Rather than consider how public policy has harmed the labor market and how reforms could strengthen it and boost worker productivity, many economists and policy makers prefer to point the finger at automation—painting productivity gains as a problem rather than a solution. "This question of technology leading to a reduction in demand for labor is not some hypothetical prospect," says Larry Summers, former U.S. secretary of the treasury and president of Harvard University. "It's one of the defining trends that has shaped the economy and society for the last 40 years."[1]

Summers's view represents conventional wisdom across the political spectrum and around the world, especially with respect to the industrial economy. Factory automation "has already decimated jobs in traditional manufacturing," said physicist Stephen Hawking.[2] The *New York Times* called automation "the long-term jobs killer"[3] and editorialized that "many economists believe that automation has had a much bigger impact" than trade on manufacturing jobs.[4] Speaking just before Brexit, former British Conservative Party leader Iain Duncan Smith attributed global political turmoil in part to "automation and technological change," to which "so many manufacturing jobs have already been lost,"[5] while Brookings Institution scholar Mark Muro said just after Donald Trump's election that the outcome was "secretly about automation."[6]

In this telling, the unstoppable force of technological progress bears responsibility for the economic duress imposed on blue-collar workers and their communities as manufacturing employment collapsed and wages stagnated. Technology has allowed us to produce more output with fewer people, displacing less-skilled workers from high-paying factory jobs into the lower-paying service sector or sending them out of the workforce entirely. Coming breakthroughs in robotics and artificial intelligence will only accelerate the trend, threatening perhaps the majority of jobs in the decades ahead. If any of this were true, productive pluralism would be fated to fail. The project of creating economic conditions in which the labor market offers opportunity to all would be a fool's errand.

Fortunately, claims of industrial employment's technology-driven demise find no support in either the data of recent economic performance or careful analyses of future labor force trends. If automation were rendering workers obsolete, we would see evidence in rising productivity, major capital investments, and a shift in the ratio of production workers to managerial workers. None of these things has occurred. If technology could render workers obsolete, the radical advancements of past generations should have done it. They did not. If this time is different, we should find evidence that a large share of current workers is uniquely vulnerable to the particular set of technologies on the horizon. We do not.

What we find, instead, is that the industrial economy has stalled. Technology-driven productivity gains have continued as in the past, if a bit slower. But whereas output used to grow at least as quickly, it now grows barely at all. The dynamic has shifted from one in which workers produce more each year, and total output rises, to one in which fewer workers are needed each year to deliver roughly the same output as the year before.

* * *

Mathematically, automation does destroy jobs. If an activity that required ten workers can, with automation, be done by five, then the economy can maintain its prior level of output with five fewer jobs. Automation is just one specific case of a more general rule: every means of increasing the rate of output per worker—measured as "productivity"—can also be understood as reducing the number of workers required to achieve the existing level of output.

This is not, generally, a problem. To the contrary, producing more stuff with less labor—whether through improved skills, more efficient processes, or better tools—is by definition how a society achieves economic progress. This means that any time we talk about rising productivity, wages, and standards of living, we are also talking about reducing the need for workers providing the current products and services.

The crucial question is what happens to output as productivity rises. If we achieve the 2.8 percent annual productivity growth that translates to a 100 percent increase after twenty-five years—the typical worker producing twice as much as a generation earlier—this also means, using the language of the automation debate, that every twenty-five years, we will destroy half of the economy's jobs. And that would indeed be the result, if output were to remain at its initial level. But if output also doubles, then everyone remains working, and material living standards can double too. This is precisely what happened from 1947 to 1972, widely seen as the golden age for American manufacturing and the nation's middle class. Economy-wide productivity increased by 99 percent; only fifty workers were needed by the end of the Vietnam War to do the work that one hundred could complete at the end of World War II.[7] The result was not mass unemployment. Instead, America *produced more stuff.* The same share of the population was working in 1972 as in 1947,[8] and men's median income was 86 percent higher.[9]

Increasing output can take different forms. Between 1947 and 1972, workers produced higher quantities of the same goods and services, which were now more affordable for more consumers. U.S. vehicle sales doubled during this period,[10] as did vehicle miles traveled per person;[11] more than 85 percent of cars and trucks were still manufactured domestically.[12] Goods and services also improved in quality—vehicles were safer and lasted longer, and some came with power steering and an automatic transmission. And with fewer workers required to produce the output of 1947, many could serve markets in 1972 that hadn't existed a generation earlier or that had been much smaller. In 1947, U.S. airlines flew 13 million passengers a combined 6.5 billion miles; in 1972, they flew 191 million passengers 152 billion miles. Fatalities per mile flown, meanwhile, fell more than 95 percent.[13]

This is how growth works. When agriculture mechanized, we didn't continue living as subsistence farmers while lamenting that nearly all our able-bodied adults were now jobless. We produced more and better food. Then we produced more of other things too. For that matter, when we introduced hundreds of thousands of ATMs across the country, we did not design welfare programs for the armies of unemployed bank tellers—*because bank teller employment never even declined*. As Boston University economist James Bessen has shown, ATMs lowered the banks' cost of doing business, and they responded by opening more branches.[14]

In theory, modern automation *could* produce different effects than in the past—if, for instance, the pace of change were to accelerate to the point that workers become unnecessary in existing roles much faster than they can find new ones. But when the *New York Times* argues that "this time may really be different" because "over the same 15-year period that digital technology has inserted itself into nearly every aspect of life, the job market has fallen into a long malaise,"[15] it is passing off correlation as causation. If we are to believe that the very process most responsible for economic progress and middle-class prosperity over the past century is now undermining those accomplishments, we should want to see some proof.

In fact, the evidence is plentiful—and it points in the opposite direction. Automation has not spurred accelerating productivity. During the second half of the twentieth century, economy-wide productivity increased by an annual average of 2.1 percent. During 2000–2016, the increase was only 1.8 percent and slowing: from 3.2 percent (during 2000–2005) to 1.9 percent (during 2005–10) to 0.7 percent (during 2010–15). In 2016, productivity *did not increase* for the first time since the early 1980s.[16]

The manufacturing sector tells a parallel story: no better progress in the early twenty-first century than the late twentieth, a steadily worsening picture, and catastrophic recent performance. During 2010–16, annual productivity growth in manufacturing averaged less than 1 percent—a period of unprecedented stagnancy.[17]

These data yield slightly different results depending on the particular metrics and time frames used—an industry's total output or only its "value added," output per worker or per hour worked, figures published by the Bureau of Labor Statistics or the Bureau of Economic Analysis. But no view alters the underlying reality that recent productivity growth is no better, and likely much worse, than it was in the past.

Might the data be misleading? Certainly measuring output and productivity is tricky. Debate rages, for instance, over how best to account for the rapid improvement in digital products. If the same workers can produce a computer processor this year with twice as many transistors as last year's, are they twice as productive? Some economists worry that taking such rapid productivity gains at face value overstates the real-world effects. After all, the ability to make faster computers this year does not mean that the prior year's computers could be made with half the workers. Nor does a computer with twice the processing power offer fully double the value to the typical user.

Meantime, other economists worry that accounting methods developed almost a century ago are understating gains by missing much of the value created by newer types of products and services. What is a smartphone worth if buying separately its camera, map, encyclopedia, music player, and so forth would have cost thousands of dollars only a decade ago, if a memory chip of comparable capacity would have cost millions of dollars?

Other indicators provide no better support for the claim that automation is spurring disruptive productivity increases. Larry Mishel and Josh Bivens of the Economic Policy Institute show that growth in capital investment generally, and in information technology particularly, has been slowing and stands well below pre-1990 levels.[18] Robert Atkinson and John Wu of the Information Technology and Innovation Foundation likewise find that the rate of labor-market "churn"—employment disappearing from some occupations or appearing in others—stands at an all-time low.[19]

Nor, within the manufacturing sector, are blue-collar jobs under particular pressure. If automation were accelerating, allowing factories to produce more with fewer people on the shop floor, the share of sector employment classified as "production and nonsupervisory" should decline. In the past, that happened. During 1947–72, the production-worker share of the workforce fell more than ten points, from 87 percent to 76 percent—or, put more dramatically, the ratio of line workers to managers fell by half, from 6.8:1 to 3.2:1. By 1982, the share reached 71 percent—a 2.4:1 ratio. Since then, for an entire generation, there has been virtually no change. In 2016, the share stood at 70 percent.[20]

Econometric studies offer a final line of evidence that explores the statistical relationship between robot installation and employment. A landmark 2015 study from London's Centre for Economic Performance found that the introduction of industrial robots corresponded to faster productivity growth during 1993–2007 without affecting overall manufacturing employment, though high-skilled workers did see some gains at the expense of low-skilled ones.[21] Another 2015 study, by the authors of the "China Shock" paper showing strong negative effects from exposure to Chinese trade, found that technological change did cause some employment shifts within sectors but did not reduce employment overall. Furthermore, while the effect of trade exposure was increasing over time, the effect of technology seemed to be dissipating.[22]

One prominent study does report a negative relationship between robots and jobs, but the magnitude of its finding is instructive. Released in 2017 by the National Bureau of Economic Research, the paper was headlined in the *New York Times* as "Evidence That Robots Are Winning the Race for American Jobs" and in the *Washington Post* as "We're So Unprepared for the Robot Apocalypse."[23] The actual effect identified: a loss of 360,000–670,000 jobs over seventeen years, of which only half were in manufacturing.[24] This amounts to a loss of only fifteen thousand manufacturing jobs per year, roughly 0.1 percent of average manufacturing employment during the period. At that rate, robots might, over a century, eliminate as many manufacturing jobs as were in fact lost during 2001.[25]

The difference this time, and the cause of economic distress, isn't that productivity is rising; it's that output is not. From 1950 to 2000, while productivity in the manufacturing sector rose by 3.1 percent annually, value-added output grew by 3.6 percent—and employment increased, from 14 million to 17 million. During 2000–2016, productivity rose by a similar 3.3 percent annually. But output growth was only 1.1 percent—and employment fell, from 17 million to 12 million. Even with all the technological advancement of the twenty-first century, had manufacturers continued to grow their businesses at the same rate as in the prior century, they would have needed *more* workers—a total of 18 million, by 2016.[26]

Faced with this reality, efforts to blame job losses on automation require the fatally flawed assumption that output is not supposed to increase. Holding output constant and comparing the past's lower productivity with the present's higher productivity will always reveal that employment would be higher but for the productivity gain. This is how, for instance, an oft-cited report from Ball State University reaches the conclusion that 88 percent of manufacturing job losses are attributable to automation: "Had we kept 2000-levels of productivity and applied them to 2010-levels of production, we would have required 20.9 million manufacturing workers. Instead, we employed only 12.1 million."[27]

But of course we're employing fewer manufacturing workers than if productivity had not increased—and the same could be said about every decade. Using this reasoning, we could say that had we kept 1960-levels of productivity and applied them to 1970-levels of production, we would have required 25 million manufacturing workers. Instead, we employed 18 million. Did automation destroy 7 million jobs in the 1960s? Maybe. But this wasn't a problem, because output rose 62 percent, so manufacturing employment was higher at decade's end. By contrast, the output of the manufacturing sector in 2016 was only 3 percent higher than it was in 2006. Single years achieved higher growth than that thirty-two times during 1950–2000, at least five times during every decade before 2010.

We want to know what has changed in our economic trends that has dislocated so many manufacturing workers and produced so much distress. The answer is not higher productivity growth; it is slower growth in output.

*   *   *

The automation question shapes debates about not only past economic trends and public policies but also those to come. President Obama, in his farewell address, warned that "the next wave of economic dislocations . . . will come from the relentless pace of automation that makes a lot of good, middle-class jobs obsolete."[28] *The Atlantic*'s cover story, "A World without Work," introduces its topic thusly: "For centuries, experts have predicted that machines would make workers obsolete. That moment may finally be arriving."[29]

The grandest visions emanate from Silicon Valley, whose technologists believe they will lead a social transformation. Many have become interested in the policy proposal known as "universal basic income," by which government would pay a livable stipend to the no-longer-employable masses. "Robots will be able to do everything better than us," warns Tesla's Elon Musk. "There is a pretty good chance we end up with a universal basic income, or something like that, due to automation....I am not sure what else one would do."[30]

Such expectations for automation get four things wrong. First, they magnify the importance of innovations at the cutting edge while taking for granted the equally fundamental innovations of the past. Advanced robotics and artificial intelligence are impressive, but so were the internet, the computer, the internal combustion engine, and electricity, to say nothing of democratic capitalism and the Industrial Revolution. Yet, as Northwestern professor Robert Gordon shows, for no period in the past two centuries has annual growth in American output per person exceeded 2.5 percent.[31] If anything, the innovative leaps of the past benefited from access to the lowest-hanging fruit. The elements of human labor easiest to replace with machines, the processes easiest to optimize, are the ones that get tackled first. In some respects, technological progress accelerates exponentially—the processing power of computer chips has been doubling every year or two for fifty years. But in others, it becomes ever harder to maintain even a constant rate of progress, as operations managers struggle to find yet another 2 or 3 percent efficiency gain on top of the last year's. Accelerating technological progress does not produce accelerating productivity; it is the minimum required to deliver even constant productivity gains.

Second, the prophecies ignore the gradual timeline on which transformations inevitably occur. Technology takes time to adapt by fits and starts to real-world conditions. And organizations take time to adapt to new technologies. Thus, for instance, the head of Google's self-driving-car project acknowledged in 2016 that the company's goal of fielding a fully autonomous vehicle by decade's end was implausible—the timeline was more like thirty years. "How quickly can we get this into people's hands?" he asked. "If you read the papers, you see maybe it's three years, maybe it's thirty years. And I am here to tell you that honestly, it's a bit of both. . . . This technology is almost certainly going to come out incrementally."[32]

And even once such new technology exists, it takes decades longer to penetrate fully its various applications. Existing vehicles will need to reach the ends of their useful lives, and new processes will have to be developed to capture the benefits. An automated delivery truck sounds wonderful, until it arrives and no one hops out to unload.

Deployment is always slow. Thomas Edison presented a lightbulb lit with power from his Pearl Street generating station in 1882, but forty years later, less than 10 percent of the nation's 6 million farms had electricity.[33] Digital is not inherently faster. Walmart took eighteen years to grow from $1 billion to $100 billion in U.S. sales.[34] Amazon, likewise, hit the $1 billion mark in 1999 but took until 2017 to reach $100 billion across North America.[35]

In manufacturing, every year will see extraordinary upgrades in some processes. But firms will have to decide how many areas they will risk changing at one time and how much capital they can devote to the effort. With each decision, they will have to balance the benefits of investment in the ideal tool for a specific task with the loss of flexibility that comes from committing to that tool and that task. Even the steel industry, a poster child for automation, required forty years to increase its per-worker output from 260 tons to 1,100 tons—an annual improvement of less than 4 percent.[36] Across the manufacturing sector globally, the Boston Consulting Group reports that the stock of installed robots grew only 2 percent to 3 percent per year during 2005–14—no faster than total manufacturing output.[37]

As robotics pioneer Rodney Brooks observed in *MIT Technology Review*, "I regularly see decades-old equipment in factories around the world. I even see PCs running Windows 3.0—a software version released in 1990." Anyone who has peered around a checkout counter to see the readout on the cashier's screen knows this feeling. Brooks continued: "The principal control mechanism in factories, including brand-new ones in the U.S., Europe, Japan, Korea, and China, is based on programmable logic controllers, or PLCs. These were introduced in 1968...I just looked on a jobs list, and even today, this very day, Tesla Motors is trying to hire PLC technicians at its factory in Fremont, California."[38]

The state-of-the-art Tesla plant has faced severe challenges, missing deadlines and postponing targets. In 2016, the company stated a goal of producing one hundred thousand to two hundred thousand of its new Model 3 sedans in the second half of 2017; in fact, it managed twenty-seven hundred.[39] *Autoweek* notes that, far from being a "temple of lean manufacturing," the plant produced only about ten vehicles per worker in 2016, across all Tesla models. By comparison, when General Motors and Toyota launched their joint venture on the same Fremont site in the 1980s, they produced twenty-six vehicles per worker in the first year; by

1997, that rate had reached seventy-four. And yes, despite productivity tripling, the plant had also doubled its workforce.[40]

The ultimate check on the rate of productivity growth is the labor force itself. Firms can adopt new technologies and processes only as quickly as they can train workers to operate and perform them. The automated factory may require a few more maintenance technicians and many fewer line workers, but if those line workers can't become technicians, where will firms turn? And even if the same workers can be retrained, instilling new skills can take years. If different workers with different capabilities are needed, more fundamental shifts in the labor market must occur. Schools must develop new programs and talent must seek other career paths; manufacturers will need to attract higher-skill talent from other industries—and those industries may have something to say about that.

The dynamic has already emerged, in the so-called skills gap that manufacturers lament. They say that they need hundreds of thousands of new workers with more advanced skills than their existing workforce can supply and present the problem as a market malfunction. On the contrary, the market is working properly, and is sending a clear signal: automation will be harder, slower, and more expensive than you may like, and to make it work, you'll have to design your processes with the capabilities of the nation's workforce in mind.

This leads to the third misconception about rapid productivity gains: that many jobs can be automated entirely. Technology often makes incremental improvements to a worker's productivity, generally leading to more and higher-quality output rather than to lower demand for her work. One reason people worry that this time may be different is that they believe robotics and artificial intelligence can now fully replicate human functioning and can therefore substitute for, rather than complement, the worker. Driving the fear of replacement are self-promotional quotes from Silicon Valley moguls about their plans for transforming society and Oxford University's much-cited 2013 study warning that 47 percent of American jobs are automatable within "a decade or two." Among the most "computerizable" of seven hundred occupations, say the study's authors, are tour guides, real estate agents, and fashion models. They rate school bus driver as among the easiest jobs to automate, along with baker and rail-track layer, and well ahead of other types of truck and bus drivers.[41]

Oxford's research usefully illustrates the limitations of such studies. From a tall enough ivory tower, or a heady corner of Silicon Valley, the claim about school bus drivers might seem to make sense. What could be easier than driving a school bus? The route is the same every day, it's short, and it gets canceled for snow. For parents, though, the idea of locking twenty kids in a self-driving vehicle for half an hour, with no adult supervision, sounds dubious at best.

These misfires point to a more general problem with automation predictions: an abstract description rarely captures the full complexity of any job. Ironically, a broad classification of jobs as automatable looks like something a computer might produce if one took such classification work as an automatable task—rote and lacking in nuance and specificity. When researchers at the Organisation for Economic Co-operation and Development tried focusing on the actual tasks required of various jobs, instead of the occupation description itself, they found that only 9 percent of jobs were automatable.[42] McKinsey and Company, likewise, finds that only 5 percent of jobs could be entirely automated with technology that has at least been demonstrated in labs, whereas 60 percent of jobs could have at least 30 percent of their activities automated; overall, the analysis forecasts that half of tasks could be automated by 2055.[43] This implies that automation could drive a doubling of productivity over forty years, or less than 2 percent annually.

Less than a year after his prediction that "robots will be able to do everything better than us,"Tesla's Musk acknowledged in April 2018 that "excessive automation at Tesla was a mistake. To be precise, my mistake. Humans are underrated."[44]

Finally, dire predictions ignore the positive. Even stipulating the unprecedented nature of future technological changes, the full implications of those changes extend far beyond automating low-skill jobs—and no law dictates that they should operate on balance to the disadvantage of workers. A tool like 3D printing, for instance, has the potential to reduce the demand for labor in large factories. But it might also spawn new industries, in which smaller businesses can perform small-scale, highly customized manufacturing with relatively little capital investment. If large factories begin to employ highly skilled and compensated robotics specialists, such specialists will relocate to the communities where the factories operate, changing demographic and economic profiles for the better.

If a truck driver can leave his cab and work from a central control facility, in which he toggles to whichever of numerous trucks requires human guidance at a particular moment, he will likely be happier, healthier, and better paid as well. If e-commerce supplants retail, the countless sales jobs concentrated in high-cost urban centers will be redistributed as logistics, delivery, and customer-service positions. Michael Mandel of the Progressive Policy Institute finds that e-commerce is creating new jobs much faster than retail is destroying them, and those jobs pay better too.[45] Anyway, employment in the retail sector reached an all-time high in 2017, with the share consisting of nonsupervisory and production workers unchanged from 1997.[46]

*   *   *

This discussion has emphasized manufacturing jobs and the "industrial economy" in part because they are the subject of much automation concern, but also because they are uniquely important. Some economists regard such a focus as anachronistic. Christina Romer, former chairwoman of President Obama's Council of Economic Advisers, worried that it derived from "sentiment and history" and "the feeling that it's better to produce 'real things' than services."[47] It does not; it derives from the very real benefits that such jobs bring to communities.

Manufacturing matters for two reasons. First, it remains among the most productive economic activities for less-skilled workers. As a share of overall employment, manufacturing has fallen below 10 percent, but in 2016, the industry still accounted for more than 20 percent of private-sector jobs in traditionally blue-collar occupations with a median wage of more than $15 per hour. The manufacturing, construction, and resource-extraction industries combined to provide almost 40 percent of such well-paying, blue-collar jobs.[48]

Take Pittsburgh, sometimes cited as a poster child for postindustrial transformation from heavy industry to health care. From 1990 to 2016, the Pittsburgh area lost forty-six thousand manufacturing jobs while gaining sixty-seven thousand health care and social assistance jobs. But while "production" jobs in the area paid a median hourly wage of $18 in 2016, in line with the area's median for all occupations, "health care support workers" earn $14 and "personal care and service workers" earn $11.[49] Over the period, the area's median household income rose at an annual rate of only 0.3 percent.[50]

Second, "tradeables"—goods and services that can be consumed far from where they're produced—are the lifeblood of local economies. Americans take for granted that they can buy what products they want from around the world. But how can someone whose work consists entirely of serving others in his community expect a firm halfway around the world to make something for him?

Consider the local physician who provides care only to those in his town. He may be well compensated, but he can't sell his work to the makers of cars or phones halfway around the world or even to the medical equipment supplier in the next state. He must trust instead that some of his patients produce goods or services that can be sent to those places and, in purchasing his medical services, give him the resources to acquire the goods that he needs. Or consider the plight of a local economy as a whole. It wishes to receive from elsewhere almost all of its food, medicine, vehicles, electronics, energy, and more. It must send tradeables of equal value. Not every individual must do so; most may work in the local services economy—but they cannot all cut one another's hair.

Tradeables can take many forms. Wall Street provides its financial services around the country and the world, Hollywood exports its movies, and Orlando sells the Disney World experience to tourists. Call-center workers are exporters too. But manufactured products represent by far the largest category of tradeables and are, along with agriculture and natural resources, the ones in which less-skilled workers and less urban locations are best suited to excel. The strength of the industrial economy dictates the fortunes of workers with a comparative advantage in physical activity and regions with a comparative advantage in open spaces and raw materials.

The importance of tradeables to a local community also helps to illuminate the vast difference between the often-equated phenomena of automation and globalization. For the worker dislocated by trade, the facility in which he once worked is likely gone, and the production now occurs somewhere else. But for the worker laid off or never hired because of automation, the facility is still operating in town, likely producing more output than before. Total demand for labor from the firm and its surrounding ecosystem is likely larger, and if capital has replaced labor, the remaining workers are likely earning more   and some other highly paid professionals may be arriving in the area with new demand for services of their own. Furthermore, while productivity gains occur bit by bit, year by year, a plant that shuts down and moves overseas is here today and gone tomorrow. In which situation might it be easier to find a new, well-paying job?

A reporter telling the story of automation speaks to a laid-off worker at a lunch counter; one telling the story of trade reports from the empty parking lot of an abandoned building. There is no one left to talk to.

What happens to a community whose economy does not produce anything that the world wants? It has one export that it can always fall back on: need. Every resident enrolled in a program of government benefits entitles the community to more goods and services from the outside world. For instance, a prominent criticism of recent proposals to cut food stamp benefits has been that it would harm not just the individual recipients but also the local economies reliant on the outside income. The U.S. Department of Agriculture promotes food stamp enrollment as a "win-win for local retailers and communities. Each $5 in new SNAP benefits generates almost twice that amount in economic activity for the community."[51] Food stamp recipients, in effect, are the community's "exporters."

Some speak of local health care systems as bright spots in depressed regions, but these industries usually indicate the government's commitment to health care as the surest way to generate hard currency for these economies. When the retiree on the front porch laments to a reporter, "When I was young we had dances at the community centers. Now they have nothing. No work around here unless you are a nurse, or a doctor, or lawyer,"[52] the list is not of especially productive professions, just those for which some government will pay. A common sight in the most dilapidated town is a sparkling occupational therapy office. The people working there are selling to the nation's taxpayers their care of the local residents on disability.

This need not be the future. Automation need not lead to deindustrialization if output continues to rise as productivity, and thus wealth, increases—and rise both should. We know already what people will buy as they become wealthier, because we can look at what those who are already wealthier buy. Households above the ninetieth income percentile spent 2.1 times more than the nationwide average in 2016, providing a picture of how the economy's spending might look as it doubles from today's.[53]

The allocation looks roughly unchanged. With 2.1 times more total spending, the top spends 2.0 times more on food, 2.1 times more on housing (including 2.6 times more on furnishings and equipment), 2.5 times more on clothing, and 2.0 times more on transportation (only 1.9 times more on vehicles but 3.8 times more on other modes, such as air travel). Entertainment and personal care do take on a relatively larger role—increasing 2.5 and 2.3 times, respectively—but those are offset by the relatively smaller role for health care, which increases only 1.9 times. Of course, higher-income households also save and invest much more, but that capital tends to flow toward other industrialized uses—housing and other building construction, for instance, as well as capital expenditures for businesses. The industry with the highest capital expenditures for structures and equipment in every year from 2006 to 2015 was manufacturing; second in most years was natural resource extraction.[54]

As people get richer, they buy more—and better—houses and cars, electronics and appliances, sofas and shirts, while investing more in physical infrastructure. They do not, generally speaking, make do with anything like the material consumption of a middle-class household while putting their newfound wealth toward yoga retreats and digital downloads. America is not within even multiple generations of exhausting what families would like to consume if their workers were productive enough to create it. For this reason, the prediction that manufacturing will go the way of agriculture is flawed. While our appetite for calories remains (relatively) fixed, our appetite for *stuff* has proven thus far insatiable. If the average American is to someday consume what the average reader of this book likely consumed last year, the potential exists for a great deal more manufacturing indeed.

The "knowledge economy," meanwhile, is not so much supplanting as layering itself atop the industrial economy. Technological breakthroughs have added countless new products and services to the economy, but what have they made extraneous? Books, CDs, and other objects whose only function was to carry information are less necessary with digital transmission. And one can always find the proverbial buggy whip that becomes obsolete. But the mainstays of the economy—food, energy, transportation, housing, and so on—remain as physical as ever, and we expect them to be more complex and reliable than ever. Furthermore, all of those digital products and services require physical hardware and infrastructure, and they have introduced a whole range of new physical devices into our lives, along with new energy demand. Likewise, the drug and device breakthroughs of the biotech industry depend on the creation of new and increasingly complex things. An industry like retail does appear to be undergoing a transformation, but most retail workers already fall into the low-skill, local-service end of the labor market, and it remains unclear whether the jobs associated with bringing goods to households will increase or decrease in quantity, become more or less productive, and concentrate closer or farther from urban centers as the interface between buyer and seller moves online.

As the retail example suggests, even the economy's geographic trajectory can take a positive turn. In *The New Geography of Jobs*, University of California, Berkeley professor Enrico Moretti argues that an ongoing "Great Divergence" between cities with the "right" and "wrong" industries is "the inevitable result of deep-seated economic forces." But such observations are true only until they are no longer true. As Moretti notes, Seattle serves today as a case study for the high-tech boom, but in the 1970s, it was "looking inward and backward, consumed by fear about the future, riddled with crime, and decimated by job losses . . . closer to today's Detroit than Silicon Valley." What changed was that two founders of a small Albuquerque start-up called Microsoft decided to move back home.[55] New York, for its part, barely avoided bankruptcy in the 1970s. In 1990, *Time*'s cover featured an "I Love NY" logo with a broken heart, accompanied by the headline "The Rotting of the Big Apple."[56]

Nobel Prize winner and *New York Times* columnist Paul Krugman believes that "smaller cities have nothing going for them except historical luck."[57] But the recent trend toward big-city growth appears already to be reversing, if it ever really began. Population growth in places like Manhattan and San Francisco has slowed every year since 2010, explains *The Atlantic* in "Why So Many Americans Are Saying Goodbye to Cities," and just as the prior generation populated the Southwest, a new generation appears headed Southeast.[58] The share of Americans living in major cities has been plummeting for decades, from 14 percent in 1950 to 8 percent in 2016 for the ten largest cities, from 24 percent to 15 percent for the fifty largest.[59] Certainly the rising congestion and cost of living caused by people coming to those places are a major part of the explanation, but that is precisely the point. Economic and population trends do not hold indefinitely until all have moved to a single massive metropolis. They ebb and flow over time in search of equilibrium.[60] Places do, in fact, get so crowded that no one goes there anymore, in the old Yogi Berra–ism.

Technological trends could help too. Moretti is correct that the enormous economic benefits of innovation will create prosperous hubs. But as noted, breakthroughs in industrial automation should in theory mean greater dispersion of highly productive workers to less densely populated areas. "For centuries, the cost of distance has determined where businesses produce and sell, where employers locate jobs and where families choose to live, work, shop and play. What if this cost fell dramatically, thanks to new technologies?" asked Bain and Company in its 2016 study on spatial economics. It noted, for instance, that greater automation will allow retailers to operate at much smaller scales, with restaurants able to operate profitably in much smaller towns and cities.

Three-dimensional printing could spur a renaissance in smaller-scale production. If e-commerce makes any product available on any doorstep in twenty-four hours, another major advantage of city living will vanish. If self-driving cars make longer commutes convenient, while virtual reality allows dispersed workforces to collaborate effectively, an exodus from inner suburbs could dwarf that from cities themselves. "A significant change in the cost of distance," Bain predicted, "would prompt millions of economic actors to rethink their strategies and investments, and cause individuals to reassess where they work, live and raise their families."[61]

The point is not that all this will happen, nor that depressed and rural areas represent the most exciting opportunities for the future. Major cities will presumably remain the nerve centers of economic activity, as they have been since antiquity. Returns to innovation, and with them income inequality, may continue to grow. But none of this requires that others' fortunes decline or that we expect or tolerate less than robust labor markets that support strong families and communities across the country. Nothing precludes productive pluralism, if we choose to prioritize it.

The question is whether innovators and investors will consider it in their interest to build American operations and invest in the productivity of American workers. This is where public policy can play a substantial role, either tying the economic fortunes of major cities and the remainder of the country more closely together or helping to dissolve existing bonds. If the bad news is that we have brought our economic distress upon ourselves and have no irresistible forces to blame, the good news is that this also means that we can do something about it. We should not allow nostalgia to point us toward efforts at re-creating the past; the future will undoubtedly look different. But whether that future has room for the American worker is up to us.

PART II

TURNING AROUND

CHAPTER 5

THE ENVIRONMENT AND THE ECONOMY

O nce every decade or so comes a day perfect for hiding the most unpopular and ill-advised policy decisions. It arrives right after a second-term president's midterm elections, when he will never again face the ire of voters, and right before Thanksgiving, when the nation shuts down and travels home to visit family. And so President Barack Obama chose Wednesday, November 26, 2014, for his Environmental Protection Agency (EPA) to announce a substantial tightening of the Clean Air Act's National Ambient Air Quality Standard for ground-level ozone (or, more commonly, "smog") from 75 to between 65 and 70 parts per billion (ppb).[1]

This obscure regulatory proposal promised substantial real-world consequences. A tighter ozone standard pushes regions of the country where the air quality met the old standard but not the new one into the status of "nonattainment zones" (NAZs), the Clean Air Act's equivalent of purgatory. The NAZ designation imposes costly requirements on pollution-emitting facilities like manufacturing plants and stalls new development in the region until air quality can be brought into compliance. Five or ten parts per billion may sound insignificant, but a shift from 75 to 70 ppb would throw cities like Atlanta, Baltimore, and St. Louis out of attainment.[2]

The action superseded Obama's own earlier decision. When the EPA first recommended a 65 ppb threshold in 2011, as the president was launching his reelection campaign, he took the unprecedented step of rejecting his own agency's proposal, citing "the importance of reducing regulatory burdens and regulatory uncertainty, particularly as our economy continues to recover."[3] This infuriated his first-term EPA administrator, Lisa Jackson, who nearly resigned over the dispute.[4] Three years and one reelection later, his determination was different. "We're using the latest science to update air quality standards," explained his second-term EPA administrator Gina McCarthy, "to fulfill the law's promise, and defend each and every person's right to clean air."[5]

How to balance "the importance of reducing regulatory burdens" with "each and every person's right to clean air"? This question lies at the heart of environmental policy and the trade-off it presents between economic activity—especially industrial and energy-intensive activity—on one hand, and environmental quality, on the other. For Obama, the calculus appeared largely electoral; pushing Cincinnati, Columbus, and Cleveland out of attainment was more palatable once Ohio's eighteen electoral votes were secured. But how should society manage such choices?

One easy answer might be that clean air and a healthy environment are nonnegotiable. This is the mind-set implied by McCarthy's promise to defend the "right" to air that is "clean" or, for instance, by California senator Kamala Harris's assertion that "the ability to breathe clean air and live in a safe and healthy environment should not be a partisan issue."[6] Such blandishments merely raise the question of what counts as "clean," "safe," or "healthy." President Clinton lowered the acceptable ozone threshold from 120 to 80 ppb in 1997; President Bush lowered it to 75 ppb in 2008.[7] President Obama settled ultimately on 70 ppb in 2015, frustrating environmentalists who wanted 65 or even 60 ppb—a level so low that NASA warned some parts of the American West might exceed it even after eliminating pollution entirely.[8] Some of America's national parks, from California's Yosemite to Maine's Acadia, exceed the 70 ppb standard.[9] Is clean-as-a-national-park clean enough?

A demand for absolute environmental quality also fails because not even those issuing it actually mean it. McCarthy apparently believed ozone concentrations above 70 ppb were unsafe, but she did not advocate shutting down all industrial activity in NAZ regions, only making rules that would bring pollution levels gradually lower. Given the potential cost, many Americans apparently did not deserve to know that the air they breathe was safe, at least not right away. Harris represents the state with by far the nation's highest ozone levels, but she does not advocate a ban on driving in Los Angeles to remedy the situation.

Even the most rhetorically passionate environmentalists are, ultimately, beholden to the core trade-off of environmental regulation. They might assign relatively higher value to environmental quality and thus tolerate relatively higher cost in its pursuit. But everyone recognizes the need to tolerate some level of pollution. Everyone recognizes the need to consider cost in determining the level.

In principle, regulators should tighten rules and standards only until they reach the point where the cost of the next marginal improvement in environmental quality exceeds the benefit of that improvement. One challenge in getting this right is identifying and measuring the costs and benefits of a rule. Another is that those factors will change across place and time. A requirement that makes sense for a booming economy with smog-choked air may be unwarranted where or when the air is pristine but good jobs are hard to find. A regulator will make wise trade-offs only if the laws he is implementing and the values he applies account for these challenges effectively.

Unfortunately, in America, they do not. The nation's environmental policy justifies itself by assigning enormous economic value to clean air and water, while refusing to consider the effects of regulation on the level, quality, or trajectory of employment. Major environmental laws explicitly reject consideration of cost in setting standards and are designed to tighten continually no matter how much environmental quality improves. The methodology used to assess a rule's costs and benefits specifically excludes effects on employment and investment in the industrial economy; the EPA claims that it cannot even determine whether the effect of new rules would be positive or negative.[10] The result: trade-offs bearing little relationship to those that would most benefit American workers.

* * *

At first glance, concern for the environment might seem the antithesis of economic piety—finally, something besides dollars and cents that counts. But that is not how the economists and other policy makers responsible for environmental protection view it. Instead, they define clean air as something that we all consume. Actions that deliver cleaner air get tallied on the ledger alongside actions that increase economic output. Even actions that deliver cleaner air while decreasing economic output can count as beneficial to consumers, if the value gained in air quality exceeds the value lost in the economy. Clean air, you see, is part of the economic pie.

The key philosophical maneuver behind this convenient conclusion is the concept of an "externality": a benefit or cost of an economic activity borne by a third party and thus not accounted for by the actors. The quintessential example is a factory that pollutes a nearby lake, killing the fish and putting the local fishermen out of business. Suppose that for every ton of steel produced, the factory generates a $10 profit for the owner but kills $15 worth of fish. The market is telling the owner to produce another ton and earn another $10. If he does so, society as a whole will be $5 poorer.

This externality is an example of *market failure*—a concept that gained prevalence alongside economic piety and that relies on the same assumptions. In 1958, MIT's Francis M. Bator defined market failure as "the failure of a more or less idealized system of price-market institutions to sustain 'desirable' activities or to estop 'undesirable' activities." Competitive markets were presumed to behave efficiently and therefore to yield the highest possible level of utility. If incomes were then "continuously redistributed in costless lump-sum fashion" to achieve the income distribution that maximizes social welfare, society could reach its "bliss point."[11] But if some malfunction caused a market not to behave efficiently, then regulators should intervene to counteract the failure, improving efficiency and thereby increasing utility.

In the steel factory example, the regulator can improve on the market outcome by restricting steel production. For most economists, the preferred solution would be to impose a $15 per ton tax on the factory. This would force the factory owner to absorb the cost of the externality; he would only produce tons that were still profitable after paying the tax, which should mean that he would produce only if the benefit in steel exceeded the cost in fish. Often, for many reasons, such a tax is infeasible or introduces inefficiencies of its own. The regulator might instead undertake a study to determine what level of pollution would make sense and simply mandate that the factory emit no more or else might identify the best available filtration technology and require the factory to install it.

The quest for economic efficiency becomes more complicated, however, if we replace the fish-killing effluent with soot emitted from the factory's smokestack. Certainly there is still pollution. But what is its cognizable cost now? We no longer have $15 worth of rotting mackerel. Likely we have only an air quality monitor showing a fractionally higher concentration of particulate matter in the atmosphere. How do we assert that the market has failed and intervention is required?

To justify concern for the air on efficiency grounds, economists monetize it. That is, they assign a dollar value to air quality, which means in turn that reducing economic welfare for the sake of improving air quality can nevertheless qualify as "welfare enhancing." This requires the perilous move of calculating how much each incremental change in air quality is worth and then presuming that those figures offer an apples-to-apples comparison with actual dollars. Get it wrong, and the economic models stop working.

For instance, in his statement rejecting the EPA's ozone proposal in 2011, President Obama promised that his EPA's other "historic steps" under the Clean Air Act would still "save tens of thousands of lives each year" and "produce hundreds of billions of dollars in benefits for the American people." Those figures do not mean what the average constituent would assume. The claim of lives saved does not represent actual lives actually saved. In fact, the EPA offers no evidence of the relevant pollutants at the relevant levels ever causing a single death. Instead, it relies on epidemiological studies showing that mortality rates tend to increase slightly (on the order of 1 percent to 2 percent in the case of ozone) on days when atmospheric pollution concentrations are significantly higher.[12] By reducing those concentrations, the suggestion goes, each person will face some minutely smaller chance of dying each day.

To determine the value of that risk reduction, the EPA then uses the *value of a statistical life*, calculated in large part from wage-risk studies that examine the wage premium given workers in high-risk occupations. For instance, as one Harvard University study sponsored by the EPA found, male blue-collar workers in higher-risk industries earned an additional $0.32 per hour.[13] This was nearly three times the equivalent premium for female blue-collar workers. Fatality rates vary by occupation and industry for white-collar workers as well, but there the researchers could find no wage premium for accepting higher risk. Statistical analysis nevertheless translated these findings into a "value" of between $8 million and $10 million per life, roughly the current figure used by the EPA.

When applied to specific regulations, the dollar values produced by such analysis lack the context necessary for commonsense evaluation. For instance, the EPA issued a 575-page "Regulatory Impact Analysis" to facilitate its choice of an ozone standard in the range of 60–70 ppb. For a 65-ppb standard, the analysis provided a low-end estimate of $6.4 billion in "monetized ozone-only benefit," based on a 0.05 percent reduction in mortality rates, avoiding 630 premature deaths annually.[14] It's hard to say whether such an estimate is reasonable.

It becomes easy, however, when the claims are viewed in aggregate. The Clean Air Act requires the EPA to report occasionally on the cumulative benefits of its regulations. With a nation of 300 million people whose lives are each worth $10 million, lowering everyone's risk of death by one one-hundredth of a percentage point is sufficient to claim "hundreds of billions of dollars in benefits." By 2010, the agency estimated that Americans were receiving roughly $4 trillion in annual benefits from the Act.[15] This would mean $33,000 per household, at a time when median household income was $54,000 per household.[16] And while income is distributed unevenly, households presumably benefit comparably from cleaner air—if anything, activists argue, lower-income households suffer more from pollution and have more to gain from its elimination. The bottom half of tax filers reported roughly $1 trillion in earned income for 2010;[17] the EPA claims to have given them environmental benefits worth nearly twice as much.

The vast majority of these benefits come from a single pollutant, called fine particulate matter—soot, essentially. The EPA values every marginal reduction of particulate matter so highly that even incidental reductions dominate the claimed benefits of rules purportedly targeting other pollutants. Thus, in the ozone rule, the $6.4 billion of claimed ozone benefit was dwarfed by a $12 billion claimed particulate-matter benefit—because, by virtue of tightening ozone standards, particulate-matter emissions were expected to decline as well.

More striking was the Obama administration's "Utility MACT" (maximum achievable control technology) rule, which mandated tight controls on mercury emissions from coal-fired power plants. The EPA predicted $37 billion to $90 billion in benefits, but only $4 million to $6 million (that's *million* with an *m*) of the projected benefits were to be achieved from the reduction of mercury and other hazardous pollutants.[18] The cleverly worded fact sheet released by the EPA highlighted the health benefits that its regulation would produce: "Until now there were no national limits on emissions of mercury and other air toxics from power plants. Uncontrolled releases of toxic air pollutants like mercury—a neurotoxin—can impair children's ability to learn."[19] Yet while it is true that uncontrolled releases of toxic air pollution can impair children's ability to learn, the anticipated improvement in children's average IQ as a result of the MACT rule was only 0.0021 points. The rest of the benefit came because the restrictions on mercury would be so tight that many coal-fired power plants would close, leading to particulate-matter reductions.

Each year, the White House's Office of Management and Budget reviews rule-making across the federal government and reports the total costs and benefits in dollar terms for major regulations issued during the prior ten years. EPA estimates for particulate-matter benefits are so high that they account for the majority of all benefits claimed by all agencies for all major federal regulations issued from 2000 to 2015.[20]

Yet America has so little particulate matter in the air that levels in only ten localities (with Fresno, California, the only city of significant size) exceed the Clean Air Act standard, already twice as strict as Europe's. Nationwide, the pollution level is on par with New Zealand's and Iceland's—dramatically below the levels in major developed economies like the United Kingdom, France, Germany, and Japan. London, Paris, Amsterdam, Frankfurt, and Munich would all be among the dirtiest cities in the United States; Brussels would be the dirtiest.[21]

Still, even with particulate-matter concentrations below the EPA's own threshold for safety, the agency continues to regard every further reduction as enormously valuable. Some argue that this should remain the case until pollution reaches zero. "The goal for policymakers worldwide should be to push down levels as far as possible," reported *Science*. "When all the research is in, [University of Southern California neuroscientist

Caleb] Finch says, 'I think [particulate matter] will turn out to be just the same as tobacco—there's no safe threshold.'"[22]

The point here is not that environmental quality is unimportant or should be ignored because it lacks a clear dollar value. To the contrary, this book's central argument is that policy makers need to attend more closely to nonmonetary outcomes if they want to make trade-offs that will lead society toward long-term prosperity. The problem arises when they focus on the wrong outcomes, or only a subset of outcomes, or assign to outcomes the wrong values.

Let's return once more to the steel factory. Weighing steel against fish seemed reasonable. Taking consideration of the air quality would too, if we could assign it a vaguely reasonable value. But in jumping from fish to air, we have crossed the Rubicon from achieving efficient outcomes within the market to pursuing nonmarket goods. Yes, we can assign a market value to air quality, but why stop there? How about the light pollution from the steel plant's night shift operation (an issue Administrator McCarthy declared to be in the EPA's portfolio[23])? Conversely, what about the nonmarket benefits of steel production? Surely the hundreds of stable, well-paying jobs with benefits for blue-collar workers have substantial value to the community. Once we unmoor the definition of economic welfare, it becomes dependent on subjective determinations of whose concerns count and what they are worth.

*   *   *

Regulatory agencies are supposed to use "cost–benefit analysis" to ensure they make their calculations well. The emphasis on these analyses began as a conservative response to unchecked regulatory excesses, though from the modern vantage point, it is hard to imagine a time when evaluating the costs and benefits of a regulation was novel. President Reagan's Executive Order 12291 initiated what (then Professor, now Justice) Elena Kagan described in the *Harvard Law Review* as "a sea change" in the administrative state,[24] requiring major rules to undergo a "regulatory impact analysis," including a cost–benefit analysis, and "determination of the potential net benefits of the rule."[25]

The approach of the National Transportation Safety Board (NTSB) in a conflict with the Federal Aviation Administration (FAA) illustrates the destructively foolish mind-set the order aimed to counteract and the valuable role a cost–benefit analysis can play. As many parents know, a child under two years old can fly without purchasing a ticket by sitting on an adult's lap. But in 1994, a DC-9 crashed while attempting to land in Charlotte, North Carolina. Thirty-seven of fifty-seven people onboard were killed, including a nine-month-old infant held by her mother. The NTSB concluded that "if the child had been properly restrained in a child restraint system, she might not have sustained fatal injuries," and thus issued a formal safety recommendation requiring that small children have their own seats and appropriate restraint systems.[26]

In response, the FAA used the number of annual aviation accidents with survivors and the share of passengers under the age of two to estimate that the proposed regulation could save no more than five infant lives per decade. With more than 6 million such infants flying each year, and assuming a ticket price of $200 per person, the cost per life saved would exceed $2 billion. Furthermore, as the FAA noted, requiring families to pay the additional cost of plane tickets for their infants would lead some to drive in situations where they otherwise would have flown, and deaths resulting from "diversions" to far more dangerous highways would cause many more infant deaths than the new rule could prevent.[27] Amazingly, the interagency battle continued for twelve years before the NTSB, without changing its opinion, "reluctantly concluded that it cannot convince the FAA to take the action recommended" and closed the matter.[28]

It is not hard to see why a president might find it necessary to order that his agencies adopt an analytical framework, apply common sense, and report upward on their decision-making processes. Cost–benefit analysis has successfully increased transparency within the bureaucracy, placed checks on the worst proposals, and forced consideration of unintended consequences and less costly alternatives. As a management tool within the executive branch, it is critical.

But the good intentions of rational governance have proved no match for the boundless ambition of determined regulators. An entire regulatory–industrial complex has sprung forth from the bureaucracies, academic institutions, and private-sector consulting firms to construct analyses that will validate whatever regulation might be proposed. The EPA not only has a dedicated team of in-house environmental economists but also utilizes external consultants for the vast majority of its largest analyses and relies heavily on hundreds of third-party research papers, of which it is often the primary sponsor. Those consultants will tend to buttress the conclusions the EPA prefers. The leading topic of economics research the EPA funds is how to assign monetary values to the environmental benefits that it claims to achieve.[29] Cost–benefit analyses have taken on the character of show trials.

Standard practice demands that analysts employ any means necessary to monetize benefits but that no such respect be afforded costs. "We start by considering how economists think about the costs and benefits of environmental protection, and how those might be measured," write Nathaniel Keohane and Sheila Olmstead in *Markets and the Environment*, the basic text of the Harvard Kennedy School's course in environmental economics. "While costs are relatively straightforward, benefits require considerable thought."[30] The ozone analysis, for instance, identified between \$19 billion and \$38 billion in annual benefits for a 65-ppb standard, as compared with \$15 billion in annual costs. But the comparison is apples to oranges. The EPA cast its benefit net widely, counting whatever public health gains it could infer from past epidemiological studies and finding two-thirds of its total not from ozone reductions but rather from the "co-benefits" of incidental reductions in particulate matter. It even counts avoidance of missed workdays for mothers staying home to care for asthmatic children, valuing each day at \$98.[31]

The cost side of the ledger, meanwhile, includes only the actual dollars that companies will spend to comply with the regulation—the cost of purchasing, installing, and operating the new pollution-control technologies. Even then, because existing technology will not be sufficient to meet the EPA's new standard, EPA analysts simply assume that better pollution controls will be developed in the future at reasonable (and declining) costs. So one-third of the cost estimate is tied to existing technologies that companies could actually purchase, and the other two-thirds comes from a hope that a better but still-affordable technology will come.[32] Are not costs deserving of "considerable thought" as well?

Thanks to the past forty years of environmental regulation, an extensive literature now documents its economic effects. For instance, a 2000 study in the *Journal of Political Economy* found that counties in nonattainment with Clean Air Act standards (as many more would be under the EPA's new ozone rule) saw the construction of new plants in polluting industries decline by 26 percent to 45 percent.[33] A study published two years later in the same journal found that, between 1972 and 1987, such counties lost more than five hundred thousand jobs and $150 billion in economic output (2016 dollars).[34] More broadly, a 2013 study in the *Quarterly Journal of Economics* found that, after the passage of the 1990 Clean Air Act Amendments, "the average worker in a regulated sector experienced a total earnings loss equivalent to 20 percent of their pre-regulatory earnings."[35]

More generally, the same industrial activities that produce negative environmental externalities also provide employment, wages, and tax payments, offering a variety of social and public health benefits to families and communities. In *Consequences of Long-Term Unemployment*, the Urban Institute provides a helpful literature review of the many findings on how unemployment leads to "declining human and social capital," "impacts on future labor market attachment," "impacts on physical and mental health," "impacts on children and families," and "impacts on communities."[36] Where, for instance, do deaths of despair fit into the calculus? Anne Case and Angus Deaton of Princeton University first reported that increased substance abuse, liver disease, and suicide among non-Hispanic whites aged forty-five to fifty-four had led to the equivalent of nearly five hundred thousand extra deaths between 1999 and 2013, affecting most dramatically those with a high school education or less.[37] They suggested that economic insecurity may be a driver, specifically "*cumulative disadvantage* from one birth cohort to the next—in the labor market, in marriage and child outcomes, and in health—[] triggered by progressively worsening labor market opportunities at the time of entry."[38] Indeed, it would be surprising if declining economic fortunes for blue-collar workers did not produce an uptick in such maladies, just as surely as an increase in pollution from industrial facilities might lead to an increase in other health problems.

Beyond the human effects within affected industries, policy makers committed to giving benefits and costs equal attention could also examine the macroeconomic implications of increased regulation. The Mercatus Center, for instance, has launched RegData, a comprehensive database quantifying industry-specific federal regulations.[39] The regulatory equivalent of studies measuring concentrations of pollution in the atmosphere, RegData allows analysts to identify relationships between regulation and outcomes like economic growth and productivity. One early study found that from 1997 to 2010, the least-regulated industries experienced productivity growth at twice the rate of the most-regulated industries.[40]

Even if policy analysts could develop usable values across all these variables, the trade-off would remain exceedingly situation specific. A struggling community with clean air and large numbers of unemployed blue-collar workers may want to accept additional pollution as the price of new factories opening near town, while a booming metropolis with a smog problem may view the marginal cost of further pollution as exceeding the marginal benefit of an additional job. A coastal enclave of educated elites may care mostly about increased traffic and an influx of new workers and thus have no interest in any new construction regardless of either job creation or pollution.

Such NIMBYism raises the further question of whose costs and benefits should count and whether distributional impacts matter. If the coastal enclave's relevant population expands to include outlying working-class communities, its analysis would change. When the costs and benefits act at different scales, managing the balance of equities becomes more difficult still. In some situations, the air pollution might spread downwind while jobs remain local, but in others, there may be regional economic benefits while only the facility's immediate neighborhood suffers the stench. Even within a given location, concentrated costs may fall on labor and capital within an industry, and on its customers through higher prices, while diffuse benefits will accrue to much broader groups.

Proper evaluation of costs and benefits thus turns the concept of "environmental justice" on its head. Social justice activists argue that low-income and minority communities suffer disproportionately from pollution, therefore aggressive regulation advances a redistributive agenda. But the cost of constraining industrial activity lands far more disproportionately on blue-collar workers than does any benefit. They are the ones asked to "pay" the most for environmental gains that high-income households value at least as highly.

Sure enough, as *Politico* reported shortly before the Obama administration finalized its ozone recommendation in 2015, "President Barack Obama's aggressive environmental agenda is running into a surprising source of opposition: Black elected leaders." Steve Benjamin, mayor of Columbia, South Carolina, and president of the African American Mayors Association (AAMA), had written a letter to the president explaining that "mayors, county officials and governors still face the challenge of curtailing ozone while expanding the industrial production, construction, and infrastructure projects that create jobs and grow our tax base." Alongside the AAMA, the U.S. Conference of Mayors, the National League of Cities, the National Association of Counties, and the National Association of Regional Councils all asked Obama to postpone any tightening of the standard.[41] Perhaps they had not read the EPA's report.

Cost–benefit analysis will get us only so far. Faced with so many challenges, the eager bureaucrat may leap into quantifying all of them. If a rule will have numerous consequences, economists can monetize them all. If circumstances vary, calculations can be made for each place and time. Tables showing the impact by income level, age, race, and gender can be populated.

Such an exercise is ludicrous on its face, because each individual quantification will be wrong and because unintended consequences will be ignored. The government mandates that children remain in bulkier car seats for more years, then discovers with dismay that families purchase larger and less fuel-efficient cars, then mandates that automakers improve fuel efficiency and promises that this will save those families money as gas prices rise, then provides large subsidies for the purchase of electric vehicles that are too small for those families and out of their price range—then watches gas prices plummet, then celebrates that gas prices are low while lamenting that they are not higher.

The good news is that such a comprehensive analysis of all relevant externalities is unnecessary, because the exercise can be approximated by asking a much simpler question: should we be improving environmental quality at the expense of economic opportunity right now, or should we be doing the reverse? This is a colloquial way of asking whether, under current conditions, the net externalities of another steel plant are negative or positive. Scientists and economists can provide data to inform this inquiry. But the trade-off is a fundamentally political one.

One can think back to the mid-1990s, under the Clinton administration, when annual emissions of air pollutants targeted by the Clean Air Act were twice what they are today. Ozone concentrations in the air were 25 percent higher.[42] That period is rightly remembered for its rising wages. It is rarely cited as a time of unacceptable environmental degradation. Conversely, the widespread enthusiasm that accompanies the announcement of a new plant's construction and the dismay that accompanies notice of an impending closure suggest that current levels of environmental regulation are out of balance with society's needs. The breathtaking array of tax breaks and subsidies that state and local governments throw at manufacturers to attract investment suggests the presence of large, positive externalities. Unfortunately, these are not determinations that the law allows or that the regulatory process will contemplate.

* * *

America remains beholden to the decisions it made in 1970, a watershed in the history of the nation's environmental policy. While the American economy was enjoying the fruits of a remarkable twenty-five-year run of growth and technological innovation, the public's concern over pollution was cresting. The prior year had seen a massive oil spill off the coast of Santa Barbara and the infamous Cuyahoga River fire in Cleveland. The first Earth Day was celebrated, the EPA was created, and, on the last day of the year, President Nixon signed the modern Clean Air Act into law.

To achieve rapid improvements without too much disruption, the Act introduced something called *new source review*. Existing pollution sources would be left alone or held to lower standards, but any new facility was expected to curtail pollution significantly. If building in a nonattainment zone, new facilities would have to install the best possible pollution controls, while also finding other facilities in the region that would make offsetting pollution reductions to compensate for any new emissions. Even if building in a region that already met all air quality standards, a new facility had to install state-of-the-art pollution controls, a requirement more stringent than what preexisting facilities had to meet. Significantly, major modifications to existing sources would cause them to be treated as "new" ones. Thus, as new facilities get built and old ones are renovated, all would be constantly required to use better controls than before.

Since then, at the behest of environmentalists, the EPA has repeatedly redefined what constitutes clean air by expanding the list of regulated pollutants and by lowering the thresholds that regions may not exceed. A region nearing a threshold one day can find it further out of reach the next; regions in attainment can be thrown out despite no change in their air quality.

If the goal is to improve environmental quality rapidly and regardless of cost—as it was at the time of passage—the Act's structure is understandable. And to that end, it has been quite effective. Between 1980 and 2016, lead levels in the air fell 99 percent, carbon monoxide fell 85 percent, sulfur dioxide fell 87 percent, nitrogen dioxide fell 61 percent, and ozone fell 31 percent.[43] These are significant achievements, and environmentalists are justifiably proud of the enormous public health benefits that have followed.

But no matter how clean the air gets, the rules demand ever more. Consider a hypothetical manufacturing plant that seeks to double in size. The expansion would represent a major modification and therefore lead to a review of the entire facility as "new." If the plant is located in an area already meeting air quality standards, it must now install pollution controls where before none were required—in both the "new" part of the facility and the old part. If it is located in a NAZ, it must install the best possible pollution controls and pay to offset its pollution. The plant's owners had wanted to create more jobs on the same basis as existing jobs, but they cannot. An investment that once looked attractive might not go forward at all.

The discrimination against new facilities amplifies other economic costs as well, and, over time, it has even interfered with environmental goals. Large businesses benefit from barriers to entry that keep newer and smaller firms out, giving them an incentive to advocate regulation that hurts them but hurts potential competitors more. Older, dirtier facilities continue to operate as they have rather than investing in upgrades that might improve their productivity while reducing their environmental impact. In some cases, shutting out new construction has led to pollution levels that are higher than they would have been if there had been no regulation at all. "This approach," writes Robert Stavins, director of Harvard University's environmental economics program, "has been both excessively costly and environmentally counterproductive."[44]

* * *

Although the EPA earns well-deserved criticism for its implementation, it is merely the messenger of a long-ago Congress's broader choices. The ever-tightening ratchet is exactly what the Act—duly passed by overwhelming bipartisan majorities in 1970 and further strengthened by overwhelming bipartisan majorities in 1990—calls for. Showing disregard for massive costs is exactly how the U.S. Supreme Court, in a unanimous opinion authored in 2001 by none other than conservative justice Antonin Scalia, has held that the Act requires the EPA to proceed.[45]

The Clean Air Act explains in its introduction that "growth in the amount and complexity of air pollution brought about by urbanization, industrial development, and the increasing use of motor vehicles has resulted in mounting dangers to the public health and welfare." That statement is out of date, and legislation premised on it strikes the wrong balance between environmental and economic concerns. But a federal statute is not a pendulum that will swing back of its own accord; it requires substantive reform. A new balance, appropriate to America's current challenges, would secure the widespread gains in environmental quality to date while prioritizing industrial expansion over further environmental improvement. It would accept the additional pollution that naturally follows from the increased output that both political parties say is their explicit policy objective.

The key reform to shift the Act's fulcrum and strike a new balance would be to eliminate new source review, ending the discriminatory treatment of new facilities. Removing heightened new source requirements would allow industrial and energy-producing facilities to expand and would also allow new facilities to be built under the same rules that older plants must follow. The EPA would continue to set air quality targets as it saw fit, but progress toward those targets would proceed more slowly. If that hypothetical factory wanted to double its size, it would be able to do so. If another firm wanted to build a competing factory with similar technology, it also would be able to do that. States would retain the authority they have today to impose tighter regulations if their circumstances or policy preferences warranted such a course.

This reform would be the economic equivalent of removing a dam. The current discrimination against new investments holds back a reservoir of capital that would surge forward were it not for the costs and restrictions now imposed. American industry sits downstream, happy to expand employment but restricted in its ability to do so. Under current law, an action like tightening the ozone standard raises the dam wall that much higher.

Eliminate the impositions on new investments and, as quickly as analysts could revise their models, a host of construction projects previously considered infeasible would become attractive. Upgrades to existing plants, shelved for fear of triggering new requirements for the plant, would go back on the drawing board. New plants, rejected because they could not operate profitably, would suddenly find willing investors. Entirely new businesses, deemed unlikely to succeed while established businesses enjoyed a sizable cost advantage, would begin hiring. Competition would increase, economic efficiency would improve, and prices would fall. New areas of the country would open up for energy exploration. And manufacturers would find themselves better positioned against international competition.

Because the policy change would remove obstacles instead of creating a new program, it would entail none of the drawbacks commonly associated with a fiscal or monetary stimulus. There would be no cost to the government and no asset bubbles created by easy money or over-investment in government-chosen sectors. No government bureaucracies would be empowered, and no markets would be distorted; to the contrary, regulations and market distortions would be removed.

The effects on air quality would follow directly from the objectives of the reform. There would be no change from the existing facilities that are the vast majority of pollution sources. New and modified facilities would not operate free of all regulation; they would simply be subject to the standards that now apply to existing facilities. Thus, although one would expect improvements in air quality to slow, overall quality could degrade only as the result of a much-needed expansion in output. Meanwhile, the competitive pressure to cut costs through improved energy efficiency would continue to usher in technological improvements that tend to reduce pollution.

Perhaps as a final touch, the introduction to the Clean Air Act could be amended to note that in recent decades, America has seen not "growth in the amount and complexity of air pollution" but significant declines instead; that it does not face "mounting dangers to the public health and welfare" but rather celebrates great improvements; and that to further the welfare of the nation, the Act will now focus on ensuring the continued use of existing pollution controls while encouraging economic development.

*   *   *

This chapter has focused on the Clean Air Act, the most prominent, aggressive, and costly of the nation's environmental laws. But the same corrosive logic of selective externalities provides the core rationale for other environmental laws as well, necessitating further reform. For instance, the National Environmental Policy Act (NEPA), signed by President Nixon on the first day of 1970, is infamous for imposing red tape on energy and infrastructure projects. The law requires the federal government to conduct a review before taking an action that will significantly affect the environment. For major projects requiring a federal permit, this means an Environmental Impact Statement (EIS), which can run thousands of pages and take years to complete—the typical EIS process runs nearly five years,[46] and delays that further lengthen the process are common.[47] Rather than concluding the matter, a completed EIS then provides an invitation for environmental groups to launch lawsuits over the quality of the EIS, occupying years more, even if no legal basis exists for objecting to the project itself.

The extent of these obstacles became obvious during implementation of the 2009 American Recovery and Reinvestment Act (known colloquially as the "stimulus"), for which Congress appropriated $800 billion with the goal of rapidly boosting employment and—purportedly—upgrading American infrastructure in the process.[48] But despite President-Elect Obama's insistence just before taking office that "we've got shovel-ready projects all across the country that governors and mayors are pleading to fund,"[49] within a couple of years, he acknowledged that "there's no such thing as shovel-ready projects"[50] and began granting waivers from NEPA's requirements to get stimulus dollars flowing.[51] As with postponement of the ozone standard, when the rubber of political survival met the road of environmental law's conflict with the industrial economy, even a historically progressive administration had to acknowledge the trade-off and concede that current law gets it wrong.

NEPA should be replaced. Countries like Canada and Germany have streamlined review processes that guarantee short, fixed timelines for review and preclude further litigation once a decision has been made.[52] Done right, such an approach could make major industrial investments far more attractive without sacrificing environmental quality. Even if the change entails some increase in environmental risk, that is a trade-off worth making.

A range of policies likewise constrains development of the nation's natural resources on behalf of environmental interests. The federal government holds lands and offshore areas off-limits and, combined with a tangle of state-level restrictions and activist lawsuits, stalls the construction of necessary pipelines. Since 2010, the use of hydraulic-fracturing technology in horizontally drilled wells ("fracking") has triggered an unprecedented boom in American oil and gas production. Yet that boom occurred almost exclusively on private land, while the federal government was aggressively slashing access to areas under its control and production in such areas was declining.[53]

Perhaps all the attractive new opportunities were coincidentally situated outside of federal control, but it's fair to ask, what if they weren't? Would the fracking boom ever have begun if it had required federal leases and permits, if the same litigation and protest tactics applied to high-profile, federally controlled energy projects like the Keystone XL and Dakota Access pipelines had targeted nascent efforts at expanding production? Certainly the decision of several states to ban fracking entirely is not an encouraging sign.

A counterfactual like this is worth consideration because it underscores the degree to which regulation's costs can exceed official estimates. If the EPA had evaluated the cost of prohibitively expensive fracking regulations prior to the boom, they would have been measured in terms of the immediate compliance costs for the small number of early drilling efforts. The impact of shutting down such efforts might have numbered in the hundreds of jobs. There would be no way to know in advance that, if investment proceeded, this was the opportunity that would create hundreds of thousands of jobs, lower energy prices by half, and spur a manufacturing renaissance in energy-intensive industries. Likewise, surveying the scene in those areas where environmental regulation has taken its heaviest toll, the specific projects canceled or scaled back or never started tell only a fraction of the story of the opportunity squandered.

Beyond specific statutory reforms, in other words, we need to change the mind-set underlying regulation. Cost–benefit analysis would be more useful, for instance, if agencies at least tried to represent regulation's trade-offs in full. "A core set of economic assumptions should be used in calculating benefits and costs," wrote Nobel laureate Kenneth Arrow and ten other economists in *Science* in 1996. "Key variables include the social discount rate, the value of reducing risks of premature death and accidents, and the values associated with other improvements in health."[54] But like those economists, agencies have neglected to include costs among their core assumptions. Just like the value of a statistical life used to monetize air quality, the federal government should establish the value of a statistical job, multipliers to translate compliance costs into reduced investment, and a direct relationship between the sheer volume of regulation and rates of investment and productivity growth. The inclusion of such estimates will not make cost–benefit analysis "work" in the sense of automating the difficult political process of making society's trade-offs; it will, though, force greater transparency within the rule-making process and some acknowledgment that trade-offs exist. There will be fewer outlandish claims that regulations create jobs or that they are delivering hundreds of billions of dollars of unmitigated benefits.

The government should also have a regulatory budget.[55] This is a fairly arcane, technical concept within regulatory-law circles, but it derives from a broader intuition that every citizen should care about. Think about the money that government actually spends in its budget each year. We don't tolerate taxing and spending without constraint, on the rationale that we are all better off wherever a congressman claims that the benefit of spending on his pet project exceeds the cost. That would be a recipe for an unsustainable explosion in the size of government. Some very good proposals may go unfunded, but everyone recognizes the need for a limit.

Why, then, should regulation be any different? Rules impose burdens on the private sector as surely as taxes do. Inviting rules without limit, anywhere a regulator can assert that benefits exceed costs, is a recipe for a comparably unsustainable explosion in regulatory costs. Each individual rule, just like each individual government program, may seem entirely justified. But at some point, for society and the private sector to function, we have to say, stop. Forcing regulators to hold total costs within some limit, and thus to prioritize among rules, would encourage a focus on those rules that would deliver the most benefit for a given cost.

And then Congress needs to involve itself. In the federal government's current model, Congress passes broad laws like the Clean Air Act with open-ended authority, which agencies like the EPA are then supposed to interpret and implement. But once the law is passed, Congress washes its hands of the question and future, fundamentally political decisions about the aggressiveness of regulation are treated as technical issues for the agency to resolve. When Congress responds to popular demand for increased regulation, it appropriately defers to bureaucratic expertise and the efficiency of the rule-making process in designing specific rules. But it should make that delegation "single serve." The agency gets to issue rules in response to the specific law, but it should await future legislation before tightening those rules or issuing new ones. A law on the books should not empower regulators to pursue new avenues of regulation decades in the future.

For instance, the Clean Air Act as passed in 1970 reflected a clear choice to increase environmental regulation at the expense of economic growth. Its amendments as passed in 1990 reflected a clear choice to strengthen regulation in certain areas. That the EPA had authority over the specifics in each instance was entirely proper. By contrast, the EPA's efforts to tighten ozone standards or address climate change in the 2010s bear no relationship to a public desire for greater regulation. The EPA is then acting on the basis of its claimed expertise in measuring externalities and cost–benefit trade-offs, whereas Congress's enthusiasm or lack thereof is a far better indicator of whether the time is right for action.

Policy makers treat regulation like a game of darts, in which they can maximize welfare by hitting some hypothetical bull's-eye. This leads them to deny the existence of trade-offs, claiming instead that they can achieve their regulatory goals while simultaneously improving market outcomes. But there is no bull's-eye in the real world, and even if there were, the regulators would not hit it anyway.

A better model for regulation is a dial. There is no discoverable, perfect setting—but policy makers can turn one direction to tighten or the other to loosen in response to society's conditions. In the 1970s, policy makers turned the dial hard to one side and have held it there ever since. If they would look outside, they would see it is long past time to turn it the other way.

CHAPTER 6

HOW THE OTHER HALF LEARNS

Aligning the work that the American economy wants done with the work that Americans can do is best approached from both sides. We have just seen how regulatory policy can influence the forms of investment employers pursue and thus the types of labor they will demand. Equally, education policy can influence prospective workers' readiness for the workforce and their productivity once in it. Doing this well is triply important: it helps to ensure that workers and employers will find mutually beneficial relationships; it increases the wages that workers can command; and if it helps to make employers successful, it can lead to demand for yet more work. The quality and reliability of a local workforce are themselves factors for employers when they decide where to set up shop.

Taking this approach too far, however, is at once hard to resist and liable to backfire. After all, emphasis on "skills" can seem like the perfect remedy to what ails the American worker. If prospective workers can learn the skills to thrive in a rapidly evolving labor market, policy makers can pursue overall economic growth without worrying unduly about the limitations of people. With higher-value skills translating to higher wages, the fruits of growth would automatically become widely shared. Plans to boost the fortunes of workers falling behind, therefore, typically start and end with transforming the workers into types who today get ahead.

The problem is that this approach does not really work. As the nation's labor market began its transformation in the 1960s and 1970s into one that favored college graduates, the education system shifted toward one designed to produce such graduates. High schools abandoned entirely, for instance, the "tracking" of less academically talented students toward vocational training. "College for all" became the goal. Spending per student in the K–12 years surged, while numerous subsidies sought to guarantee the affordability of higher education. Yet by 2016, fewer than half of young Americans were successfully completing community college, let alone earning a bachelor's degree.[1]

The result is the worst of all worlds. Policy makers ignore the importance of a healthy labor market for workers lacking postsecondary education by instead claiming universal college completion as a plausible goal—even though it has proven *implausible* for *most* Americans. In pursuit of that end, they direct the education system away from the pathways that most people will ultimately travel. The types of schooling that would most benefit the people confronting the most challenges wind up abandoned in favor of more investment in pathways for those least in need of assistance.

Consider a single cohort of American students, who, having marched single file through years of education, climb onstage at their senior year's end to receive high school diplomas. Their experiences to that point will have been remarkably similar for so diverse a group of 3.5 million minds; the objective of college enrollment will be almost universal. Yet, after shaking hands with the principal, their paths will diverge sharply—as if separate staircases lead down the stage's other side.

Roughly speaking, one-fifth of all students were already off-track and did not join their classmates crossing the stage. Another fifth will move from their senior year to something besides further schooling. The third fifth will enroll in college but fail to complete it. Yet another fifth will complete some form of college but land in jobs that don't require the degrees they just earned. Despite decades of reform in teacher training, student testing, and standards, as well as school choice and hundreds of billions of dollars in new annual education spending, only a final fifth will successfully navigate the path—high school to college to career—that is our education system's ideal.[2]

An alternative to the current approach would be to accept instead that students' roads to the future will inevitably diverge and to help each excel on her trajectory. This requires the reintroduction of tracking, a term with various definitions in education-reform circles but used here to denote the separation of high school students into educational programs that seek different outcomes. One could lead toward college enrollment, another toward occupational training that leaves a twenty-year-old with serious work experience, a marketable skill, and $30,000 in a savings account.

The obstacle to this alternative is philosophical, not practical. Compared with the futility of our efforts to boost academic achievement, helping students translate their demonstrated aptitudes into gainful employment is a far more achievable course. It is already the model employed in virtually every other developed country. But it would require Americans to change their conception of what schools can accomplish and to relinquish some cherished egalitarian ideals that do more harm than good.

Politicians have shown zero interest in moving in this direction. Mentions of "apprenticeships" and "vocational training" sprinkle their talking points and budget proposals, true, but few seem to have contemplated the implications of elevating such programs beyond their second-class status. We need to acknowledge that college is not just "not for everyone" but in fact not for most, that those who are not college-bound deserve to begin their preparation as early as those who are, and that our education policy and allocation of resources should prioritize those headed down the rockiest paths instead of those already holding a golden ticket.

* * *

Perhaps the best way to understand our misplaced zeal for college is to consider what blogger Mickey Kaus calls "the most important chart around when it comes to explaining contemporary politics."[3] The chart shows the average hourly wages of Americans based on educational attainment, with separate lines tracing the progress since 1970 for each level, from less than high school to advanced degree.

Higher levels of education have always corresponded to higher wages, but whereas the lines moved in parallel through the 1970s, they veer apart after 1980. Wages of college graduates rose over the past generation, while those of high school graduates did not—depending on the inflation adjustment one uses, they have remained flat or have fallen by 15 percent. In 1979, median weekly earnings for those with at least a bachelor's degree were 38 percent higher than for those with only a high school diploma; by 2007, the premium had doubled to 77 percent. Advanced degree holders did better still, high school dropouts worst of all.[4]

The diverging lines invite two very different interpretations. In one, the lines depict educational experiences, which cause different outcomes: attending and graduating from college leads to higher earnings. In the other, the lines reflect preexisting characteristics that correlate with different outcomes: whatever academic talent and other endowments make one a college graduate also tend to make one a high earner. These two interpretations suggest very different policy responses. If the first is correct, the education system should indeed try to get everyone into college—moving people from lower lines to higher ones. But if the second is closer to the truth, the system should focus on maximizing the fortunes of those headed toward each outcome—and especially on shifting the lower lines upward.

Americans of all political stripes naturally gravitate toward the first, more egalitarian interpretation. We want to believe that anyone given the opportunity to pursue a college education can gain the prosperity that blesses college graduates. And so we expect that an education policy that aims squarely at smoothing every student's path to college will be to the benefit of all.

Unfortunately, experience has not borne this out. Most high school seniors are unprepared to succeed in a college environment, and the K–12 system has shown limited capacity to change this. Even as per-pupil spending has doubled since the 1970s,[5] average National Assessment of Educational Progress scores for seventeen-year-olds in both reading and math have remained flat.[6] In states where almost all high school seniors take the SAT, only about one-third achieve scores that would indicate a likelihood of maintaining a B minus average at a four-year college.[7] Nationwide, SAT scores have fallen, suggesting that for those who do plan to pursue college, the average level of preparedness is actually declining.[8]

For many years, these disappointing results were reflected as well in flat to declining high school graduation rates. The share of public school students earning a diploma within four years of beginning the ninth grade fell from 79 percent in 1970 to a low of 71 percent in 1996, before recovering to 75 percent in the mid-2000s—barely treading water after almost forty years of reform and investment.[9] The Obama White House trumpeted unprecedented progress on this metric, achieving a rate of 83 percent by 2016,[10] but those gains increasingly appear to have been a mirage—caused not by improved performance but rather by declining standards and outright fraud.

Numerous states, it turns out, watered down or eliminated their testing requirements.[11] California claimed to achieve the nation's most impressive gains—a stunning fourteen-point improvement from 69.2 percent in 2006 to 83.6 percent in 2013[12]—but a 2018 report by the U.S. Department of Education concluded that the state's measurements "did not provide reasonable assurance that reported graduate rates were accurate and complete." An in-depth audit of the classifications for forty-five students in the Los Angeles Unified School District found that more than 10 percent had been mischaracterized as graduates.[13]

In the nation's capital, the *Washington Post* headlined with a straight face that the "Entire Senior Class at D.C.'s Ballou High School Applies to College," even though the school's graduation rate the prior year had been only 57 percent and fewer than 5 percent of its students had passed the citywide standardized exams.[14] A National Public Radio investigation discovered that half the graduates missed at least three months of senior-year classes and that teachers had faced overwhelming pressure to pass failing students. More than one-quarter of the teaching staff quit during the year.[15]

How could so many reforms and so much money have accomplished so little? Because, as far as we can tell, school quality may not be the big factor in academic achievement that many people believe it is. In 1966, the Coleman Report, which was called for by the Civil Rights Act, concluded that, when socioeconomic factors are controlled for, "differences between schools account for only a small fraction of differences in pupil achievement."[16] Revisiting the question fifty years later, Johns Hopkins researchers found that "expenditures and related school inputs have very weak associations not only with test scores in the sophomore and senior years of high school but also with high school graduation and subsequent college entry." As they concluded, the results "are mostly in line with the whispered result that has become the apocryphal characterization of [the Coleman Report]: 'It's all family.'"[17]

This might overstate the case—certainly there is evidence that good schools and good teachers can lift achievement. But such results often come with the caveat that we do not know how to replicate them. For instance, while some charter schools serving disadvantaged students have had notable success, Bruno V. Manno and Chester E. Finn Jr. highlighted in *National Affairs* the "painful tradeoff states face between charter-school quality and quantity."[18] Likewise, at *EducationNext*, Jay Greene described a "general disconnect between test scores and later life outcomes."[19] Better test scores, that is, do not necessarily extend to higher graduation rates or college enrollment, let alone college completion. We should keep striving to improve our K–12 schools, of course, but we should not be under the illusion that, for example, higher spending will yield higher achievement or expect nationwide college preparedness to jump anytime soon.

The experience of college enrollees further confirms what the high school data predict. Only 40 percent of enrollees at four-year colleges graduate from their first school on schedule; only 30 percent at two-year schools graduate in even three years. Those figures are closer to one-half if transfers and delayed graduations are included, but reliance on such circuitous routes does not indicate a system functioning well.[20] While discussion of Ballou High School focuses generally on its implications for high school graduation, perhaps the fraud's most distressing dimension is that 100 percent of seniors not only earned diplomas and applied to colleges but also that 100 percent were *accepted* to colleges. The story is not one of a single high school run amok, in other words, but of a high school–to–college pipeline disconnected from reality. Policy makers continue to emphasize college attendance, but when enrollment bears no relationship to qualifications or completion, the result is often wasted years and burdensome debt.

A 2017 report from the Brookings Institution put it bluntly: "Although college attendance rates have risen steadily in the United States for the past two decades, bachelor's degree attainment has not improved at all." The percentage of twenty-five-year-old Americans with at least a bachelor's degree was lower in 2015 than it was in 1995.[21] The story looks slightly better if including degree attainment among twenty-five- to twenty-nine-year-olds, but a divergence between the sexes also comes into play. While women have made substantial progress, this owes at least in part to changing social norms rather than the education system's effectiveness.[22] For men, "college completion reached 27 percent in 1976 and 1977, but subsequently fell, and did not rise above 27 percent again until 2011," reports the U.S. Census Bureau.[23] As of 2016, it remained below one-third.

If it seems that America's colleges and universities are poorly suited to the average American eighteen-year-old, perhaps that's because they were never designed to serve him. We think of the post–World War II GI Bill boom as having opened college to the masses, but even at its 1949 peak, only 20 percent of men between the ages of eighteen and twenty-four were enrolled in higher education.[24] It would be an extraordinary coincidence if a program designed decades, if not centuries, ago for the edification of the wealthy and the training of a narrow segment of the population also happened to meet the needs of a typical 2010s workforce entrant.

The disconnect is on stark display in the massive gap between these institutions' self-perceptions and the demands of the public. In Gallup's 2017 survey of more than seven hundred college and university presidents, only 1 percent strongly agreed with the statement that "most Americans have an accurate view of the purpose of higher education"; overall, they were four times more likely to disagree than agree.[25] College presidents believe their goal is to help students "become educated citizens, be exposed to new points of view, to become lifelong learners," said Terry Hartle, senior vice president at the American Council on Education, to *Inside Higher Ed*. As for the general public, "often all they care about is jobs."[26]

Indeed, a 2015 survey by the think tank New America found that the top three "reasons to go to college" for prospective students were "to improve my employment opportunities" (91 percent), "to make more money" (90 percent), and "to get a good job" (89 percent).[27] Unfortunately, college presidents have been successful so far in resisting such bourgeois priorities: a separate Gallup survey found that only one-third of Americans believe that college graduates are well prepared for success in the workforce[28]—and that's if you are fortunate enough to graduate.

*　*　*

If our education system has not shown the ability to move a significant share of the population into the ranks of college graduates, we must give more credence to the second interpretation of the income–by–education level chart. Most Americans' educational trajectories appear to develop independently of their school experiences, which places the onus on our schools to meet students where they are and help them prepare for success with the academic outcomes toward which they are headed.

Such a conclusion can become emotionally charged if read as a negative judgment of those on the lower lines. But it needn't be read that way. The factors that influence an individual's trajectory might be any combination of innate and environmental. Blame society if that helps. For education policy, what matters is that we have not found the school-based tools that will consistently reshape trajectories. One can argue for early-childhood interventions or for antipoverty programs—but while our schools await success on those fronts, we need a different plan of attack.

The critical component in this shift should be tracking: offering dramatically different programs of secondary education depending on whether the student will proceed next to college or directly to a career. This model, again, is standard elsewhere in the developed world but roundly rejected in America. For instance, a chart by the Organisation for Economic Co-operation and Development (OECD) shows that most developed countries have between 40 percent and 70 percent of their secondary school students in vocational and technical programs but excludes the United States entirely. A footnote explains that the omission is because of "the rather different approach to vocational education and training in U.S. high schools."[29]

Americans have long resisted tracking. In 1892, Harvard University president Charles W. Eliot exclaimed, "I refuse to believe that the American public intends to have its children sorted before their teens into clerks, watchmakers, lithographers,…and so forth, and treated differently in their schools according to their prophecies of their appropriate life careers. Who are we to make these prophecies?"[30] When the nation pioneered universal secondary education in the early twentieth century, its "comprehensive high schools" emphasized a broad education in the liberal arts.[31] During the 1960s and 1970s, in keeping with so many other areas in which idealism trumped practicality at the expense of the purported beneficiaries, the notion of tracking was squelched entirely.[32]

This particular bout of American exceptionalism is a mistake. What sense does it make to treat the vast majority of high schoolers as if they were prospective college graduates when they are not, to pretend that the sudden divergence of outcomes after high school graduation did not in fact begin long before? Indeed, the best way to understand the American system is not as trackless but rather as committed to a single track tailored toward those most likely to succeed anyway.

One common objection to tracking is that a career track will be disproportionately populated by students from disadvantaged backgrounds. But this is a description of society and an implicit condemnation of the current system, not a plausible criticism of tracking. After all, students best suited to a career track are precisely those least well served by its absence and experiencing the worst outcomes today. A tracked system could offer them a better chance at economic success, increasing in turn the odds that their own kids land on the college track a generation later. It will speed social progress and improve countless lives along the way.

A tracked system also will unavoidably place some students on a career track who might have done well in college. But the career track is not a death sentence. It can lead in many cases to a more fulfilling (and even more remunerative) career than might the college track, especially for its most talented students. And individuals would have opportunities to shift tracks both during their education and much later; as the *New York Times* notes, "it is not uncommon to find executives in Europe who got their start in apprenticeships."[33] No public education system will serve every student well, but the share finding themselves mismatched will be far lower if programs at least try to meet the needs of the majority.

Society must choose between proceeding with a charade and acknowledging honestly the limitations it faces. Pretending against all evidence that every student should prepare for college sustains the fiction that government programs can compensate for various background disadvantages and thus deliver "equal opportunity," defined as equality of life chances. Pushing every student in that direction yields the occasional Horatio Alger story, which warms the heart and stands for the proposition that the same could happen to anyone, even though its rarity in fact underscores the opposite. The approach is most useful to those least affected by it, who benefit from innate and environmental advantages, who can flourish in college, and who can now justify a broad array of economic policies that further benefit themselves by claiming that everyone else can follow their path too. It is most harmful to those already disadvantaged, who must now navigate a system that has proven repeatedly its inability to meet their needs.

To make progress, society will need to embrace a less ambitious definition of opportunity. The goal should be to ensure that every person, no matter her starting circumstances, can find a vocation that allows her to support a family, live in a community where she can build a good life, and then give to her children even greater opportunity than she had herself. When we say that we want everyone's opportunity to be "equal," we should abandon the conceit that this could mean an equality of life chances (and thus, by implication, randomly distributed outcomes) and focus instead on eliminating any public impediments that deprive people of opportunities they might otherwise pursue.[34] The sad irony is that, in our effort to deliver equal opportunity, we have built an education system that more resembles an impediment to opportunity.

If our commitment to opportunity were more realistic and less focused on correcting for differences between individuals, we could give our schools a more achievable task.

* * *

In practice, tracking would begin in ninth or tenth grade, at which point each student could elect a college or career track. Critically, while the school would provide a recommendation, the choice would be the family's. No high-pressure test dictates the future; no institutional discrimination tramples on the judgment of those who know the student best.

While the college track would look much like today's high school, the career track would be very different. Further academics would be compressed and then placed in a curriculum that emphasized practical skills, offered opportunities to explore different industries, and instilled in students the flexibility to adapt and learn as their careers progress. By eleventh grade, time might be evenly divided between classroom learning and vocational training; twelfth grade would generally be replaced by the first year of an apprenticeship.

Such things are easier to describe than to implement. Schools would require new curricula, new teachers, and new facilities. But models in other countries suggest that this can be done, and they offer a place to start. In Switzerland, roughly two-thirds of students go the vocational route, choosing from more than two hundred occupations. A three- to four-year program begins in the tenth grade, with students splitting time between employers, industry groups, and the classroom.[35] Germany's apprenticeship system offers recognized qualifications in 350 occupations, and 80 percent of its young adults are employed within six months of completing their education, compared with 48 percent in the United States.[36]

Presumably, the United States cannot and would not want merely to replicate some other country's system; the point is that reform in this direction is neither untested nor implausible. Already, isolated programs in the United States are validating the concept. In *City Journal*, Steven Malanga has described a variety of experiments under way, including efforts in New York City that now reach twenty-six thousand students. Siemens has created a four-year program for high school seniors in North Carolina, in partnership with a local community college, that leaves each student with an associate's degree in mechatronics, no student debt, and a job paying more than $50,000 per year. But it is no coincidence that Siemens is headquartered in Munich; "compared with Europe, America has few firms that participate in apprenticeship and other job-training programs," reports Malanga.[37] Nor should policy makers be surprised that American firms have shown limited enthusiasm for such programs when efforts promoting them are not accompanied by the reforms that would elevate their status and position them to succeed.

Direct employer engagement is critical to success, but it requires a dramatic change in mind-set. Rather than collaborating, the public and private sectors in America apparently prefer pointing fingers over the disconnect between what students learn and what employers consider valuable. Employers insist that they want to hire more and pay better but that they cannot find enough qualified workers. Policy makers retort that if an employer needs better-trained employees, then it should invest in training them. Both sides have a point.

Employers are correct that they cannot and should not bear the full cost of training. For one thing, the time and money spent improving a worker's skills and productivity generally accrue more to the benefit of the worker than to the trainer. The worker will expect to be paid commensurately with his newfound value, and if his current employer won't pay, he can go find another who will. If society wants its workers to be more productive and thus better paid, it needs at least to help with footing the bill. And of course, that's exactly what it does on behalf of employers who hire high-skilled college graduates. Why should *those* employers get the benefit of a worker trained for years at his own or the public's expense, while firms hiring less-educated workers are on their own?

Employers also face the realities of operating in a global economy, where other countries invest in exactly the sort of workforce preparedness that America has neglected. If hiring in America comes with more costly training requirements, global firms will hire elsewhere instead. Domestic firms will face higher costs than their foreign competitors. America's economic success in part depends on it matching the workforce invest-ments of its competitors.

This does not mean, however, that employers can sit back and await a flow of fresh talent. The government may have the resources, but it lacks the knowledge and pressure to deploy them well. Just look at the track record of existing job-training programs. In 2011, the U.S. Government Accountability Office found that the federal government was spending $18 billion annually on forty-seven overlapping programs. Studies of effectiveness had been conducted on only five of the forty-seven, and those "generally found that the effects of participation were not consistent across programs, with only some demonstrating positive impacts that tended to be small, inconclusive, or restricted to short-term impacts."[38] In 2016, a "gold standard" review of Workforce Investment Act programs initiated by the U.S. Department of Labor found that participation in job training did not increase earnings or employment more than a full year after initiation.[39] In Janesville, Wisconsin, where a major General Motors plant closed down in 2008, laid-off workers who enrolled in com-munity college had fewer steady jobs and earned less; those who made it to graduation saw the sharpest losses.[40]

The government controls unrivaled resources, countless facilities, and—perhaps most importantly—the *time* of prospective workers in the years prior to their first jobs. But only employers know what training is needed, and only if they have "skin in the game" can they be counted on to put time and effort into protecting their investment. A successful model must marry the two, as in the Siemens program described earlier. In Kentucky in 2005, Toyota—another foreign transplant—launched its own advanced manufacturing technician (AMT) initiative in collaboration with the Bluegrass Community and Technical College. The new campus was established on a Toyota manufacturing site, and Toyota employees served as the first two campus directors. By 2017, AMT was being operated by a multiemployer collaborative called the Federation for Advanced Manufacturing Education, with 305 employers sponsoring students on twenty-two campuses in nine states.

Community colleges bid to become program sites and offer a two-year AMT associate's degree. Employers sponsor students, who spend two eight-hour days in the classroom and three eight-hour days working for their employers each week. Students get paid for their work hours, they graduate debt-free with substantial work experience, and more than 90 percent of graduates proceed directly to full-time positions with their sponsors in jobs paying $50,000–$75,000 in the first year. Crucially, it is a central tenet of the program that "the employer is the primary customer"; employers fund the program, but they get to define it to meet their needs.[41]

Bringing the same model to high school students will require similarly intensive employer engagement. In San Antonio, Texas, Lockheed Martin, an employer facing a skills shortage, collaborated with the city and the local community college to create the Aerospace Academy in 2001. Now there are Alamo Academies in Aerospace, Information Technology, Manufacturing, Health, and Heavy Equipment. In their junior and senior years, students spend their mornings taking community college courses that earn both high school and college credit. In the intervening summer, they work as interns at sponsoring companies. The community college provides the facilities and instruction, school districts provide transportation and textbooks, employers pay intern salaries, and the city funds operating costs.[42]

A major benefit of a tracked vocational system is the additional resources it makes available because students are simultaneously learning and working. In the existing American system, a student might move through eleventh and twelfth grades at a cost of $15,000 per year, then spend two years in community college at an additional cost of $10,000 per year, and then at the age of twenty begin looking for a full-time job. He will then have consumed $50,000 in public resources and forgone substantial earnings of his own. By contrast, a German on a career track has much of his training cost funded by the company at which he works, on top of which he might begin to earn wages.[43]

With no net increase in education spending, America could offer every tenth grader additional classroom learning, a subsidized three-year apprenticeship for which he might also be paid, and a savings account with $20,000 to $40,000 awaiting him upon completion. Ultimately, the education system should commit to spending at least as much on a fifteen-year-old whose next seven years will be spent in a combination of school, apprenticeship, and employment as it spends on one headed to a four-year public university. If anything, given their respective earnings horizons upon completion, it is the career-tracked youngster who deserves the more generous support. That offer might not appeal to the one-fifth of students headed down the idealized path today. But the other 80 percent would be wise to consider it, and we owe them that option.

Reforms in this direction would begin with the elimination of federal standards, mandates, and funding streams that treat academic achievement and college enrollment as primary goals. Career tracks should be presented as equally worthy, evaluated on their own terms, and eligible for at least comparable per-student funding. The impermeable barrier between secondary and postsecondary education must be breached so that students can access programs and funding when they need them. Partnerships with private employers should be not only permitted but encouraged and, where appropriate, subsidized with public education dollars.

Within such a framework, success would depend, too, on motivated employers who recognize such engagement and investment as in their own best interest. This requires policies that push employers to use the domestic workforce already available, encourage them to collaborate with workers in ways that boost productivity, and make the employment relationship as economically attractive as possible. The following chapters discuss each of these issues further.

CHAPTER 7

OF BORDERS AND BALANCE

Practical objections to "globalization" tend to be quite narrow. Few people, for instance, take umbrage at globalization's original conception: McDonald's and Coca-Cola selling their products worldwide or, for that matter, Pret A Manger opening on every other street corner in New York City.[1] Nor do they mind global entertainment culture's homogenization or the cross-pollination of tastes in food and fashion. They aren't sick of the tourists, feeling overrun by invasive species, or fearful of some exotic pathogen triggering a pandemic. Even trade, broadly speaking, is not the issue. Exports are fine; so are imports of novel goods and services unavailable in the domestic market. Rather, when American pundits, politicians, and voters decry "globalization," they mean two very specific things: immigrant workers and imported substitutes, especially when produced by American firms that have moved operations overseas. In other words, they are upset about globalization's warping of the labor market.

The connection between immigration and the labor market is straightforward. People who move to the United States obviously join its labor market, increasing the supply of whatever labor they can perform. But goods and services entering the United States actually have a similar effect, allowing work that otherwise must be done by someone inside the country to be performed instead by anyone in the world. When the set of cars available to Americans goes from those made domestically to those made anywhere, the supply of labor available to meet U.S. car demand shifts from prospective autoworkers living within the nation's borders to all prospective autoworkers worldwide.

Both immigration and trade have the potential to boost demand for American work too. After all, immigrants are consumers as well as workers. And the same trade agreements that enable foreign workers to produce for the domestic market are supposed to enable domestic workers to produce for foreign markets. Trade and immigration can also promote economic dynamism and innovation through greater competition and more business creation. Immigration affects the communities into which immigrants move, tax collection and welfare spending, and long-term demographic trends. Trade delivers lower prices to consumers as well as geopolitical stability. And immigration and trade help determine millions of foreigners' economic prospects.

Thus people's views about trade and immigration policy depend on which outcomes they emphasize, the interests they prioritize, the time frames they consider, and the trade-offs they accept. This complexity strains the standard American political coalitions. Republicans have traditionally been more supportive of open trade, while Democrats have emphasized open immigration, but sharp splits have emerged within both parties on both questions. Some, seeking to elide the complexity, strike absolutist positions, claiming, for instance, that unconditional free trade always benefits Americans, regardless of whether other nations reciprocate, or insisting on "open borders" that welcome an unlimited number of immigrants.

The emphasis on labor-market outcomes that I've advanced in this book offers a distinct perspective for understanding globalization's effects, in which matching the nation's supply of workers to the demand for their work becomes the primary policy-making goal. From this perspective, the skill level of immigrants becomes a crucial question, while trade becomes a question of balance. And policy makers, it becomes apparent once again, have gone badly off course.

*   *   *

Reporting on the expected return of unskilled immigrants from the United States to Mexico in the wake of Donald Trump's election, and the anticipated impact on the Mexican economy, the *Washington Post* managed to encapsulate perfectly (if inadvertently) the economics and politics of the immigration debate: "More returnees means lower wages for everybody in blue-collar industries such as construction and automobile manufacturing, where competition for jobs is likely to increase, economists say."[2]

No prominent American newspaper would *ever* include such a nonchalant observation in a report about the U.S. labor market. But stripped of the fraught emotional context surrounding domestic immigration debates, the pressures of competing interest groups, and the imperatives of various political agendas—when the itinerant workers flood into another country's market, that is—describing the dynamic proved unproblematic. Neither reporter nor editor bothered to include caveats or highlight countervailing benefits. There was no need even to put any particular economist on the record. *Of course* a sharp increase in the supply of unskilled labor would force blue-collar wages lower.

Several months later, when Senators Tom Cotton and David Perdue introduced a Trump-endorsed proposal, the RAISE Act, to reduce immigration and prioritize admittance of highly skilled immigrants, outrage quickly coalesced around the negative effects on *total* GDP.[3] Former chief economist for Vice President Joe Biden and *Washington Post* columnist Jared Bernstein reacted by writing, "This move is completely inconsistent with Trump's aspiration to generate faster GDP growth, of which labor force growth is a key component."[4] He then provided a table from the Congressional Budget Office forecasting lower GDP growth for 2017 to 2027 than occurred from 1950 to 2017, driven in part by lower productivity growth but primarily by a slower expansion of the labor force. "The key point on why the RAISE Act is so misguided," he continued, was that the slowdown in labor force growth "is the part of the slowdown we can actually do something about, through welcoming immigration policy."

This distinction between the effect of immigration on individual incomes (and thus *per capita* GDP) and its impact on total GDP was highlighted in a *Wall Street Journal* analysis of Arizona's experience as its illegal-immigrant population fell 40 percent over the past decade.[5] The labor force was smaller, and so GDP declined, which should surprise no one—and means little unless Arizona were preparing for war with a neighboring state. What happened to the remaining Arizonans, especially those lower on the income scale? Wages on farms and in construction jumped 10 percent to 15 percent in just four years. Starting wages for some new hires rose by 40 percent to 60 percent.

The immigration debate is ultimately about America's priorities. If overall GDP growth is the goal, then all forms of immigration might make sense. If reducing consumer prices is the goal, then welcoming as many workers willing to work for as little as possible might indeed be the right choice. But if improving labor-market outcomes for the nation's less-skilled, lower-wage workers is the central objective, the economic case for unskilled immigration collapses.

The skill-based distinction is critical to understanding immigration's aggregate effect on the labor market. The economy has no fixed number of jobs that immigrants might "take" from native workers, nor do higher or lower levels of immigration necessarily lead to higher or lower wages. Immigrants are both producers and consumers, so their presence increases both the supply of labor and the demand for it. But we should expect immigrants who compete in a specific segment of the labor market to suppress wages of existing workers in that segment.[6]

This is because each immigrant's economic footprint is asymmetric. All people have somewhat similar consumption patterns, regardless of their skill and income levels. High-income households consume more overall, and more of luxury goods in particular, but everyone uses housing and transportation, food and health care, education and entertainment. So every new immigrant adds demand for many types of goods and services provided by many types of workers. On the other hand, each immigrant is himself only one type of worker. A worker with only a high school diploma contributes far more to the supply of such workers than to the demand for such work; a highly skilled worker, by contrast, adds at least somewhat to the demand for less-skilled work while adding to its supply not at all.

Defenders of "immigration" as a general phenomenon miss this point when they argue that recent waves have not been responsible for wage declines.[7] They may be right about that, but they are answering the wrong question. The issue is not whether immigration has been or will be better than no immigration; it is whether we are admitting the appropriate mix of immigrants. The counterfactual to ponder is how different things might look had we welcomed highly skilled immigrants but more tightly restricted the entry of those who compete directly with less-skilled native workers—or even had we simply enforced the immigration laws on the books, which are flouted predominantly by less skilled immigrants and their employers. Going forward, regardless of the policy adopted for immigration in the highly skilled segment of the labor market, lower-skilled American workers will do better if their segment of the labor market has relatively fewer of them.

In fact, the United States has been adding millions of unskilled immigrants to its workforce. After passage of the Immigration and Nationality Act in 1965, the immigrant share of the U.S. population nearly tripled, from less than 5 percent in 1970 to almost 14 percent in 2015, or more than 43 million people—most of whom hold no more than a high school degree.[8] In 2016 alone, the U.S. government granted lawful permanent resident status (issued a "green card") to more than 1 million people.[9] While educational attainment among immigrants has risen as Asians have surpassed Hispanics as the largest incoming demographic, most new arrivals still lack a four-year college degree.[10]

The effect on the labor market is large and concentrated. In 2016, more than one-quarter of American workers with no more than a high school degree were foreign born, as compared with just 14 percent of those with at least some college.[11] Immigration has pushed the labor market much further out of alignment than it might otherwise be; every additional unskilled immigrant, whatever other benefits he might bring the nation, compounds this problem.

Nor are these less-skilled immigrants filling "jobs Americans won't do," as proponents of the current approach often claim. The U.S. Bureau of Labor Statistics reports that both native- and foreign-born Americans work in all twenty-two of its occupational categories and that native-born workers represent the majority in every one.[12] The Pew Research Center went a level deeper, examining workforce composition across hundreds of detailed occupation categories, and found that immigrants accounted for more than 50 percent in only five; in no occupation did they exceed a 65 percent share. The majority of grounds maintenance workers, meat processors, and dishwashers are U.S. natives.[13]

Anecdotal evidence does suggest that farms struggle to fill certain jobs requiring intensive manual labor. For instance, the North Carolina Growers Association reports that even in 2011, with the state's unemployment level above 10 percent, it could find only 268 native applicants to fill

6,500 positions. Farms hired 245 of the 268, but only 163 came to work the first day, and only 7 stayed on for the year.[14] In South Carolina, a peach farm hired 483 native applicants during 2010–12, but only 31 lasted the season.[15] Such stories are representative of neither immigrant workers nor agricultural employment, however. Fewer than 3 percent of immigrants work on farms, and nationwide, the majority of farmworkers are natives.[16]

When employers argue that, even if some native workers are on hand, they nevertheless need foreign labor, the question always looms, what is the alternative? One might be to offer more attractive wages and working conditions to lure enough native workers. Another might be to mechanize processes and employ fewer but more productive native workers. Illustrating its reporting in Arizona, the *Wall Street Journal* described a farmer struggling with the loss of illegal-immigrant employees who would pick jalapeños by hand for $13 per hour. He invested in machinery that he hoped (many fewer) native workers would operate at $20 per hour. This would lower total employment, yes, but if those illegal immigrants previously working the lower-wage jobs have left the country, the labor-market outcome is suddenly sunnier. People in the market will more likely have jobs, and those jobs will be better ones.

That response to a farmworker shortage is just one example of a broader principle: workers in the labor market benefit when employers have no alternative to them. A strange facet of the modern immigration debate is the tendency of the same pro-business interests that typically wax lyrical about free-market dynamism to lament in apocalyptic terms the prospect of a limited supply of labor. But the result of such limit is not, generally, economic ruin. Instead, businesses reorient themselves toward using the labor that is available. Investment goes toward making jobs more attractive and boosting productivity. In 2018, fearing that a shortage of construction workers would slow spending on new homes, Home Depot announced a ten-year partnership with the Home Builders Institute to invest $50 million in training twenty thousand additional workers.[17] The shortage and its emerging solutions are not evidence of a market failing; they show how the market can work.

* * *

For policy makers, an emphasis on labor-market health points toward a fairly straightforward principle for immigration policy, based on current and forecasted labor-market conditions: the United States should limit increases in its supply of unskilled immigrant labor. This new approach would require first and foremost that criteria for allowing entrance into the country emphasize education level—attainment of a college degree, in particular. While proposals to do this are predictably decried as "racist," they reflect the immigration policies employed in countries like Australia and Canada, which few see as bastions of oppression.[18] Implementation would also require a robust enforcement mechanism to prevent people from entering and working in the country illegally.

That requirement helps to explain opposition to a skills-based approach, because it leads inescapably to the question of what do with the roughly 10 million illegal immigrants living in the country already. Any effort to prevent future illegal entrants from working will equally affect past entrants, unless they are granted some legal status. From the perspective of the labor market, the answer is again straightforward: require unskilled illegal immigrants to leave. This would improve labor-market outcomes nationally, as it did in Arizona. The best case would be a steady, predictable transition that avoids sudden disruptions, which could do more harm than good to labor-market outcomes—for instance, bankrupting employers reliant on suddenly vanished immigrant labor faster than they can invest in alternative production processes or find other workers trained or compensated in new ways.

But at stake as well are other values and the fates of millions of people who have built their lives and raised their families as members of American communities. If the ultimate objective is strong families and communities, tearing either apart would be counterproductive. Recognizing the labor market as the most important policy consideration but not the *only* one helps to make the trade-offs concrete. Politicians should at least be honest, though, when arguing that illegal immigrants should stay: this would impose real costs on their struggling constituents.

A labor-market emphasis also suggests a prioritization: putting future immigration policy on sound footing is more important for the economy than dealing with past illegal immigration in one way or another. A compromise on the past, where there are no good answers, coupled with a strong policy for the future, where the right answer is clear, is a far superior outcome than the current impasse. The one caveat for any compromise is that the promise of future enforcement must be credible. If the world believes, based on how the United States deals with its existing population of illegal immigrants, that future illegal entry will be rewarded as well, the nation will never have control of its labor market.

All these factors point toward a possible approach that has received little consideration from either side of the immigration debate: *last in, first out* (LIFO). Under LIFO, the longer that an illegal immigrant has been in the country, the longer he can remain. Those who have only just arrived, or migrate frequently across the border, would be barred from the labor market immediately. Those who have already resided in the country several years would be issued a work permit that expires several years hence. And those the United States has allowed to settle in the country over a decade or more would be granted a decade-long work permit leading to citizenship, on condition that the more transient groups have left as scheduled. Approximately two-thirds of illegal immigrants have resided here for more than ten years and might ultimately stay.[19] But this would happen only after others had left and the nation had demonstrated firm control over its borders.

This compromise places the labor market on a trajectory toward tighter supply at the lower end and creates time for the economy and employers, on one hand, and immigrants who will need to depart, on the other, to adjust—in direct proportion to how entrenched their situations have become. It lays the groundwork for a stable, enforceable, forward-looking policy.

*　*　*

Immigration can feel uniquely disruptive. But in economic terms, both the benefits and the costs of international trade are potentially much larger. Whereas anyone is a potential immigrant to the United States, relatively few make the move. Once they do, they subject themselves to American regulation, the American cost of living, and so on. When the United States opens its markets to the world, by contrast, workers everywhere gain the opportunity to produce things for sale to American customers. And they do so while remaining in local economies whose laws and norms may be radically different and where $1 per hour may be a livable wage. Meanwhile, gaining potential access to the 95 percent of people living beyond America's borders represents an enormous opportunity for American firms and workers.

Trade delivers its benefits in several ways. The standard mechanism, taught in Economics 101, is specialization. Where two parties have capabilities that make them better at different types of things, they can both be more productive (and create more output for consumption) if they specialize where they are relatively better equipped. This is true of next-door neighbors where the accountant does both households' taxes and the carpenter does both households' repairs, and it is true of the United States and Mexico, where one nation's climate is ideal for growing wheat, the other's for growing avocados.

A second benefit, which many economists now believe is more important in the international context, is scale. Think of the carpenter, who must buy a full set of tools even if just to maintain his own house but would prefer, via trade, to deploy his talents and equipment throughout the neighborhood. Likewise, Microsoft can expect far greater revenue and invest more in product development if its software will be bought not just in the United States but around the globe.

The third benefit is technological diffusion. When producers come in contact, they can learn from each other, and competition can force both to become more effective. If the carpenter can work all around town instead of just in his neighborhood, he will likely discover superior techniques some of his peers use and seek to improve his time per job to match what they offer, especially if they will be doing business in his neighborhood as well. Although the stiff competition from international automakers dealt harsh blows to Detroit, it introduced products and processes that over time led to better domestic cars too.

Through all these channels, workers can become more productive while consumers can benefit from greater choice, lower prices, and more rapid innovation. Thanks to these effects, the elimination of trade barriers and increase in international trade in the second half of the twentieth century produced gains throughout the world, above all in certain developing countries. In the 1960s, less than one-quarter of global economic output traveled across international borders. By 2003, that share had reached half; as of 2015, it stood at nearly 60 percent.[20]

Yet trade is not without costs. The parties trading almost certainly gain—it is, after all, their choice to make an exchange. If one measured prosperity solely in terms of consumption, this might be the end of the story. People and firms who once could buy things only on the domestic market now can also buy from the larger international market. What's not to love? But as social theorist Irving Kristol once observed, "where is it written that the welfare of consumers takes precedence over that of producers?"[21]

If the goal is productive pluralism and the focus is labor-market outcomes, the calculus changes. In isolation, opening the U.S. market to a global supply of labor could be cause for serious concern. Trade needs to be *balanced* for the net effect on the labor market to be positive, with the world roughly buying as much from the United States as we buy from the world, so that workers not only face greater competition but also enjoy greater opportunity.

That balanced outcome is by no means guaranteed. If trillions of dollars of foreign goods are flowing into the United States, then Americans must send back *something* in return. But other countries might impose obstacles to American producers selling in their markets and instead acquire U.S. assets like stocks, bonds, and real estate. For instance, what if China sends $50 billion worth of electronics to the United States and we send $50 billion worth of U.S. Treasury bonds back to China? In colloquial terms, China has sent the goods on credit. U.S. production is lower and government debt is higher. Such an imbalanced exchange is far from the model of prosperity-enhancing free trade taught in economics classes. It can reduce opportunities for workers, lower the trajectory of their productivity, and diminish the nation's real prosperity.

Just such an imbalance has emerged in recent decades. For instance, in 2017, the United States traded $3.89 trillion in goods: $1.55 trillion of exports and $2.34 trillion of imports, which resulted in a roughly $800 billion deficit, offset only in part by a $240 billion surplus on $1.32 trillion of services trade. Of that $3.89 trillion in goods, about 20 percent was in goods dependent on agriculture or natural resources, where differing national endowments would make one country or another an obvious importer or exporter. Trade of this type was balanced: $394 billion of imports against $339 billion of exports; forty-three product categories with net imports and forty-three with net exports.

By contrast, for the 80 percent of trade in manufactured products, Americans bought $1.60 of imports for every $1 of exports sold overseas—$1.86 trillion in imports against $1.16 trillion in exports overall; 120 product categories with net imports and 53 with net exports. Of the twenty-two product categories with a surplus or deficit of at least $10 billion, twenty-one ran deficits. The *only* manufactured product of which the United States exports significantly more than it imports is airplanes.[22]

The U.S. trade deficit in advanced technology is particularly stunning. Balanced trade might include a large deficit in unsophisticated manufacturing that relies heavily on low-cost, unskilled labor, offset at least in part by U.S. exports of more sophisticated products. Yet the United States is a net importer even of what the U.S. government designates as "advanced technology products," importing $464 billion against $354 billion of exports in 2017.[23] In addition to airplanes, U.S. exports do exceed imports in weapons and flexible manufacturing tools. But the nation is a net importer of biotechnology, life sciences, computers and electronics, advanced materials (including semiconductors), and even nuclear technology.

This imbalance has not happened by accident. Countries like South Korea, Taiwan, and Japan achieved rapid growth in part through mercantilist policies that aggressively subsidized and promoted their strategically important industries on the global stage, while preventing foreign (for instance, American) producers from selling in their markets. Today, China is the primary practitioner of this mercantilism, and its gargantuan scale is producing unprecedented economic distortions. Its approach to the international economy differs in both degree and kind from its predecessors' and incorporates brazen practices like widespread intellectual property (IP) theft. With its "mercantilist campaign to dominate advanced industries by flouting the rules of the international trading system," explained Rob Atkinson, president of the Information Technology and Innovation Foundation, "China has been kidney-punching its competitors."[24]

Although China's commitments through the World Trade Organization limit the official tariffs it can impose on imports, they do not prevent it from placing exporters at other insurmountable disadvantages when trying to sell into the Chinese market. China designs regulations and establishes technical standards that its domestic producers can more easily meet, provides direct subsidies to give those producers a financial advantage, and slows the approval of foreign products. It establishes "local content" requirements that force foreign firms to set up shop within the country and enter into joint ventures with local companies rather than manufacturing at home and exporting the finished goods to China. And it ensures that government procurement gives preferential treatment to local firms—no small matter in a state-run economy where the government is often the primary consumer.

Even when American companies do have the opportunity to enter the Chinese market, they are often reluctant to do so for fear of falling victim to the pervasive IP theft that the Chinese government permits and, in many cases, facilitates. It is official Chinese policy to promote "indigenous innovation" by forcing foreign firms to transfer their technology and trade secrets to local Chinese companies as a condition of doing business in the country.[25] The U.S. Chamber of Commerce called the policy "a blueprint for technology theft on a scale the world has never seen before."[26] Meanwhile, the government provides little to no enforcement of protection for foreign firms that find their patents and trademarks ignored by their Chinese counterparts.

China's market distortions and IP abuses have an impact on the U.S. domestic market as well. A subsidy that advantages Chinese firms in China gives them a similar edge when they export across the Pacific. And China is actively pursuing an unprecedented global campaign of industrial cyberespionage, targeting thousands of U.S. companies, including Google, Coca-Cola, and the *New York Times*.[27] The issue rose to the top of the United States–China economic dialogue as centrally coordinated Chinese cyberattacks seized hundreds of billions of dollars' worth of IP, while giving Chinese firms access to their competitors' strategies.[28] General Keith Alexander, former head of the National Security Agency and the U.S. Cyber Command, and Dennis Blair, former director of national intelligence, have called the theft "the greatest transfer of wealth in history."[29]

As the *New York Times* reported early in 2017, "China has charted out a $300 billion plan to become nearly self-sufficient by 2025 in a range of important industries, from planes to computer chips to electric cars." The so-called Made in China 2025 program "would provide large, low-interest loans from state-owned investment funds and development banks; assistance in buying foreign competitors; and extensive research subsidies."[30] Already rolling off the assembly line: China's C919 commercial aircraft, a direct competitor to Boeing's 737, built conveniently through "at least 16 joint ventures for avionics, flight control, power, fuel and landing gear."[31]

The C919 made its first test flight in May 2017 and, by early 2018, had accumulated almost eight hundred orders.[32]

In June 2017, Tesla announced that it would build its second electric vehicle plant in Shanghai, not the United States, supported by a 50 percent investment from the Chinese government that would include free land. A research-and-development center and a second "gigafactory" for batteries may follow.[33] Tesla believes China could become its biggest market; but apparently, a market for U.S. exports it will not be.

* * *

Why has the United States tolerated this state of affairs? To the untrained observer, it might seem self-evidently harmful both to send away the labor-intensive industrial employers that sustain communities and to forfeit leadership in the industries that might play such a role in the future, especially if the result is to become increasingly more indebted in the process.

Unfortunately, the standard position on trade, held by many economists and adopted by many policy makers, is that trade is always good and that more is always better. This conclusion stems from the error of evaluating trade primarily by its effects on immediate consumption. In the short run, a consumer would obviously prefer having the opportunity to purchase something from abroad over not having that opportunity. A trade deficit created by the United States importing more from other countries than it exports, on this view, would be unimportant or even beneficial. "The idea with international trade is to import the largest volume of goods and services for any level of exports," writes columnist Simon Constable, a fellow at the Johns Hopkins Institute for Applied Economics. "The more goodies you get rather than give, the better off you are."[34] In this thinking, if other countries are willing to send us more than they demand we send in return, it is they who are the patsies. If, rather than purchase U.S.-made goods, other countries choose to purchase U.S. Treasury bonds or companies or houses, that's a demonstration of confidence in the American economy and the desire of foreigners to invest here.

Concern for the long term falls by the wayside in this perspective, assuming away differences between industries in employment profiles, growth trajectories, opportunities for productivity improvement, and spillovers to broader research ecosystems and supply chains. Writing in the *New York Times*, Council of Economic Advisers chair under Obama Christina Romer observed, "American consumers value health care and haircuts as much as washing machines and hair dryers." Or as Michael Boskin, chairman of George H. W. Bush's Council of Economic Advisers, reportedly said, "computer chips, potato chips, what's the difference?"[35]

This consumerist focus is myopic, as adopting a production lens makes clear. In aggregate, at the national level, imbalanced trade places the economy on a lower trajectory. In the short run, it reduces productive capacity. It also allocates both human and physical capital away from industries that hold most potential for the future, and it builds industrial ecosystems and supply chains outside the United States, which will make future efforts to regain a competitive foothold more difficult. "The products a country makes today," explains *The Economist*, describing research conducted by Harvard professor Ricardo Hausmann and MIT professor César Hidalgo, "determine which products they will be able and likely to make tomorrow, through the evolution of their capabilities."[36] What begins as a distortion or imbalance becomes genuine advantage as supply chains and know-how embed in the countries that have seized them. The United States, meantime, has become a prominent exporter of garbage (not just bad pop music but actual refuse).[37]

Individuals and their communities feel the labor-market effects directly. Harvard professor Greg Mankiw assured his *New York Times* readers that "full employment is possible with any pattern of trade. The main issue is not the number of jobs, but which jobs. Americans should work in those industries in which we have an advantage compared with other nations, and we should import from abroad those goods that can be produced more cheaply there."[38] But which jobs do Americans lose and which do they gain if trade is imbalanced and other nations are dominating the most promising industries? Presumably, other jobs have not been available to them all along in which they could have been working more productively. The new jobs could well be ones in which workers are less productive and which will provide less opportunity for gains over time.

Furthermore, where unbalanced trade reduces the American economy's output of the "tradeable" goods and services that can be produced in one place and sold to another, the suggestion that workers shift into the services economy is unhelpful. As we saw in chapter 4, everyone can't just serve each other coffee. Notwithstanding the views of those economists who regard attachment to manufacturing (and manufactured goods make up a disproportionate chunk of tradeable goods) as an exercise in pointless nostalgia, a very good reason exists for the average citizen to place special value on such activity. Every community, defined by its local labor market, must produce a sufficient quantity of tradeables to exchange for what it needs from the outside world. Yet that tradeable sector is, by definition, the one exposed to the most withering competition.

Economists are gradually acknowledging that trade is not always an unmitigated good. An influential 2016 paper by MIT professor David Autor and colleagues found that the economic shock of China's entry into the global trading system caused the net loss of more than 2 million American jobs between 1999 and 2011, roughly half in manufacturing and half in other industries. Affected low-wage workers saw the largest proportional declines in earnings and were most likely to exit the labor force entirely.[39]

Another 2016 paper, by former Harvard University president and U.S. secretary of the treasury Larry Summers and colleagues, observed that under conditions of "secular stagnation," characterized by low interest rates, slow growth, subtarget inflation, and excessive unemployment,

> neo-mercantilist policies—policies that attempt to improve one country's net foreign asset position relative to another or run persistent current account surpluses—are beggar-thy-neighbor. Neo-mercantilist policies alleviate the secular stagnation of the country pursuing them by exporting savings, but at the expense of the trading partner.

They conclude, "Economists and policymakers need to give substantial weight to the possibility that secular stagnation [and thus the dangers of neomercantilism] will be the defining economic challenge for macroeconomic policy over the next decade."[40]

Yet when confronted with this problem, many supporters of the current approach to trade shrug and say nothing can be done. This resignation comes in three forms: first, they say, even if past policies were misguided, the die has been cast, "the jobs aren't coming back," and the unique "China shock" will never repeat. (It's worth noting that the same consumer-focused advocates who dismissed the strategic value of retaining industrial strength now also dismiss the possibility of restoring industrial strength, on the ground that it has become too firmly entrenched elsewhere.) Second, they contend, trade imbalances are merely a symptom of underlying savings imbalances, and trade policy is powerless to intervene. Finally, any disruption of the status quo or confrontation with countries whose policies hurt Americans, they warn, risks a "trade war," which would cause an even worse situation. None of these positions is correct.

Better policy can still have an enormous impact. Technological advances will transform ever more goods and, especially, services into tradeables. Behind the 1 billion Chinese, another 4 billion citizens of the world are eager to produce their way out of poverty and would happily follow a mercantilist path steamrolled with impunity by China. That path to development must be foreclosed. Effective policy would also go beyond the prevention of future harm and help to reverse recent losses. The garment factories of early twentieth-century New England will not roar back to life. But more of the products still designed in the United States and produced by U.S.-based firms—from aerospace components to pharmaceuticals and medical devices to, yes, iPhones—could be made here as well.[41]

The *Harvard Business Review* highlighted one firm's decision to make stainless steel trash cans in the United States instead of in Asia, with a more automated production line that employs seven to ten workers versus the equivalent eighty overseas.[42] The seven to ten new workers don't care that somewhere else the total might have been eighty; nor do the other employees working to support the domestic plant, nor their families, nor their communities. "Its medium-term goal—if its first U.S. facility is successful," reports the *Review*, "is to add as many as three more U.S. manufacturing sites. In the longer term, the company might supply global demand from the United States."

These transformations will not happen overnight. The massive advantages of entrenched supply chains and built expertise, which policy makers wrongly ignored and allowed America to give away, now stand as obstacles to future U.S. growth. But the same forces that warped global supply chains away from the American worker can straighten them again, at a similar pace. In many cases, the choice to move production overseas is a close call, and relatively small policy changes can have large effects in terms of preventing further departures and encouraging returns. If trade would start operating as its proponents promise, the United States should even be a place to which other countries offshore their own production in some instances. The domestic petrochemical industry has experienced just that, as falling natural gas prices began to shift businesses calculations: in Iowa, one can now find an Egyptian fertilizer plant; in Tennessee, a German polysilicon plant; in Texas, a Taiwanese ethylene plant and an Austrian steel-precursor plant that sends one-third of its output back to Austria.[43]

Americans should likewise be unsatisfied by claims that the trade deficit is an inevitable side effect of the nation's low savings rate. Yes, a country consuming more than it produces will—by definition—run a trade deficit. But that merely invites the question, *why* is it doing this? Unless one prefers a reductive (and some might say stereotypical) analysis that "those spendthrift Asians will always be savers, while those cowboy Americans will never be able to hold on to a dollar," policy choices must surely be playing a role—and could surely play a different one.

The issue gets confused, once again, by the dominant emphasis on the American consumer, which leads to descriptions of the trade deficit as excess American consumption. But view it instead as a problem of insufficient production: why isn't the American economy producing more? In exchange for the goods that foreigners send to the United States, why are these foreigners taking back American assets—stocks, bonds, and real estate—instead of American goods? The American consumer is only one variable in this equation. The policies of U.S. and foreign governments that discourage foreigners from buying American products are responsible too—and those policies can be changed.

Are such fights worth picking? Even after conceding that some trade is harming American workers, that jobs could come back, and that trade policy matters, skepticism remains that any policy changes would strengthen the American position. Such assertiveness, the thinking goes, would spark a "trade war" in which other countries respond with further protection for their own producers, matters escalate, and the international trading system shudders to a halt.

But that trading system is not self-enforcing. It is a reciprocal construct, in which only the prospect of benefits denied compels each nation to play by the rules. If large economies so fear the possibility of a trade war that they would rather surrender preemptively—tolerating the abuses of others and forgoing opportunities to advance their own interests—then more and more countries will flout the rules more and more aggressively, imbalances will persist, and domestic frustration will grow. Such appeasement is not a sustainable arrangement, nor is it truly free trade.

The alternative is for the United States, in partnership with other developed nations facing similar challenges, to make clear that it will no longer tolerate the status quo. China today, and other nations plotting their own mercantilist strategies, would then need to decide whether to settle on a peaceful equilibrium, in which everyone plays by the rules that benefit everyone, or to persist on a path that would undermine the international economic system. Given only those two options, following the rules would seem the obviously more attractive one for all involved. That is the hope and the goal—not actually to retaliate but rather to create conditions in which abuses are no longer contemplated. But the crucial point is that if some nations in fact prefer an open trade war to genuine free trade, then the collapse of economic relationships is inevitable.

Accusing those who would defend American economic interests of "starting a trade war" represents a form of economic pacifism. The trade war has already started, but only one side is fighting. The question for the United States is whether to respond or to surrender, bearing in mind that a response has a good chance of defusing the conflict, whereas surrender will only embolden nations with no commitment to free markets, undermine the health of the trading system as a whole, and leave the committed free-traders to fight on far less favorable ground.

*   *   *

This is not to advocate protectionism or to suggest that anyone voicing skepticism about current conditions must be on the right track. For instance, President Donald Trump made opposition to free trade a centerpiece of his campaign. His policy prescriptions, to the extent that they were fleshed out, emphasized the renegotiation of trade deals and imposition of tariffs aimed at reversing bilateral trade deficits. But no particular bilateral deficit is necessarily problematic, so long as the nation's aggregate volumes of imports and exports remain balanced—in a well-functioning system of global trade, countries might run deficits with some partners and surpluses with others. Furthermore, within the undifferentiated aggregate of exports and imports, some elements of trade may be constructive, while others are destructive. And further still, free trade agreements (FTAs) reached by the United States with other countries have tended to improve its terms of trade—from 2001 to 2015, for instance, the U.S. trade deficit in goods has fallen by one-third with its FTA partners, while more than doubling with other countries.[44] The Trans-Pacific Partnership (TPP), from which Trump withdrew the United States upon taking office, aimed squarely at promoting a more idealized model of trade, while assembling a coalition of free-market economies to combat the unfair trade practices of nations like China.[45]

A middle ground exists between the refusal to countenance affirmative trade policy and the desire to throw weight around indiscriminately. For instance, the *Wall Street Journal*, known for its aggressive opposition to protectionism and fear of trade war, editorialized in 2017 that

> Mr. Trump brandished big sticks in the campaign by promising to declare China a currency manipulator and impose punitive tariffs. But this would hurt the U.S. as much as China. U.S. officials now concede that a better approach is to target areas where China fails to grant Americans the market access that Chinese enjoy in the U.S.
>
> So if China declares internet industries off-limits to foreign investors, Chinese companies will be blocked from buying similar American firms. If Tesla is hit with high tariffs on its U.S.-made cars, then Chinese cars will face higher duties in the U.S. Exports from firms that receive state assistance under the "Made in China 2025" industrial-policy plan could be blocked or subject to countervailing duties.

"Such a policy," the editorial concluded, "would address the reality that after benefitting from access to Western markets, China in the past decade began to harass or close its door to foreign companies."[46]

A policy that fully occupies this middle ground would focus on four objectives: first, building strong American advantages in the tradeable sector; second, deterring unfair foreign practices that undermine free markets; third, addressing financial imbalances that contribute to trade imbalances; and fourth, providing support to the less-skilled American workers who disproportionately bear trade's costs. Let's look at each objective in turn.

BUILDING AMERICAN ADVANTAGES

The idea of government offering advantages to segments of the private sector offends many pro-market policy makers. It appears an invitation for government to "pick winners and losers"—something bureaucracies do extremely poorly. But that framework is not quite right where international competition is concerned, because the task does not require determinations of which firms should be given a boost. Improving American competitiveness elevates the nation's domestic firms and industries at the expense of competitors overseas, a distinction that policy makers are well suited to make.

The condemnation of government intervention also presumes a marketplace that would be free but for a proposed policy, but the United States doesn't decide on its own whether the international marketplace will be "free" or "distorted"; other nations have their own say, and they have stated loudly their preference for the latter. Under those conditions, a choice to reduce trade barriers and expose the domestic market to foreign competition is by definition a choice to introduce greater distortions into the domestic market. The choice for American policy makers, if they wish to leave barriers down, is whether to push American producers onto an equal footing or leave them to flounder.

Efforts at boosting the competitiveness of American producers (and making the United States an attractive place for foreign firms to locate production) need not mimic the government-led mercantilism on display elsewhere.[47] The United States can leverage its own strengths by focusing government support on innovation, infrastructure, and education. If policy makers were to acknowledge the enormous social value of domestic production, they would direct resources accordingly. As one concrete example, public funding for research in manufacturing—advanced materials, robotics, logistics, and so on—should be on par with that given to the National Institutes of Health.[48]

Many other policy areas acquire greater urgency and new priorities in this context. Reforms to organized labor and vocational training, discussed in other chapters, would make important contributions. The same goes for regulatory reform, which should be expedited especially for infrastructure investments, such as pipeline construction and port upgrades, that might have the greatest global effect. The American advantage in cheap and abundant energy that has developed over the past decade, thanks in particular to new oil and gas supplies unlocked by hydraulic fracturing, must be embraced and extended.

DETERRING UNFAIR PRACTICES

The logic of international trade, built on reciprocity, leads toward tit-for-tat retaliation as a means of conflict resolution. But that is rarely constructive and can leave a country taking action that hurts itself as much as its target. To deter unfair practices that contribute to unbalanced trade, the United States should develop asymmetric tools that hurt trading partners without hurting itself and can therefore be credibly threatened.

Where other nations deny American producers access to their markets with nontariff barriers like discriminatory regulations and local content requirements, the United States should respond in areas where its own advantages give it the greatest leverage—for instance, by limiting access to American student visas, advanced medical technologies, and capital markets. Denying any of these to a foreign country would hit its ruling class hardest, while doing little damage to its lower-income population or to American households.

The goal in developing such tools ideally is not to have to use any of them. America should not want to exclude foreigners from its schools, deprive them of lifesaving drugs, or quarantine them from American investors. But developing these tools is every bit as important as developing the next generation of military technologies, and being prepared to use them is every bit as important as it is in the realm of peace and war.

Theft of IP poses a particular threat to the United States because so much of its potential advantage in the international market derives from its superiority in IP development. The United States should designate foreign industries that use stolen IP as *personae non grata* and prohibit importation of their products. Furthermore, it should attempt to build a coalition of developed economies that together prohibit their firms from transferring sensitive IP to any country with a track record of IP theft or forced IP transfers—essentially, imposing IP sanctions, in similar fashion as they do with sensitive military technology.[49] One way to prevent China from inducing Tesla to set up shop in Shanghai is flatly to prohibit the move; if Elon Musk would prefer to proceed as a Chinese firm partly owned by the Communist Party without access to the U.S. market or investment, he is welcome to make that bet.

Short of banning IP transfers, and perhaps more effective in the absence of international cooperation, the United States could bar the import from China of products that contain IP in its first five years of protection under a U.S. patent. The IP could only have gotten into the product if an American firm transferred it or a Chinese firm stole it. If neither action is in the American interest, then neither is the subsequent import. This approach would be less draconian than IP sanctions, because American firms could still enter the Chinese market and do business there; but it would insulate the American market from reverberations back across the Pacific. This parallels the U.S. policy of banning drug reimportation from Canada. American firms can develop drugs here and then sell them in Canada, where that nation's government aggressively distorts drug prices. But once the drug passes through that distortion and gets sold at a below-market price, it cannot be brought back into the United States, because doing so would bring the Canadian policy back with it.

ADDRESSING FINANCIAL IMBALANCES

The truism that a trade deficit reflects a lack of national savings—that is, national consumption in excess of production—says nothing about causality and does not justify a claim that the former is merely a by-product of the latter. The policies described herein, by increasing the relative attractiveness of consuming-by-importing-from-the-United-States as compared with saving-by-acquiring-U.S.-assets, would likely reduce both trade and savings imbalances. However, the truism is helpful in highlighting another lever for addressing undesirable imbalances in the international economy: not only trade policy but also financial policy can influence the trade balance. If the purchase of U.S. assets becomes less attractive to foreigners holding U.S. dollars, the purchase of U.S.-produced goods and services will become relatively more attractive. Any number of policy tools could discourage foreign acquisition of assets, but the most straightforward would be simply to block it. As with technology transfers, the United States already blocks various corporate acquisitions deemed not in the national interest. A foreign government boosting its own economy's production at the expense of America's by sending goods on credit should qualify for such treatment.

The United States would find an enthusiastic partner here in Germany, which saw the value of Chinese acquisitions rise more than eightfold in 2016. "It's not on that Germany sacrifices its companies on the altar of free markets, while at the same time our own companies have huge problems investing in China," complained Vice Chancellor Sigmar Gabriel. According to *Politico Europe*, "trade experts warn that a recent spending spree by Chinese companies—many of them supported by the Chinese government—will harm the competitiveness of European business in the long-term," but "China has a major advantage: It has a plan. Germany doesn't. Neither does the European Union."[50]

Beyond scrutinizing specific high-profile transactions, the United States could more broadly reduce the attractiveness of assets to foreigners by taxing acquisition of them. Some nations assess such taxes, which both raise revenue and have the effect of making their produced goods relatively more attractive.[51] Whether such a tax would also impose economic drag depends on whether one believes that the free flow of capital adds significant value to begin with. As Jagdish Bhagwati observed in "The Capital Myth," a seminal 1998 essay in *Foreign Affairs*, "even a cursory glance at history suggests that these gains [from free capital mobility] may be negligible. . . . It is time to shift the burden of proof from those who oppose to those who favor liberated capital."[52] *The Economist* agreed.[53]

SUPPORTING AMERICAN WORKERS

Conspicuously absent from this agenda is tariffs, which would be largely duplicative of the other efforts advanced here in combating mercantilism and boosting competitiveness. A tariff might deter foreign distortions, but the United States can accomplish that deterrence far more effectively with asymmetric tools that cause greater pain abroad and less at home. A tariff might insulate domestic firms from competition, but that is a poor substitute for boosting their own capabilities.

And tariffs come with a substantial set of drawbacks. If generally applied, they are overly broad, slowing trade indiscriminately. If targeted, they become political prizes for domestic industries to chase. Congress is unlikely to choose which industries to target in a neutral or efficient manner, and even to the extent it succeeds, a well-placed tariff can be easily counteracted with another well-placed subsidy from the other side. By contrast, both asymmetric deterrents that target blatantly unfair practices abroad and measures to enhance American competitiveness can be applied economy-wide from the American side, forcing politicians to focus on the most economically beneficial measures.

One market intervention would be constructive, however: a "wage subsidy" that recognizes the social value of employment and gives a boost to domestic workers facing competition from foreigners willing to accept far lower wages. This policy, and its implications for international competitiveness, is discussed at length in chapter 9.

*   *   *

Even if costly to Americans in some circumstances, trade has undoubtedly provided enormous benefits to far poorer workers in other countries; indeed, the trade costliest to American workers probably has been the most beneficial elsewhere. In addition, the interdependence that trade fosters may deliver significant geopolitical benefits. Traditionally, trade proponents cite these external benefits as peripheral by-products. As a result, little scrutiny is applied either to the genuine value of those benefits or to the degree to which status quo trade policy is the lowest-cost way to achieve them. But if the economic case for trade weakens, these other factors become crucial. And, as in the immigration debate, such factors raise the philosophical question, who counts?

For American policy makers, the nation's political community is the group to whom long-run prosperity should be delivered. Democracy in general, and certainly the American constitutional republic, is built on the expectation that each elected official serves the interests of his constituents or can at least be held accountable by them. The hope is that compromises struck among these officials on behalf of their various constituencies achieve the best approximation of a government that its people agree to live under. Ask officials to represent instead other interests, to whom they are not accountable, and both the accountability and the legitimacy of the system erode.

If American policy makers want to promote global prosperity, they should start by ensuring that America is itself building from the strongest possible foundation. If they get that right, they will find far greater domestic support for policies that benefit people around the world, open opportunity to them, and welcome them to our shores.

CHAPTER 8

MORE PERFECT UNIONS

Early in season 1 of *Friends*, Rachel Green brandishes her first-ever paycheck to the gang, rips open the envelope, and then puzzles, "Who's FICA? Why's he getting all my money?"[1] If only she knew the half of it.

For every dollar deducted from her check by the Federal Insurance Contributions Act (which collects the "payroll taxes" for Social Security and Medicare), her boss at the coffee shop had to pay one to the government as well. And employing her carried countless other costs, which, depending on Central Perk's policies, might include vacation days and paid leave, health and disability insurance, and legally mandated contributions to unemployment programs and worker's compensation funds. By 2017, wages accounted for just two-thirds of the direct cost of employing an American worker.[2]

Government rules both increase the costs and reduce the value of an employee. Employers try to hold schedules below forty hours per week to avoid paying time-and-a-half or below thirty to avoid the mandates of the Affordable Care Act. The Occupational Safety and Health Administration (OSHA) ensures compliance with lifesaving procedures but also requires that stairrail systems serving as handrails be "not more than 37 inches nor less than 36 inches from the upper surface of the stairrail system to the surface of the tread, in line with the face of the riser at the forward edge of the tread."[3] The Americans with Disabilities Act facilitates broader inclusion in the workforce but also expensive lawsuits over accommodation for a bridge maintainer's fear of heights and a teacher's fear of children.[4]

Nearly everyone supports the broad objectives underlying these policies, and that is the ground on which they are often debated: isn't a forty-hour workweek a good thing? Aren't you for workplace safety? Do you support discrimination? Lost in this kind of framing are the unavoidable trade-offs. After all, we could eliminate workplace injuries entirely if every worker were accompanied at all times by a licensed personal-safety supervisor. But no one considers that a reasonable approach.

More protections mean higher costs for employers, and that usually means lower wages and fewer jobs for workers. Each new requirement inserts another small wedge between how much the employer must spend to have the work done and how much the employee can earn. Each makes relatively more attractive the alternatives of automating the work, doing it overseas, or abandoning it entirely. From 2005 to 2015, the United States added almost 9 million of the independent-contractor, on-call, and temporary jobs that enable employers to avoid various regulatory burdens, while traditional employment did not grow at all.[5] Yet there remain times when employment regulation makes good sense. If an employer stops providing eye protection to machinists for the sake of raising wages by a few cents, that is no more sensible than the licensed-personal-safety-supervisor plan.

A balance must be struck; the critical question is, who decides? Federal regulators increasingly dictate the terms and conditions of the workplace, but they are badly handicapped in carrying this out in two respects. First, they do not know the preferences of those for whom they are dictating. How can they divine whether a janitor prefers a mandated break every few hours or an extra $50 at the end of the week? Second, they cannot offer the tailoring and flexibility that a diverse national economy requires. Even if they knew the answer for a particular janitor, could they find an answer right for all janitors, let alone all low-wage service workers?

The alternative would be to let employers and employees reach their own arrangements. The employer knows the cost in lost productivity of breaks at a given interval; the employee knows how much he values those breaks. Presumably, the result of their bargaining will not be individualized schedules for everyone. But each employer has a strong incentive to offer the package of pay and benefits to its workforce that delivers the greatest value at the lowest cost, and job seekers have a similarly strong incentive to find the packages that best meet their needs.

The system will not be perfectly efficient, but the question is whether it will be *more* efficient than a series of edicts delivered from Washington. Skeptics may doubt that workers will have a good sense of the parameters of an employer's operation, especially for something as intangible as, say, safety conditions. But in fact, workers tend to seek higher wages to compensate for more dangerous jobs—so consistently that, as we saw in chapter 5, economists actually use the relationship between higher wages and higher workplace fatalities to estimate how much an average American values his own life. Every time someone justifies a new regulation by quoting the high value of reducing deaths—whether from traffic accidents, air pollutants, or hospital infections—she is endorsing the idea that workers manage to get themselves compensated fairly for the risks they incur.

The stronger objection to leaving employers and employees to their own devices is that the two sides have uneven bargaining power. A given worker with a particular skill set in a specific location may not have many job options from which to choose and, once on the job, may not have a credible option just to quit. But before asking the federal government to impose labor arrangements with no chance of striking the right balance between the parties, we should ask whether we might position the two sides to negotiate effectively themselves.

"Organized labor" claims to do just this, of course. Unfortunately, the American system of organized labor is a relic of the Great Depression, woefully incompatible with the demands and opportunities of the modern economy and actively harmful to both workers and firms. Private-sector union membership has been plunging for decades, from 36 percent of the workforce in 1953 to less than 7 percent in 2017.[6]

As its economic relevance has waned, Big Labor has mutated into a predominantly political force. Of $2.1 billion spent by the thirty largest federal-election donors from 1990 to 2014, public- and private-sector unions accounted for more than $1 billion—and directed 97 percent of that largess to Democrats.[7] Such one-way spending is at odds with union-member ideology, which aligns 26 percent "liberal," 44 percent "moderate," and 30 percent "conservative"—only slightly left of the general population.[8]

Democrats prize union bosses' Midas-like ability to transform the dollars and energy of a bipartisan workforce into homogenous left-wing support. Thus their response to plummeting union membership isn't to promote substantive reform that might make organizing more attractive to workers but instead to push for procedural changes to help unions bring more workers into the existing system and ensure that donations keep flowing. Republicans seem content to frustrate such efforts and watch the system continue to wither.

What a missed opportunity. Organized labor is neither inherently partisan nor inherently counterproductive economically. In theory, an arrangement by which workers "bargain collectively" and offer "mutual aid," as the National Labor Relations Act (NLRA) establishes is their right, can be a neutral or even positive part of a flourishing market economy. Other countries have implemented labor systems sharply different from—and more effective than—the American one. Even within the United States, examples exist of organized labor's potential to operate more constructively.

A better form of organized labor could push labor markets toward healthier outcomes by making workers more valuable and their employment more attractive. It could provide a superior alternative to government regulation of the workplace by brokering agreements that reflect the balance workers really want between protection and pay. It could also take a leading role in workforce preparedness and job training. More broadly, by performing functions like these, it could reassert itself in civil society, strengthening solidarity and offering a local mediation between government programs and recipients. Community health would benefit.

Appreciating the good that organized labor could do, however, requires first understanding the damage it has done.

* * *

It's an image deeply embedded in American culture: management sitting on one side of the table, its representatives wearing suits and looking perhaps a bit standoffish, and labor sitting on the other, its members tailored less elegantly and looking insistent, even angry. The confrontation has a long history, but the terms on which the two sides now negotiate have changed dramatically from the days of strikebreakers and labor goons. Today, when a private-sector union and an employer first negotiate, the union issues all the demands, offering in exchange only more of the labor peace that the employer presumably already enjoys. The best that a company can achieve in this scenario is to placate the union at minimal cost. To a labor organizer, the question "what's in it for the employer?" might seem bizarre—the whole point of organizing, after all, is to improve labor's position against capital. But even if shifting power toward labor is desirable for organizers, browbeating management into making concessions may not be wise. At a minimum, the effectiveness of such an approach will depend on economic and social conditions.

Those conditions may have been favorable in 1935, when Congress passed the NLRA—guaranteeing the right of private-sector workers to unionize and bargain collectively for better pay and working conditions—but much has changed in eighty-some years. The union movement's strategy under the NLRA of trying to organize whole industries—which harmed economic dynamism, even as it penalized consumers through higher prices and discouraged new workers by limiting job opportunities—proved unsustainable. Furthermore, employment regulations, by embedding traditional areas of bargaining directly into the standard law of the workplace, have undermined the entire premise of the NLRA. Meantime, the plunge in private-sector union membership has exposed unions' minimal value to workers. The total employee share of national income—66.1 percent at the start of 2016—is actually higher today, with a fraction of the union presence, than it was during the unions' 1950s zenith (64.5 percent).[9]

Union organizers locate the NLRA's primary shortcoming in its failure to protect workers' "free choice." As they see it, the law's requirement that they conduct an open campaign before any unionization vote within a firm invites the employer not only to inform workers about potential drawbacks of joining a union but also to intimidate them with illegal tactics that the law tries, but fails, to deter. Thus, say organizers, the appropriate remedy is to tilt the organizing process in their favor with rules that sideline employers—such as "card check," which enables a union to show majority support in a workplace simply by collecting enough employee-signed pro-union cards, dispensing entirely with secret-ballot elections.

It's pretty clear, though, that workers don't like unions much these days. In a landmark 1994 survey of more than twenty-four hundred nonmanagement workers, Harvard professor Richard Freeman and University of Wisconsin professor Joel Rogers primed respondents with various questions couched to make organizing seem attractive and then asked those not in a union already whether they'd vote for one if offered the chance. Only 32 percent said yes. When respondents had the option of joining a union or participating on a cooperative management–employee committee for discussing problems, union support fell to 23 percent; the committee concept proved more than twice as popular.[10]

While pro-union sentiment has ebbed and flowed nationwide in the intervening years, little evidence suggests that workers have become more inclined toward organizing. In 1994, when the survey was conducted, 57 percent of Americans viewed labor unions favorably. That figure fell as low as 41 percent during the Great Recession, before rebounding to 60 percent in 2017.[11] In 2010, constitutional amendments seeking to bar card-check campaigns won approval in four states.[12] From 2012 to 2017, right-to-work laws weakening union power expanded into the former labor strongholds of Indiana, Wisconsin, Michigan, West Virginia, Kentucky, and Missouri and now encompass the majority of states.[13]

In a controversial 2013 essay, longtime organizer Rich Yeselson argues that efforts to reinvigorate the labor movement through new organizing campaigns are futile. "Smart union strategists," he acknowledges, "can't compensate for a mostly (though not entirely) uninterested working class."[14] Thomas Geoghegan, a veteran labor lawyer who sought the Democratic nomination for a Chicago congressional seat in 2009, admits that even he, even in that political environment, "lost [his] nerve" to campaign in favor of organized labor. "As we know, most Democrats just won't say, outside of a union hall, 'You ought to join a union,'" writes Geoghegan in his 2014 book on the future of organized labor. "Yes, of course I think they should say it, but they won't. So let's deal with it. Like it or not, the word 'union' brings up too many mixed feelings."[15]

Chattanooga, home to a Volkswagen manufacturing plant with more than fifteen hundred hourly workers, is the Waterloo of 1930s-style organized labor. VW decided to support the United Auto Workers (UAW) in what would have been the first successful campaign to organize employees of a foreign auto manufacturer in the American South. For two years, management coordinated public statements with the union and let organizers into its facilities to meet with workers. The majority of workers gave organizers signed cards signaling support. But when the secret ballots were counted in February 2014, the unionization drive lost, 712 to 626.[16]

What workers understand, but labor organizers apparently do not (or will not), is that the NLRA's model of hyperadversarialism offers them much less upside than it once did and lots more downside, guaranteeing a conflict-ridden relationship with their employers and producing only short-term "gains" that over time reduce workers' value and opportunities. Among the most telling findings in Freeman's 1994 survey: given choice of representation either by an organization that "management cooperated with in discussing issues, but had no power to make decisions" or by one "that had more power, but management opposed," 63 percent of workers preferred cooperation and just 22 percent an adversarial stance. These results held even among active union members.[17]

What's changed is the background against which labor law operates. In 1935, workplaces were largely unregulated, the Great Depression had pushed the working class to the brink, and widespread labor unrest was causing severe economic and social disruption. The NLRA's objective was not only to empower workers but also to end what Senator Robert Wagner, the law's sponsor, called "a procession of bloody and costly strikes, which in some cases swelled almost to the magnitude of national emergencies."[18] Section 1 of the NLRA accordingly finds that "experience has proved that protection by law of the right of employees to organize and bargain collectively safeguards commerce from injury, impairment, or interruption, and promotes the flow of commerce by removing certain recognized sources of industrial strife and unrest [and] by encouraging practices fundamental to the friendly adjustment of industrial disputes."

Given the chaotic alternative, an employer might have seen real value in its employees organizing and bargaining peaceably under the new rules. But since 1935, regulations have made superfluous most of the basic terms and conditions of employment that were the basis for collective bargaining. Federal law now provides a safety net of benefits for the elderly, disabled, and unemployed; a forty-hour workweek, paid overtime, and a minimum wage; prohibitions on discrimination; workplace safety standards; personal leave; and a mandate that employers provide high-quality health insurance. Yet unions must still find something to deliver their dues-paying members. If the political process dictates (via regulation) those practices of highest value to workers, and funds (via taxpayers) the basket of resources and protections that society seemingly wants citizens to enjoy, what's left to bargain over?

Thus comes the prevalence of destructive work rules, circuitous grievance procedures, and counterproductive seniority systems in collective-bargaining agreements. With most sensible restrictions already legally mandated, employers have two options: make wage concessions that will impose higher costs now or make peripheral commitments that will be felt only later. Codifying new work rules tends to cost little at first, because the parties usually design them aware of the limits of current operations—but unaware of how market demands and production technologies might change over time. Forcing managers to retain incompetent workers costs little—until a critical mass of bad workers accumulates. Promising seniority doesn't hurt, either—until layoffs become necessary and better workers get let go. Bestowing lavish pensions is painless too—until they have to be funded. The longest-tenured and least-effective workers are usually the union's strongest supporters, which makes such provisions ideal from their perspective as well. The result: shortsighted agreements that best serve each side's immediate interests but can have considerable long-term costs.

In 1936, after a summer that saw hundreds of deaths from poor working conditions in Michigan auto plants, GM workers in Flint launched their famous sit-down strike to achieve recognition for the UAW. Among their demands: permission to speak in the lunchroom.[19] Seventy years later, GM had converted the site of the sit-down into a "rubber room" where laid-off union members earned salary and benefits for doing nothing, as part of an industry-wide "jobs bank" that cost nearly $1 billion per year.[20]

As the declining value of collective bargaining eroded the NLRA's foundation from one side, the growing burden of its costs caused significant damage from the other. Throughout the postwar boom, when oligopolies controlled large swathes of an American economy isolated from foreign competition, multiemployer negotiations between an industry's major producers and a union representing all the industry's workers were common.[21] Collectively bargained terms that applied to all industry producers would maintain the competitive balance among them; if costs rose, they would raise prices together, preserving profit margins.[22]

This translated into higher prices, lower output, and slower innovation for the economy as a whole—and weaker job growth, harming prospective employees. Union members were also consumers, of course, which meant that they were often negotiating against themselves—balancing their desire for higher wages and benefits against their desire for lower prices. If nonunion consumers were the deal's real losers, well, then, that was all the more reason to join a union.

In recent decades, the collectively bargained concessions that unionized firms have adopted often put them at a disadvantage against foreign competition as well as against new, nonunionized domestic rivals. Unionized firms, as a consequence, have sought to shift their capital toward plants, regions, and countries where they can operate free of union constraints. Even if an industry remained insulated from foreign competition, the cumulative effect of operating for decades in an environment that muffles competition, constrains output, and stalls innovation has tended to leave it smaller and less productive than it might otherwise have been. Over time, the NLRA has burdened unionized facilities within a firm, unionized firms within an industry, and unionized industries within the economy.

The trend in manufacturing is illustrative. Union defenders cite a trade- and automation-driven employment collapse in that sector, a natural base for organized labor, as a no-fault explanation for the dwindling relevance of manufacturing unions. But this confuses cause and effect. Yes, unionized manufacturing employment plummeted from 7.8 million to 1.3 million from 1973 through 2017. But the drop accounted for more than 100 percent of the decline in manufacturing jobs during that period; nonunion manufacturing employment actually increased from 12.3 million to 13.3 million.[23]

The NLRA is clearly not accomplishing its goals. Yet, rather than contemplate how organized labor might function better, union leaders and their political allies just keep the emphasis on getting more workers to join unions.

* * *

Collective action by workers under a different framework could help address some of America's greatest challenges in ways that policy makers across the political spectrum should consider.

Call the new organizations "co-ops." One potential path for this new kind of organization, taken by unions operating under the "Ghent system" of many European countries, is to establish relationships with workers and provide benefits to them outside the employment context. In Denmark and Sweden, for instance, unions administer an unemployment insurance system that workers join independently of their employer. Those countries don't require workplace elections, good-faith bargaining by employers, or compulsory dues payments, yet a majority of workers are union members.[24] While the scale of the American labor market may seem dissimilar, management of most social insurance—including unemployment, disability, and health—has devolved already to the state level. Co-ops can plausibly supplement or supplant state-level programs, with the relationship perhaps differing based on a state's economic profile.

"In the Danish system," explains SUNY Buffalo professor Matt Dimick, "the employer's freedom to hire and fire is explicitly linked to the robust unemployment insurance guarantee in its vaunted program of 'flexicurity.' Hence, just as the official slogan of Swedish Social Democracy proclaimed in the 1950s and 1960s, Denmark's model of flexicurity is described as providing 'employment security, not job security.'"[25] Remarkably, the American conservative Yuval Levin offers a prescription for twenty-first-century America that echoes the central tenet of mid-twentieth-century Swedish social democracy. Supports for workers, he writes, "will need to help make a diffuse labor market more secure, rather than trying to reverse its diffusion."[26] Co-ops could help do this.

Co-ops representing workers in negotiations with an employer could also provide a market-based alternative to the government's employment regulation. The need for such regulation stems largely from the premise that individual workers lack the leverage to protect their interests—an obsolete consideration when an organized workforce can bargain collectively. Why shouldn't a co-op be allowed to accept wages below the federal minimum, perhaps for apprentice-level workers enrolled in job-training programs?

While a co-op, when negotiating with an employer, would never be forced to accept terms or conditions below the federal standard, it could have the option of doing so if the employer offered something compelling in return. Workers could substitute their own judgment for that of federal bureaucrats about what they value most. A retail chain and its workers, for instance, might benefit from an hours-scheduling system that created certainty and eliminated "on-call" time, while lowering overtime pay below time-and-a-half. A regulatory adjustment, voluntarily agreed to by employer and co-op, could reduce employer costs and boost worker satisfaction.

Treating employment law not as ironclad but as a default rule from which the parties can agree to depart also gets rid of the problem of one-sided bargaining. Instead, workers in a given firm would have the choice between a federally regulated workplace and one overseen by a collective-bargaining agreement. Such bargaining could still be adversarial, in the way any business negotiation involves two sides seeking to maximize their own gains, but it would not be zero-sum; the outcomes could deliver significant benefits to both sides. Imagine the first day of negotiations opening with the employer dropping an inch-high stack of rules on the table and asking "how much do you want if we can get rid of this?"

Another promising avenue for co-ops would be to partner with employers to improve the job readiness of new hires and offer job training for all workers. When business leaders complain that they can't find enough qualified employees, the solution seems self-evident: if they need a better-trained workforce, perhaps they should invest more in training. But the economics of human capital are complex.[27] If an employer improves a worker's skills, the worker can demand to be compensated accordingly—or leave for another firm. The employer might design its training so that the worker's skills are inapplicable elsewhere, but this leaves it far more vulnerable to an organizing campaign and strike; if its specially trained workers walk out, in other words, they can't easily be replaced. The depressing alternative is for employers to design processes that require the least skill and make workers most interchangeable.

Employers would like to hire highly skilled workers whom they don't pay to train, just as workers would like to acquire more skills and work in systems that value them accordingly. But how to get there? Co-ops could fund and conduct training programs, negotiate with employers to share costs and provide access to apprenticeships, and draw on government education programs as well. Although workers would pay for a portion of their own training via co-op dues, they would benefit from substantial employer and government support—as well as, eventually, the full value of their improved skills.

Such schemes raise the prospect of twentieth-century corporatism, with established employers, unions, and government collaborating to drain a slush fund of other people's taxes and dues—but in this case, the correct participants, sources of funds, and incentives are in place to minimize that risk. Placing worker-controlled and -funded co-ops at the center of training initiatives should keep them focused on the interests of workers. Even if co-ops get "captured" by self-interested leadership, that self-interest should point toward maximizing the skills, earnings—and, therefore, dues—of as many workers as possible. For their part, employers will have to negotiate for access to the co-op pools that offer the highest-quality talent and should seek out those that can accomplish this at the lowest cost.

This approach would be superior to the nation's largely ineffective current network of job-training efforts. Decision-making would shift from government agencies and well-meaning nonprofits to employers and workers—who need each other, understand their requirements best, and will measure their return on investment by how many high-productivity jobs result, not by "enrollment" or "graduation," as is typically the case with government and nonprofit plans. Co-op-led training would also introduce a fair, insurance-like support mechanism, whereby dues from the currently employed help pay for the unemployed to learn new skills.

Examples of union-led training already exist. North America's Building Trades Unions, for instance, operate sixteen hundred joint labor-management training centers, funded by more than $1 billion in annual dues and employer contributions.[28] The Las Vegas Culinary Workers Union's Culinary Academy, created in partnership with the Las Vegas hotels, is another example, providing basic job training to recruit new workers into the trade and then ongoing training to help them advance in their careers.[29]

But these arrangements come with all the baggage of an NLRA union. In Las Vegas, for instance, the culinary union is also known for "cutthroat, guerilla tactics" and its years-long assault on the nonunion Station casinos.[30] Station was ranked by *Fortune* among "the Top 100 Best Companies to Work For" nationwide in four consecutive years, from 2005 to 2008.[31] But it committed the unforgivable sin, in the eyes of the union, of refusing a demand to forgo secret-ballot elections and permit organization via card check. Reminiscent of the classic story in the film *Ocean's Eleven* of a casino mogul who sought revenge against a cheat by "bankrupt[ing] his brother-in-law's tractor dealership,"[32] the union has gone so far as to have its New York affiliate pressure that state to maintain a ban on mixed martial arts' Ultimate Fighting Championship because the league's owners also own Station.[33] Valuable training partnerships notwithstanding, such dynamics are not ones any employer or industry is likely to tolerate.

Less tangibly, but no less importantly, co-ops could be mediating institutions that help to strengthen civil society for poorer and less-educated Americans. Formal organization increases the chance that a workplace also becomes a nexus of community. It establishes the infra-structure for workers to build relationships, access resources, and provide mutual aid. It creates space for the "solidarity" that David and Amber Lapp of the Institute for Family Studies emphasize is critical to the social health of working-class individuals and communities. "John Paul II," they note, "described [worker associations] as essential, 'not only in negotiating contracts, but also as "places" where workers can express themselves.'"[34] Such institutions can also play a role in the broader community and offer a point of contact for those outside the workforce who need to enter. Policy makers generally agree on the importance of rebuilding mediat-ing institutions and social capital but find few levers to pull on behalf of phenomena like family and faith. Reforming organized labor, by contrast, is an appropriate and plausible government intervention.

Within the workplace, co-ops could build collaborative relation-ships with management. From the workers' perspective, the opportunity to raise concerns and suggestions from within the protection of a group has inherent value and is likely to lead at least sometimes to positive change. From the employer's perspective, such communication can pro-vide useful feedback, which could help improve the experiences of both employees and customers. Furthermore, regular interaction between the two sides—as equals committed to (and essential to) the success of the enterprise—should contribute to more autonomy and innovation on workers' parts and also to the emergence of more empathetic cultures within and beyond the workplace. That's something most employees want, as Freeman's survey showed.

Such arrangements exist in many countries as company-specific "works councils," most notably in Germany, where they're present at almost 90 percent of firms with more than five hundred workers and have significant authority not just to hold discussions but also to make operational decisions.[35] They're at present prohibited in the United States by section 8(a)(2) of the NLRA, which treats their formation, absent a formal union, as an unfair labor practice.[36]

The failure to reform this provision offers another reminder that union and worker interests don't invariably align. Unions rightly fear that companies and workers would embrace this alternative form of organized labor. (Volkswagen cooperated with the push to organize its Chattanooga plant chiefly because it wanted a works council.) Works councils, says former AFL-CIO president Lane Kirkland, are "sham organizations designed to prevent real worker empowerment."[37] Big Labor's vocal endorsement of "free choice" does not, it seems, extend to choices other than joining Big Labor.

Finally, co-ops could extend employment-like benefits and training functions to sectors of the economy with no traditional employer. The NLRA delivers the worst of both worlds—pushing employers to avoid worker relationships that could trigger collective-bargaining obligations but offering little to the growing mass of less than fully employed workers this helps create. Co-ops do the opposite, increasing the value of employment relationships and providing nontraditional workers with some of the infrastructure they otherwise lack.

The "gig economy" introduces efficiency and dynamism into certain markets, while offering valuable flexibility to workers. But as George Mason professor Tyler Cowen observes, that kind of labor-market flexibility implies that "more workers will have to teach and train themselves, whether for their current jobs or for a future job they might have later on. I submit many people cannot train themselves very well, even when the pecuniary returns from such training are fairly strongly positive."[38]

Given the burdens of current employment regulation and labor law, the transportation-network firm Uber is understandably reluctant to engage with its drivers as employees or to risk collective bargaining. But what if its drivers were to form co-ops, independent of their relationship to Uber, to support one another and discuss with the firm arrangements like human capital investment, which might benefit both sides?

Like the guilds of the past, co-ops could provide structure to otherwise free-floating careers and a valuable signaling mechanism to prospective employers. They would also give workers the scale and security to negotiate with buyers of labor in the marketplace. To take an ambitious example from *Grand New Party*, written by *National Review*'s Reihan Salam and the *New York Times*'s Ross Douthat the year before Uber's founding,

> in the long run, unions might evolve into enormous talent agencies with an economic stake in increasing the wages of members by, for example, taking some small cut of any salary increase and then reinvesting the money into providing workers with the resources to move from sluggish labor markets to booming labor markets. Whereas traditional unions have an interest in keeping workers in one place, new model unions would encourage them to be footloose, all while maintaining strong ties to their fellow workers.[39]

Any proposed labor reform should be guided by a question: will it facilitate such imaginative futures, or frustrate them?

*　*　*

The smoothest path to reform may be not to update or replace the NLRA but to leave it in place and go around it. A union whose members are satisfied can continue to represent them, and an organizer who believes an NLRA union would win majority support in a workplace should be free to pursue such a campaign. But other options should be available too. Over time, especially if co-ops proved their value, membership in NLRA unions would decline toward zero as capital departed unionized firms, remaining workers voted to change their organizational form, and few new organizing campaigns succeeded. If workers chose to give NLRA unions a fresh look, they could still do that. This is what real employee choice would look like.

Effective reform would have four elements. First, the NLRA must no longer have exclusive jurisdiction over relationships between employers and organizations of workers. Its definition of a covered "labor organization" must narrow from all organizations of employees whose purpose is "dealing with employers" to only those established for the purpose of using NLRA-defined rights and processes. The 8(a)(2) prohibition on nonunion collaboration between employers and workers must go. None of these changes affects the ability of a union to operate with its current model—to the extent that workers choose it.

Second, the government should formally recognize the existence of the "labor cooperative": a nonprofit controlled by its dues-paying members for the purpose of advancing their employment and creating value in the labor market rather than merely reallocating it. Co-ops will be held to governance and financial standards appropriate to their potential roles and be eligible to partner with government in delivering benefits. They will also have the capacity to earn recognition as the collective representative of employees in a given workplace, but their existence will not depend on such recognition.

The government should also recognize the works council—a group of worker-selected employees responsible for representing employee interests to management, including the ability to bargain collectively. An employer could support the creation and operation of such a council, but checks must exist on any possible employer domination of its decision-making. For instance, employees might have recourse to a snap "vote of no confidence" in a council that they felt wasn't fully representing their interests.

Fourth, a recognition process similar to that existing for NLRA unions should allow a co-op or works council to become the exclusive representative of employees for negotiating a collective-bargaining agreement with an employer—but that bargaining process will differ from the NLRA's. Applicability of most employment regulation should be negotiable. Multiemployer bargaining should be banned. Any defined-benefit pensions should be set explicitly outside the protection of federal insurance—if workers want to make such a bet on employer solvency, they should do it on their own initiative. These changes improve the position of the employer by design, with the goal of creating a space for mutually beneficial agreements.

Co-ops could take several forms in such a framework. Some might be specific to a company, community, industry, occupation, or combination thereof. A works council might choose to form a co-op for its own employees and ultimately expand further into the community, or a nonprofit might incubate a number of co-ops within a city. An employer and a community college might partner to get a co-op started. Benefits to scale and expertise sharing will emerge, but the importance of local relationships and community engagement should place a high premium on local control. Some of these hypothetical arrangements will undoubtedly prove impractical, while many more alternatives not yet conceived will emerge if employers and workers have the freedom to innovate outside the NLRA's sclerotic confines.

Unlike with unions, membership and dues payment would always be voluntary, meaning that the path to success would entail effective provision of services, not an accumulation of political power and victories in contentious workplace votes. Organizations would have to behave more like employee-owned service providers than like the national machines of Big Labor. The act of "organizing" would look more like selling gym memberships than like sidewalk picketing.

Social safety-net reforms could allow properly constituted co-ops to receive funding for programs like unemployment insurance, job training, and community college. Current proposals like wage insurance and subsidized apprenticeships should consider what role co-ops might play in delivery. Where employers do not provide health insurance, co-ops could serve as an alternative before workers shop for individual plans.

Last, co-ops must be kept from redirecting funds toward political advocacy. "There is nothing in the nature of unionization that requires the bundling of economic and political functions," says Harvard professor (and former Service Employees International Union assistant general counsel) Benjamin Sachs. "Bundling is instead an artifact of history and, more to the point, of law."[40] After all, unlike unions, co-ops will potentially receive funding not only from member dues but also from employers, nonprofits, and the government. The restriction on advocacy is consistent with that applied to 501(c)(3) organizations (including those engaged in public policy debates), which does not raise First Amendment concerns. Co-ops will be free to create, and fund-raise for, separate PACs, as many nonprofits do today. But their worker-representation and political functions would remain separate.

It's not crazy to suggest that organized labor focus on delivering economic benefits to workers instead of campaign contributions to politicians or to imagine that workers might benefit more from collaboration than from conflict with their employers in the modern economy. Workers themselves seem to believe this. Good policy could help to achieve it.

*   *   *

A decision to leave the terms and conditions of employment in the hands of workers and their employers departs dramatically from the current trend in policy making, which seeks to identify and impose the package of benefits that policy makers themselves prefer. Such efforts to override the labor market demand two types of scrutiny, which the contrast with market-based bargaining throws into sharp relief. First, who pays? Second, who is constrained?

When government chooses to provide a benefit itself, the financial transaction is transparent. Funds come from taxpayers and go to beneficiaries. The cost appears clearly in the annual budget. When government instead mandates that someone else, like an employer, provide a benefit, the dynamic is murkier. No "spending increase" occurs. Yet, just as surely, the force of law is used to take resources from some people for the benefit of others.

The minimum wage, discussed further in the following chapter, provides a classic illustration of the phenomenon. A minimum wage may be free to taxpayers, but someone must put the additional money in each paycheck. Maybe it is the employer; maybe it is other employees; maybe it is customers. A theory of who is paying goes a long way toward explaining whether the policy is fair and whether its influence on the labor market will be beneficial.

Generally speaking, government-mandated benefits must be borne in some combination by employers and workers. This makes them doubly unattractive. First, the policy is regressive, imposing a higher burden on people relatively less able to pay, at least as compared with the high-income taxpayers whom society has chosen to fund its social programs.

Second, by raising the cost of the employment relationship, the policy pushes labor markets away from the desired outcome of more jobs at higher wages.

If a policy maker does believe a benefit is so important that all workers must receive it, regardless of the agreements they reach with their employers, he should propose to provide it via a standard government program, funded by taxpayers. Benefits provided in this way operate as subsidies for employment and thus boost rather than hinder employment relationships. The policy maker would predictably complain that no funds are available for such a program, but that is the point. If he would not countenance a tax increase to fund his idea, he should not countenance a law that has no "tax" but orders private actors to incur comparable costs just the same.

Recognizing mandates as a form of taxing and spending, then, highlights the second question about constraints: if government is to raise and spend funds on behalf of workers, why not just give them the funds via a wage subsidy? Why force them to spend it on the policy maker's chosen benefit?

The bipartisan push for paid parental leave is a perfect example. The concept of parental leave enjoys broad support, and ensuring that lower-income households can continue to pay their bills while away from work would seem an obvious prerequisite to making the opportunity universally available. But the policy can be disaggregated into two independent components: the financial payment and the absence from work. For instance, a man with a $30,000 salary who takes six weeks of paid leave receives a $3,600 payment and six weeks off.

What if, especially facing the costs of a newborn on a shoestring budget, that family decides the man should work during those six weeks, allowing him to receive his $3,600 paid-leave payment *as well as* $3,600 of salary for the period? If the goal is to provide financial resources to the family, this outcome should be as welcome as the one in which he takes his leave.

By instead conditioning the $3,600 paid-leave payment on *not* working, the government asserts an explicit goal of having the man spend time at home. That presents an awkward quandary. If the government has already decided it has the $3,600 available to spend on helping this family, and the family has decided the man's best use of time in those six weeks is working for pay, does the policy maker have a legitimate basis for overruling the family's determination?

More often than not, government-mandated benefits are borne by the wrong payers, deliver the wrong benefits, and push toward the wrong labor-market outcomes. Empowering workers to assert their own interests and find arrangements mutually beneficial to themselves and their employers holds far greater promise for delivering the outcomes we need.

CHAPTER 9

THE WAGE SUBSIDY

In July 2017, the Taiwanese electronics supplier Foxconn, assembler of iPhones, announced that it would build a $10 billion manufacturing facility in Wisconsin. Annual payroll would exceed $700 million—thirteen thousand workers at an average salary of more than $50,000, plus benefits—and Wisconsin expected the plant to generate annual state and local tax revenue of $181 million and lead to the creation of twenty thousand additional jobs. To attract this investment, the state offered Foxconn approximately $3 billion in tax incentives over fifteen years, conditional on the firm achieving the promised levels of investment and employment: up to $1.35 billion for capital investment, up to $1.5 billion for job creation, and $150 million in sales tax exemptions.[1]

To some, the deal stunk of corporate welfare. "Foxconn could get up to $200 million in cash a year from state residents for up to 15 years," the *Milwaukee Journal Sentinel* lamented.[2] "Wisconsin taxpayers should not be subsidizing private corporations at the expense of our children, schools and roads," Democratic state representative Jimmy Anderson complained.[3] "This is buying jobs at a very high price," Carl Davis of the Institute on Taxation and Economic Policy told the *New York Times*. "And it's certainly not small government. This is not stepping out of the way and letting the market do what it does."[4] MSNBC host Chris Hayes responded via Twitter with a nonplussed "Wut."[5] (The *Urban Dictionary*

explains that this word is "used in response to an unclear or absurd statement when seeking to clarify it or expose said absurdity."[6]) In response,
Wisconsin's Republican governor Scott Walker fired back, "That's fine,
but I think they can go suck lemons."[7]

This kind of subsidy defies conventional analysis. Is it liberal?
Conservative? Free market? Statist? Pro-business? Pro-worker? Under
the strain of a global economy pulling from one side and a social safety
net pulling from the other, the meanings of these words are colliding. If
other countries offer such packages to attract manufacturers, does the U.S.
government promote a "free market" by refusing to go that route—or by
doing the same? The free-market supporter might prefer an undistorted
market, but by endorsing free trade with mercantilist economies, he has
already allowed the distortions of foreign governments into the United
States. For the unemployed Wisconsinite, "smaller government" is poor
consolation when a firm chooses to hire workers in some other country
because *their* government provides it a subsidy, while *his* would not.

Meanwhile, a household with no income may already receive more
government aid than it would cost Wisconsin to have Foxconn provide
gainful employment. An eligible family of four in Wisconsin receives
health care and food stamp benefits worth more than $15,000 annually.[8]
If an unemployed adult exited the workforce entirely and began collecting disability insurance, he might get an additional $10,000.[9] By paying
Foxconn a lesser amount to offer that family a good job with benefits,
does the government grow or shrink?

The Foxconn deal illustrates another way policy makers can influence the labor market. If we want more well-paying, blue-collar jobs in
America, on this view, we can just buy them. Numerous social benefits
would accompany such purchases, reminding us why we care about
labor-market outcomes in the first place. The state and local tax payments
would nearly equal the incentives paid out, on top of which the federal
government would pull in tax payments as well. Welfare payments would
decline. More than thirteen thousand households would have a worker
with full-time employment and benefits. Foxconn's operations would
likely spill over into increased investment and employment elsewhere in
the local economy.

Wisconsin's approach is half right—paying for jobs makes sense.
How they've gone about it, however, does not.

*   *   *

At present, America generally does not pay for jobs. In fact, federal and local governments impose large taxes on them. Every dollar an employer pays to a worker is subject to tax, as is any profit the employer earns from the worker's activity. Good reasons exist to use income taxes as the primary means for funding government, but any discussion of how public policy influences the labor market must acknowledge that the result of this taxation is to insert a substantial wedge between worker and employer. A task for which a worker would accept as little as $10 per hour and an employer would pay as much as $10 per hour won't translate into a job, for example, because paying the worker $10 leaves him, after taxes, with less than $10.

In theory, for lower-wage workers in particular, the income tax system's progressivity should avoid this predicament. The government tries to raise most of its tax revenue from higher-income households, applying no income tax to a worker's initial earnings and only very low tax rates until he reaches the middle class. Households with $50,000 to $75,000 of income, for instance, pay an average income tax rate below 4 percent.[10]

The problem is that America also has payroll taxes, intended to finance Social Security and Medicare. These are paid at the same rate by all workers, beginning with their first dollar earned (and while the employer pays a portion of the tax formally, economists generally presume that the worker bears its full burden). Until 1950, payroll taxes claimed only 2 percent of income. By 1990, they exceeded 15 percent.[11] Over that same time period, while individual income taxes consistently accounted for between 40 percent and 45 percent of total federal revenues, payroll taxes rose from an 11 percent share to a 37 percent share. Corporate income taxes, conversely, fell from 27 percent of federal revenue to just 9 percent. Those figures then held relatively steady through 2017.[12] This tilt in the federal tax burden from corporations and their shareholders on to lower-income households, over a period when the former's fortunes surged and the latter's sagged, seems inexplicable.

Except that it is easily explained by the interests of the two political parties. For Democrats, payroll taxes are the one source of revenue tied irrevocably to funding entitlement programs. Tax rates rose along with the cost of Social Security and Medicare; holding them down would require either restricting the growth of entitlement spending or else funding that growth out of general tax revenues. Such a funding shift would expose the reality that these old-age entitlements are in fact welfare programs that pay many retirees far more than they paid in, potentially undermining their popular support. Protecting the entitlements has been the Democrats' priority, even when it comes at the expense of low-wage workers.

Republicans, meantime, prioritize tax cuts that they expect will produce the largest gains in business investment and thus economic growth. This leads them to focus on lowering rates for corporations and high-income households. Other things held equal, they might support lower payroll tax rates as well. But if forced to choose, most would regard the tax-burden shift that occurred from corporations onto low-wage workers to be the more attractive, pro-growth option. If the goal is merely faster GDP growth, that may be the best approach. If the goal is a healthy labor market, though, aiming the tax code at promoting investment and growth is overbroad—that is, much of its effect is disconnected from the purported goal—and paying for corporate and high income tax reductions with higher taxes on low-wage labor is counterproductive. The implicit message to the market is "try to grow rapidly with as little labor as possible." The market appears to have listened.

The Foxconn deal errs in a different way. By identifying a specific employer that would provide the specific jobs lacking in the state's labor market, Wisconsin cannot be accused of an overbroad policy. Its offer amounts to a single-user tax cut, eliminating tax liability for a particular investment contingent on it creating the desired jobs. That may be defensible in isolation, but as public policy, it is unwise. Why should Foxconn pay lower taxes than Wisconsin's many other manufacturers? Why should it pay lower taxes than the many other businesses that will be located in the same town? Maybe, in a perfect world, the government could carefully calibrate a precisely appropriate tax rate for each employer—the idea recalls the environmental regulator's dream in chapter 5 of accounting for every externality. In the real world, this kind of case-by-case winner picking introduces significant distortions into the labor market and places investment decisions under political control. Soon politicians will be horse trading to steer employers to their own districts, boost politically popular industries, and play at venture capitalism as they guess which investments hold the greatest promise for the future.

Programs and proposals abound to split the difference between a generic tax cut and the company-specific handout. For instance, the federal Work Opportunity Tax Credit provides businesses with a tax credit of 25 percent to 40 percent of a new hire's first-year earnings if he falls into a category such as veteran, welfare recipient, or ex-felon.[13] During her 2016 presidential campaign, Hillary Clinton proposed a $1,500 tax credit for every apprentice a business hired, with an additional bonus for providing opportunities to young people.[14] As with the Foxconn deal, these measures sound appealing in isolation but are problematic for the wider labor market. They encourage employers to discriminate in hiring, churn rapidly through workers, lobby for new provisions and exceptions to benefit themselves and harm competitors, and in general adapt their business practices to the particulars of the tax code. Workers in turn get steered toward the behaviors that their prospective employers will be rewarded for seeking out.

No, if the goal is to create a corporate tax code that pushes the economy toward more labor-intensive development, the best way to accomplish that would be to lower the tax burden of firms with relatively more workers. We could create a standard, per-worker exemption, just as the individual tax code had for children up until the 2017 tax reform. For every full-time worker employed for the entire year, a firm could subtract, say, $10,000 from its taxable profits at year's end. To raise the same revenue as before, the corporate tax rate would need to be higher—yet firms that generated profits through the productive employment of workers would benefit at the expense of firms that did so through other means. For entrepreneurs, the kind of business that makes use of the workers available in the country would become more attractive.

Still, even a simple and straightforward attempt to mold behavior with tax incentives faces the challenge that the tax code is a mess and yet another tweak will only make it messier. Business tax credits generally work only if the business has profits (and thus taxes) to be credited. Different types of businesses get taxed at different rates and thus see different value in reducing their taxable income. The temptation for financial engineering and other manipulation inevitably proves overwhelming, in this approach: hiring sprees would be timed before the start of a calendar year and mass layoffs concentrated after its end, for example. There is a simpler way.

If we really want to "pay for jobs"—and we should—then we should do it *directly*. Recall Rachel Green's reaction to opening her paycheck and discovering that FICA had deducted a percentage. What if another line, titled "Federal Work Bonus," showed that the government had put an additional $3 into her check for every hour she had worked? That would be a wage subsidy.

* * *

The premise of any subsidy is to encourage economic transactions that would not otherwise occur. The subsidy provider in effect pays a seller to accept a price he would otherwise consider too low or pays a buyer to make an otherwise too-expensive purchase. If the federal government wanted Americans to buy larger televisions, for example, it could offer consumers or manufacturers $50 for every fifty-inch flat-screen sold. Without the subsidy, a consumer willing to pay only $450 for a television that costs $500 would decline to buy it. With the manufacturer subsidy, the seller gladly accepts the $450 that the consumer will pay, but he still gets the $500 he originally sought, after the government pitches in. Or, with the consumer rebate, the buyer gladly pays the $500 asking price because he ultimately spends only the $450 with which he was willing to part.

A wage subsidy produces the same effect in the labor market. Workers unwilling to sell their labor for less than $12 per hour may be worth only $9 per hour to an employer. No job will emerge in that scenario. With the insertion of a $3 per hour wage subsidy, by contrast, the employer can pay the $9 per hour that the work is worth and the worker can receive the $12 per hour that he demanded. Thus will appear a job where none existed before.

Furthermore, a wage subsidy is doubly beneficial because we care not only about how many transactions occur but also about how much workers receive. We may be indifferent to the TV manufacturer earning $500 versus $450 per TV, but we are pleased when families see their household incomes rise. If a worker earning $9 per hour can take home $12 per hour instead, we may have lifted him out of poverty.

The federal Earned Income Tax Credit (EITC) already operates something like a wage subsidy, offering low-income households large tax refunds that can exceed what they paid in taxes to begin with. In 2017, 27 million households received an average of $2,445 through the program;[15] for a married couple with two children and income of $25,000, the credit would exceed $5,000.[16] But the EITC gets paid long after the income is earned—at tax time the following year—based on an opaque formula. It creates none of a wage subsidy's immediate, transparent effect in the labor market. How many people, after all, realize that the federal minimum wage is not really $7.25 per hour because, counting the $5,600 credit for which he is eligible, the parent of two children working full time at that wage eventually ends up with more than $10 per hour worked?[17]

The EITC also skews its benefits heavily toward households with children. A single person working full time at minimum wage would get a credit of $41, less than 1 percent of what his colleague with kids can expect. As an antipoverty initiative, such targeting may be defensible; as a labor-market intervention, it is not. In many cases, the single, childless worker is precisely the person whom policy makers should be most eager to connect with a job.

As in the $9-per-hour example, the ideal wage subsidy would instead operate as a per-hour payment to the worker, based on his market wage. The value of the subsidy would be set relative to a "target wage" of, say, $15 per hour, and close half the gap between the market wage and the target. A worker would initially receive a subsidy of $3 per hour, in this case, equal to approximately $6,000 per year if he worked full time.

This differs from most programs that transfer resources to lower-income households, including the EITC, which phase out as the household's total income rises; for every additional dollar earned by the household, the worker loses some of the benefits he was receiving. With the direct wage subsidy, the worker receives the same subsidy for every hour worked at a given wage, no matter how much total income he earns. He can take a second job and earn the subsidy for each of those hours. His wife can take a job and earn her own subsidy too. The value of the subsidy only declines as workers become more productive, earning promotions and raises.

Administration of such a program would be straightforward, in fact, because the government and employers already do it, in reverse.

To operate the payroll tax system, almost every employer must calculate for each pay period, for each employee, a tax owed; deduct that amount from his paycheck; and send it to the U.S. Treasury. The subsidy requires a comparable process, but with money placed into the paycheck instead of taken out. All workers would be automatically eligible based on their hourly wage (for salaried employees, on a per-hour equivalent). If overtime hours get paid at a higher wage, those hours receive less or no subsidy.

As chapter 7 briefly alludes, subsidizing wages is a particularly well-tailored response to the challenges that globalization presents for American workers. First, the wage subsidy is the appropriate mechanism for redistributing gains from the economy's "winners" to its "losers." It comes closest to doing this directly, by taking tax revenue drawn from higher earners and inserting it directly into the paychecks of lower earners. As a result, it demands the least of government and introduces the fewest opportunities for inefficiency and distortion. Perhaps most importantly, it ties the redistribution to productive employment rather than to its absence.

Second, the wage subsidy offsets subsidies given to foreign producers and moves the cost to employers for domestic workers closer to parity with what firms pay foreign workers living in sharply different social and economic contexts. The benefit is largest for industries where the work is most labor intensive and relies on the lowest-cost labor—in other words, the industries under greatest pressure from globalization. But it does this through a *neutral structure*, not through politicians choosing when to intervene.

Third, the wage subsidy helps to sustain communities that lose their tradeable sector. A community lacking the ability to export (even to the rest of the nation) must rely on government-transfer payments to fund the resources it requires from the outside world—the community is literally exporting need. The existing American safety net conditions those transfers on very low incomes—often, no work at all—and channels them primarily toward consumption of health care services. With a wage subsidy, work, rather than unemployment, draws government support, and that support can flow to a fuller range of productive activities in the community. In this model, a services economy can still thrive disconnected from a tradeable sector—not an ideal arrangement but one far better than today's.

This invites the question, isn't the wage subsidy just another form of redistribution from the wealthier beneficiaries of growth? Yes and no. Yes, it is redistribution. And yes, high-income taxpayers will finance it. But unlike with government assistance disconnected from work, productive pluralism is not diluted if the productive job through which someone supports her family and contributes to her community yields a paycheck into which the government has put in more than it takes out. Certainly a society of thriving and perfectly self-sufficient families would be preferable. But America is nowhere near such a reality today, and for some people, it may never happen. If we can at least make redistribution a tool for creating jobs and promoting work, we will be moving the labor market in the right direction and delivering better outcomes for those who need support.

Indeed, a key benefit of the wage subsidy, discussed at length in the next chapter, is that it can *supplant* parts of the safety net rather than adding yet another layer. Antipoverty programs already transfer vast sums—far above what the wage subsidy would require—to low-income households. Unfortunately, they do this in ways that discourage work and thus tend to trap people in poverty rather than lifting them out. Reallocating funding into paychecks for those who can work would boost the labor market and improve the quality of the safety net, at no additional cost to taxpayers.

* * *

Wage-subsidy proposals have existed for decades, emerging from disparate points on the political spectrum. In 1974, the Urban Institute's Robert Lerman—then a congressional staffer—prepared a report for the Joint Economic Committee that proposed one.[18] In 1997, Nobel Prize–winning economist Edmund Phelps published a book that proposed one.[19] In 2017, Senator Marco Rubio proposed legislation to implement one in Puerto Rico.[20] Yet the mainstream of both political parties has preferred to retreat behind firmly entrenched positions.

True, the EITC already exists. But it began as a temporary program in the 1970s, expanded in fits and starts, and, as described earlier, is poorly suited to the task of subsidizing wages. Both parties profess support, but neither will contemplate any sacrifices to bolster it. In 2014, President Obama and Representative Paul Ryan both proposed expanding the meager credit offered to childless workers, but Obama would not agree to shifting money from any other program to fund the expansion, and Ryan would not agree to raising any taxes.[21] In 2017, Representative Ro Khanna, the Democrat representing Silicon Valley, proposed more than doubling the credit at a cost of $1.4 trillion over ten years. Lest anyone think him serious, he explained neither how to pay for this nor how it makes sense to deliver assistance to a family with $20,000 of annual income in the form of a $10,000 check the following year.[22]

For many Republicans, any wage subsidy remains a form of redistribution and thus inherently suspect. Furthermore, it intervenes in the market, encouraging employers to hire workers whom they otherwise wouldn't under current market conditions. They might accept a subsidy as a replacement for existing safety-net programs, but if cutting safety-net spending is on the table, many would prefer to spend that savings on a growth-generating tax cut.

This became eminently clear in debates over the 2017 tax reform package, which ultimately increased the ten-year federal deficit by $1.5 trillion for the sake of reducing the corporate tax rate, while failing to deliver even the small EITC increase for childless workers that now-Speaker Ryan had once championed.[23] Indeed, while the Khanna proposal in its 2017 form is not a serious one, even it could have been implemented more cheaply than the tax reform that ultimately passed. The deficit spending would have been equally costly, but at least the labor market and its low-wage workers would have been the chief beneficiaries.

Democrats, for their part, remain suspicious of a wage subsidy because it links assistance to work, something most steadfastly resist. Furthermore, their instinct is to reject as "cuts" any proposal to repurpose funds from existing antipoverty programs, even if total spending remains the same and the new use is far more constructive. How else could President Obama in 2014 fail to find *any* spending *anywhere else* in the government that he would have preferred to spend on the childless EITC, which Republicans wanted to expand too?

What really infuriates Democrats, though, is the possibility that employers might benefit. Factually speaking, they have a point. If the government offers a $3 subsidy atop a $9-per-hour job, the result will not necessarily be a $12-per-hour job. The employer might instead cut the market wage to $8, to which the government would add $3.50—half the $7 gap to the target wage of $15—leaving the worker with $11.50. Both worker and employer are better off than without the subsidy, but the entire benefit is not the worker's. How workers and employers respond to the subsidy will vary based on labor-market conditions. What we do know from studies of the EITC and a similar program in the United Kingdom is that, in those instances, roughly 75 percent of the financial benefit accrued to workers.[24] In general, employers have to benefit at least somewhat. A central premise of the wage subsidy is to pull more prospective workers into the labor force. Other things held equal, if the supply of workers increases, then employers will be able to offer lower wages—even as, thanks to the subsidy, workers take home more.

Democrats don't like this because they view low-wage employers as culpable in creating the conditions that necessitate the support to begin with. In 2015, economists at the University of California's Berkeley Center for Labor Research and Education reported that federal and state governments spend more than $150 billion annually on working families.[25] "This is a hidden cost of low-wage work," the center's chairman told the *New York Times*, which called such benefits "a huge subsidy for employers of low-wage workers." The *Times* described efforts in Connecticut to assess a fee on large employers per worker earning less than $15 per hour and in California to publish the names of companies with more than one hundred employees on Medicaid and "how much these companies cost the state in public assistance."[26] (Rounding out one of the less coherent agendas in recent memory, Representative Khanna has highlighted the Berkeley Labor Center's study and proposed—along with his massive EITC expansion—a tax on low-wage employers that would "levy a direct fee equal to the public assistance each corporation's employees are eligible to receive."[27])

But this badly misunderstands how public assistance affects the labor market. Welfare programs cannot subsidize low-wage employers because they do not increase in value when low-wage employment relationships are formed. To the contrary, all those benefit recipients would be receiving the same *or higher* benefits in the absence of their low-wage employment. If anything, public assistance operates as a tax on low-wage employers because workers are likely to lose a share of every dollar earned as their benefits phase out with higher income. The exception to this rule would be the EITC, or, better, an actual wage subsidy, which subsidizes work by increasing in value as workers take jobs and earn more.

This leads to the more important point: to the extent that a government program *does* subsidize low-wage employment, and employers share in the benefit, *that is a good thing.* Remember, the wage subsidy's goal is not only, or even primarily, to transfer resources into the pockets of low-income households. It is also to connect more workers with employers in permanent jobs. The task requires employers to do the hard work of hiring and training certain employees whom they otherwise would not, and this benefits society greatly. A central premise of the wage subsidy is to reward employers sufficiently so that they choose to do more. By contrast, just wishing that firms would create more and better jobs when they have no economic incentive to do so is futile; it has zero bearing on what will happen in the actual labor market.

Note that this need to create incentives for the employer is no different from what happens in any other effort at assisting low-income households in a market economy. When people use food stamps at the supermarket, the supermarket benefits. When they use housing vouchers to pay the rent, the landlord benefits. Unless the government wishes to produce everything itself, or order market participants to take actions against their own interests, efforts to deliver results that the market will not deliver for low-income households always benefit the businesses that choose to participate in the transactions. Otherwise, they wouldn't participate! It is a strange consequence of our commitment to individuals as consumers that we unthinkingly pay hundreds of billions of dollars each year to hospitals and universities to provide treatment and education to customers whom they otherwise would turn away but shrink from the idea that society might pay anything to an employer to hire someone he otherwise would not.

*   *   *

Just as the Republican Party's relative disinterest in the labor market is made apparent by its preference for a tax cut over a wage subsidy, a good distillation of the Democrats' core attitude toward the labor market emerges from comparing a wage subsidy to their preferred approach: the minimum wage. Raising the minimum wage is the quintessential left-of-center labor-market policy. Unsatisfied with the market outcome, Democrats suggest decreeing a different one. The outcome it professes to deliver is widely desired. It seems "free." And then it damages, rather than strengthens, the labor market.

The minimum wage and the wage subsidy both aim to raise the earnings of low-wage workers. Whereas the wage subsidy asks taxpayers to make up the difference, the minimum wage asks employers to. Who pays matters a great deal. For the wage subsidy, taxpayers pay. This is good, because the tax code collects money from across society in accordance with the allocation that society has chosen for funding its most important objectives—generally, a highly progressive one that places most of the burden on high-income households. If connecting more people to better-paying work is a national priority, we can be confident that the federal tax base is an appropriate place to look for funding.

Economists debate who exactly pays the minimum wage's cost. Some part is eventually borne by employers, described in political campaigns as anonymous "corporations" but often small businesses or franchise owners trying to make ends meet. If they and all their competitors face the same increases in labor costs, they may respond by raising prices, in which case it would be consumers—themselves often from the low-income households the policy is intended to help—who put the extra money in the paychecks. Some employers might also rearrange their cost structures, lowering the pay for slightly higher-wage workers to accommodate higher pay at the bottom.[28] If society is committed to raising low-wage paychecks, handing the tab to taxpayers is a far better choice than leaving it to any of these other groups.

"Who pays" is not only about fairness; it also dictates what happens in the labor market. The wage subsidy injects funds from outside the labor market to boost the formation of employment relationships and encourage greater investment in labor-intensive businesses. The minimum wage does the opposite, operating as a tax on low-wage employment that employers have to pay for every low-wage hour they use. We should expect them to respond by employing fewer low-wage workers. Maybe not right away—changing a business model takes time, and investments already made cannot be undone. Rather than immediately cutting back or closing down, it often makes sense to raise some prices, accept some lower profits, and try to recoup fixed costs. A small minimum-wage increase won't trigger a sudden surge in unemployment.

But if the law's effect is to tax the employment of low productivity workers, it will influence which business models succeed, which investments get made, and thus the trajectory on which the labor market evolves. If the minimum wage is $12 per hour instead of $8, an employer must decide whether to boost the productivity of his $8-per-hour workers by 50 percent, seek different workers who are already more productive, or find a way to make do without those positions. The higher the minimum wage is, the less likely it is that the low-wage workers will benefit. Capital will move away from businesses that employ them and toward ones that use different workers, implement different processes, or operate in different countries.

Evidence is already emerging that substantial minimum-wage increases come at the expense of the very workers they are designed to help. On June 2, 2014, the city council of Seattle, Washington, voted unanimously to approve an ordinance that would raise the city's minimum wage for large employers to $11 per hour in April 2015, $13 per hour in January 2016, and finally to $15 per hour in January 2017.[29] The city then contracted with a research team at the University of Washington to conduct detailed analysis on the labor-market effects.

An initial review of the 2015 increase found positive and negative effects roughly canceling out. Wages increased slightly, employment decreased slightly, and the total earned in low-wage jobs was roughly unchanged.[30] The effect of the 2016 increase was quite bad. Average wages rose little, but hours worked in "low-wage" jobs (defined by the researchers as less than $19 per hour) fell by 7 percent, reducing annual earnings per worker by almost $900.[31]

* * *

Without a focus on the labor market, public policy will continue in its present pattern. Republicans will prioritize tax cuts and Democrats will prioritize minimum-wage hikes and welfare programs. When the economy grows, but in ways that don't benefit the typical worker, Democrats will seek to impose yet more rules, and Republicans will press for further tax cuts. If we want the market to work for everyone, we will need to do more.

PART III

BEYOND THE MARKET

CHAPTER 10

FOR THOSE WHO CANNOT WORK

The paradox at the heart of antipoverty policy is this: every dollar spent to reduce the suffering of an impoverished person reduces the incentive for that person to improve her own condition by earning an income. This happens not only because her need has become less pressing but also because the system will in fact punish her for any success by taking the dollar away once she earns a few of her own. A social problem compounds the economic one. If the government offers to provide for a worker's family roughly as well as he might on his own, it deprives his work of the meaning associated with achieving self-sufficiency. If it provides for families throughout a community in this way, it eliminates self-sufficiency as a norm and thus the pride associated with fulfilling that expectation and the shame associated with failing. The "handout" is locked in perpetual battle with the "hand up."

Such concerns are often misunderstood as indictments of the poor. The suggestion that someone might prefer to collect benefits instead of working sounds like an accusation of laziness; describing a "culture of poverty" built on dependency implies the bad character of those enmeshed in it. To the contrary, the point is that people struggling to enter the labor market and make ends meet *are* like everyone else. They, their families, and their communities are just as reliant on work to thrive. They, like everyone else, face a swirl of economic and social pushes and pulls as they choose how to use their limited time and money. Where they differ is that society has chosen to take away specifically from them, the group for whom it is most important to take the first step into a perhaps unattractive job, many of the pushes and pulls in that direction. For those who could be working, a generous safety net is not just ineffective; it is destructive.

Yet for others, the safety net is indispensable. Not everyone can work, and not everyone who can work can meet his family's needs. There are children, the elderly, the disabled. Life is full of pregnancies, ailing relatives, unforeseeable disasters, and addictions. Sometimes, in an economic downturn, no job is available. America possesses the wealth to alleviate some of this hardship, and all Americans benefit from a policy of doing so. It insures everyone against her own bad fortune. It promotes public order by reducing the blights, such as crime and homelessness, that accompany desperation. And it fulfills people's desire to live in a society that is inclusive and compassionate. Ideally, "antipoverty policy" would mean two entirely separate things: for those capable of earning an income, a labor market with adequate opportunity and wages for all; where self-sufficiency is not possible, a safety net.

Unfortunately, no such bright line exists, and government cannot draw one. The labor market and safety net are inextricably linked because people pass frequently between them and often participate in both at once. What level of physical or mental impairment, for instance, prevents someone from engaging in "any substantial gainful activity"—the Social Security Administration's threshold for receiving disability benefits? How much income does a family need before it can afford its own food? When is work unavailable versus when is the worker's alcoholism making him unemployable?

Nor, if such lines could be drawn, would society enforce them. America long ago committed to providing for the basic needs of all its citizens through public assistance, for reasons of not only compassion but also common sense. We still want emergency rooms to treat acute injury and illness, regardless of the patient's ability to pay. We still want to offer food and shelter to the indigent and hope that they will accept it rather than living on the streets or turning to crime. When children are involved, the imperative to provide assistance becomes stronger still. Even if somebody simply refuses to work (and almost never is it so simple), those commitments remain.

To balance the competing goals of providing resources to meet immediate needs and pushing people toward work that might eventually lift them out of poverty, the safety net must be positioned at the right height—safely above the rock-hard floor yet still well below the tightrope. The value of the baseline government benefits provided to someone not working must be significantly lower than the income that person could earn in an entry-level job. That "income gap" is necessary to maintain both the economic and social reward for work, encouraging people to self-sort toward working to the extent they are able.

Accomplishing this requires a safety net that providers can tailor to the needs and abilities of individual beneficiaries. Historically, the institutions of civil society—families, charities, and churches—that provided assistance to the poor could apply *judgment* to their efforts. Sensitive and subjective determinations about the nature of people's needs could allow unconditional support to reach people with no alternative, while focusing any assistance for prospective workers on getting them onto their feet and into jobs.

Where they can, some organizations still do just that. For instance, Catholic Charities of Fort Worth (CCFW) has a goal to get ten thousand families out of poverty in the next ten years, which it defines as a job that pays a living wage, no government assistance, no inappropriate debt, and three months of savings. Each family meets weekly with a case worker, often for a year or more, to make progress toward those goals. CCFW deploys its resources strategically, helping with financial stabilization and other immediate obstacles for the family, but its support is contingent on their continued engagement in the program. Heather Reynolds, the group's CEO, tells the story of a family who realized that they needed a second income and wanted the mother to start working. The mother was hired quickly, but then quit. She took another job, but quit again. The problem was that the family could not afford to start their child in adequate daycare. CCFW agreed to pay the first and third month of childcare expenses; if she stayed employed for six months, CCFW would reimburse her for months two and four as well. That's just what happened, and more than a year later, she remained steadily employed and her family had achieved self-sufficiency and its three-months-of-savings goal.[1]

For some, the immediate reaction to this story may be that government should provide subsidized childcare. Problem solved. But that won't do, for three reasons. First, it badly misallocates resources. Childcare is a crucial need for some people, but for many others, it isn't. A family member or neighbor may be available to take care of the kids, an affordable daycare may operate nearby, or the parents may have the option to work different hours. Subsidized childcare will be popular if it is offered, but for many who use it, the real need might be a car repair or a security deposit on an apartment closer to work. We can't just start saying, "Well, then, give everyone those things too." Furthermore, the subsidy would operate indefinitely, leading families to take that support for granted and build their budgets on top of it. CCFW could provide an initial four months of childcare assistance to nine times as many people as a government program that was still subsidizing this one family three years later.

Second, the program will itself drive the cost of care higher. Childcare providers will respond to the introduction of a subsidy by raising prices. Regulators will try to define what constitutes high-quality childcare that should qualify for the subsidy, what training the providers should have, and what standards the facilities should meet, forcing costs higher still. (Washington, D.C., where monthly "tuition" already averages $1,800 per month, among the nation's highest levels, has recently established a requirement that childcare workers earn college degrees.[2]) Perhaps all of this sounds admirable—who opposes high-quality childcare? But that wasn't the question. We were trying to allocate our finite resources toward moving as many households as possible toward self-sufficiency.

Third, unless we wish to pay for *all* the nation's childcare, we will need the subsidy to decline as household income rises. For every additional dollar the family earns, we will take some of their support away. The more programs we create—health care, housing, food, now childcare—that operate in this way, the more of each additional dollar vanishes. The lifestyle afforded by low income and generous government support begins to look eerily similar to that of middle-class self-sufficiency.

Even if CCFW's short-term cost of supporting a family is quite high, its assistance looks nothing like a permanent handout. It is targeted to a specific, demonstrated need. It is time limited. It is designed to move the family out of poverty, not maintain them in it. No one would mistake the support provided by CCFW as a substitute for self-sufficiency or an acceptance of dependence, even if a family relies heavily on assistance for some time. This allows the safety net to become more generous with fewer undesirable side effects. We can provide much greater support to people genuinely in need if we can trust our programs not to provide the same to someone else whose genuine need is for a wake-up call.

In the twentieth century, and especially since 1965, government gradually supplanted civil society as the safety-net provider. This has advantages: government can bring greater resources to bear in the regions and at the times of greatest need, exactly where and when civil society's resources may be scant. More checks exist to prevent abuses of power, arbitrary and unfair decisions, and discrimination. But the same generalized rules and procedures that prevent invidious discrimination also tend to prevent much-needed differentiation between individuals. The distant bureaucrat who rules impartially on every case does not have, and anyway must ignore, the context that a local pastor or case manager might consider. Only with careful design and great reliance on local flexibility can policy makers hope to establish a benefit-delivery system capable of distinguishing those who can work from those who cannot, and one that maintains a substantial income gap among those who can work that favors those who do.

* * *

Unfortunately, economic piety has led to precisely the opposite. Beginning in the 1960s with President Lyndon Johnson's launch of the War on Poverty, the United States embraced fully a transactional model for alleviating poverty by transferring resources to the poor. From 1965 to 1975, federal, state, and local spending on programs targeting low-income households nearly quadrupled, from roughly $75 billion to $270 billion (in constant 2015 dollars). From 1975 to 1995, the total doubled. From 1995 to 2015, it doubled again, so that annual spending exceeded $1 trillion[3]—more than the nation spent on national defense, on public education, on Medicare, or on Social Security. It would be enough to send every American below the poverty line a check each year for $20,000—a single mother with two children could receive $60,000, placing her household's income well above the national median.[4] Yet the 2010s poverty rate exceeded the average level of the 1990s, which in turn exceeded the 1970s level.[5]

While this outcome may seem inexplicable, it is entirely consistent with the design of the nation's safety net, whose programs operate primarily to maintain people in poverty rather than to help them climb upward. Providing 20 million households in need an average of $3,000 in food stamps each year is an effective way to guarantee access to food.[6] Offering Medicaid or an insurance subsidy to households with up to $100,000 of income is an effective way to guarantee access to health insurance coverage.[7] Indeed, counting the full range of federal benefits as "income" to low-income households leads to a substantial reduction in the poverty rate.[8] But it does not reduce the number of households who will need that support again next year.

As the economic prospects of low-income households declined and the potential value of their government benefits grew, the income gap eroded—for some, it vanished entirely. Not all of the $1 trillion spent annually goes to typical poverty alleviation. For instance, a lot is spent on long-term care for the low-income elderly population.[9] But even focusing specifically on the full package of benefits a welfare-eligible single mother with two children could receive, the Cato Institute has shown that in 2013, the value in most states exceeded the earnings from a minimum-wage job. In half of all states, the benefit package would bring the family up to at least 80 percent of the state's median salary.[10]

As a family earns money, the benefits are taken away. In 2015, the Congressional Budget Office reviewed the impact of key federal programs and found that a hypothetical single mother with one child would receive $18,000 of after-tax income (from government benefits) if she earned $0 in wages but $30,000 of after-tax income (from both earnings and benefits) if she earned $20,000 in wages. From her perspective, she receives $12,000 in reward for her $20,000 of work—the equivalent of a 40 percent tax rate. If her earnings climbed from $20,000 to $40,000, she would find her after-tax income rising only from $30,000 to $35,000—the equivalent of a 75 percent marginal tax rate as she tries to move from poverty into the middle class.[11] State-level benefits compound the problem: in Pennsylvania in 2012, a hypothetical single mother with two children but no earnings might have received $45,000 in benefits, comparable to the after-tax income she could expect with a $50,000 salary.[12]

The issue here is not whether taxpayers are spending "too much" on support for lower-income families. The issue is not even whether welfare benefits are "better" than entry-level jobs. The problem is that with such high baseline benefit levels—benefits that fall away as the recipient begins to earn income—the income gap is too low. The lowest-income households end up facing what in effect are extraordinarily high marginal tax rates, meaning they receive far too little additional take-home income for each dollar they earn and thus face relatively little incentive to earn any income at all. Entry-level jobs are often just stepping-stones to better opportunities for workers who develop skills and a track record of performance. But that upward mobility requires that the initial leap into the workforce be made. Without a sufficient income gap, it may never be.

Recent trends only compound the problem. Society's definition of a minimum standard of living is expanding to include higher education, health coverage for everything from birth control to the most advanced therapies, and even cell phones and broadband internet access. As discussed earlier, many would include childcare as well. A *Washington Post* analysis expresses concern over "a little-discussed gap in the social safety net: Currently, there is no federal program that helps low-income people care for their pets."[13] Ensuring that every American has access to these things is an admirable goal, but if every American is *entitled* to them, then those who work hard to earn a middle-class living will find themselves doing little better than those who do not work at all.

At the same time as expectations rise, the standard of living offered by low-skilled work continues to decline. In 1970, the median income for a male with a high school degree amounted to more than double the poverty line for a family of four. In 1990, it exceeded the poverty line by only 60 percent. In 2016, it cleared the threshold by less than 40 percent.[14] For entry-level positions specifically, those numbers drop even lower.

As the range of potential benefits expands and the attractiveness of entry-level work declines, maintaining an income gap that favors work and encourages labor force participation becomes more challenging and more important. Unfortunately, the current antipoverty infrastructure makes it nearly impossible. The alphabet soup of federal agencies through which $1 trillion flows each year from taxpayers to beneficiaries appears designed to stifle reform, increase spending, expand bureaucracy, and avoid accountability.

The core assistance programs were created through different pieces of legislation and are administered by different agencies, with different eligibility requirements, incentives, and procedures. Medicaid is an entitlement program within the Department of Health and Human Services

(HHS). Disability operates within the Social Security Administration. The Department of Agriculture (USDA) controls food stamps through legislation incorporated into the farm bill; the Department of Housing and Urban Development (HUD) controls housing assistance; and the Department of Education controls education programs. Unemployment insurance relies on a hybrid state- and federally financed trust fund, administered by the states, with oversight from the Department of Labor, backstopped by additional federal funds. The Internal Revenue Service administers the EITC and the Child Tax Credit through the tax code. And so on and so forth for dozens of smaller programs, from the School Breakfast Program to the Weatherization Assistance Program.

Implementation is sometimes, but not always, assigned to the states; sometimes, but not always, with matching state funds; sometimes, but not always, with state-established income thresholds. From the states' perspective, little can be done but to replicate the structure of an array of federal programs and play by the perverse rules set from above. The tangle of strings attached to each program prevents any harmonization or consolidation among programs. Matching funds reward higher spending in some instances, while block grants attempt to curtail spending in others. State-level programs get layered on top of federal programs rather than integrated with them efficiently. Individuals end up facing wildly different incentives depending on their specific circumstances, sometimes encountering so-called income cliffs where small increases in their earnings will disqualify them from benefits and leave them worse off than before.

The 1996 "welfare reform" is widely regarded as an inflection point for the safety net, abandoning unconditional cash transfers in favor of a system that required states to hold at least some of their recipients accountable for meeting work requirements. But welfare reform was actually quite limited, replacing the traditional Aid to Families with Dependent Children with the new Temporary Assistance for Needy Families (TANF). TANF is not even among the top five federal anti-poverty programs in either expenditures or enrollees. Medicaid, SNAP ("food stamps"), the EITC, Supplemental Security Income (SSI, commonly referred to as disability), and even Pell Grants for higher education are larger.[15]

For policy makers, the system defies analysis, let alone substantive reform. The USDA is an illustrative microcosm: in 2012, the agency spent $114 billion on fifteen different nutritional programs, each with a separate legislative authorization. Its Inspector General's Office expressed concern that the agency "may be duplicating its efforts by providing total benefits that exceed 100 percent of daily nutritional needs," explaining that the agency "has not fully assessed its food safety net as a whole to determine the impact of providing potentially overlapping nutritional benefits through multiple programs."[16] Now multiply the absurdity across more than one hundred different programs spanning numerous agencies and objectives.[17]

No one even considers how best to allocate funds across types of assistance or types of beneficiaries. Medicaid spending climbs higher, crowding out funding for other types of programs regardless of whether a marginal dollar is best spent on health care. Even if health care is the most important funding priority in aggregate, does that same priority hold everywhere? Some states might prefer to reduce health spending but work their housing waiting lists down to zero, say, or to shift funding from college tuition grants to job training, or even to let the individual recipient decide whether what he really needs to get back on his feet is health coverage, housing, or a used car. Under federal control, states have no say; they must all take roughly the same allocation.

Year after year, the entrenched bureaucracies of separate agencies shovel their separate funds down separate chutes, each striving to secure the largest possible shovel for next year by establishing just how acute is the need for its program. None are required to show the reduction in demand for their services that actual success would entail. Here comes another year, there goes another trillion dollars, and the poverty rate is unchanged.

* * *

Consider housing. The federal government, through HUD, spent about $50 billion on low-income housing programs in 2014, with $37 billion of that total subsidizing the rents of 9.8 million people in 4.8 million households. This subsidy amounted, on average, to $3,800 per person, or $11,300 for a single mother with two children.[18] Simply mailing these families a check in that amount would have brought them more than halfway to the poverty threshold.

Nothing so simple happens, however. HUD doesn't actually operate its housing programs itself. Rather, it establishes extensive standardized regulations for them, addressing everything from permissible eligibility criteria (consideration of marital status strictly prohibited) to "discretionary pet rules" ("project owners may limit the number of four-legged, warm-blooded pets to one pet in each dwelling unit or group home").[19] Then it disburses funds to an array of state, local, and nonprofit public-housing authorities (more than twenty-five hundred nationwide), which must implement the regulations.

The program works poorly, to put it mildly. Housing support becomes a way of life for many recipients and not a temporary lift up. The annual turnover rate among participants in New York City's public housing is only 2.6 percent, meaning that over a decade, fewer than a quarter of residents are likely to have moved on.[20] Subsidized housing's rules perversely work against two of the most effective paths for escaping poverty—geographic relocation and workplace promotion; moving can mean returning to the back of the line for a subsidized apartment, and earning too much money can make one abruptly ineligible for a subsidy—and unable to pay the rent. In Seattle, for instance, after a minimum-wage hike, some workers found that higher pay threatened their housing eligibility, and they requested fewer hours to keep earnings down.[21]

In part because recipients stay put so long, the eligible population for housing subsidies in most areas vastly outstrips the available vouchers and public-housing units, leading to years-long waiting lists. Nationwide, only 25 percent of those technically eligible for the programs get to use them.[22] New York City's backlog is so large that it has not even accepted new applications since 2009.[23]

The dynamic not only serves individual families poorly; it also undermines communities. HUD's Fair Market Rent, applying uniformly to entire metropolitan areas, dictates the size of a voucher that a housing authority can offer. Neighborhoods with rents at the requisite low level become magnets for impoverished voucher recipients, concentrating poverty. The vouchers, as the head of one community-development corporation in Baltimore described them, act as "a catalyst in neighborhood deterioration and ghetto expansion."[24] *The Atlantic* reported in 2015 that in New York City, "the Fair Market Rent for a one-bedroom is $1,249, a price that would relegate voucher-holders to the neighborhood of

Brownsville in Brooklyn, one of the most dangerous places in the city, and where the most public housing is located."[25]

The federally designed rules for housing support work differently from those of other federal welfare programs, introducing further inefficiencies. The head of household for a family of three living in New York City needed an income below $23,350 to qualify as "extremely low income" for housing purposes, but move a few miles north to Westchester, and the cutoff jumped to $28,550. Move east to Nassau, and an income up to $29,450 remained eligible for benefits.[26] Meantime, though, the federal SNAP sets statewide thresholds, so in any of those counties, a separate $26,124 cutoff would determine receipt of that benefit.[27]

Some of these flaws arise from poor program design; others, however, flow almost unavoidably from the federal government taking too extensive a role. The federally designed eligibility rules, applied to widely varying economic conditions and without reference to actual budgeting, create demand for benefits far in excess of the supply of funds—because Washington makes no attempt to close the gap between the cost of the programs and the appropriations made for them. The resulting waiting lists both prevent the aid from reaching those who would benefit most and strengthen the incentive for those who do get in to stay. Furthermore, the federally calculated municipal "market" rents for housing vouchers often run at cross-purposes to local aid initiatives, such as minimum-wage increases and urban-development plans. And misaligned poverty definitions from one federal program to the next leave individuals confused and underscore the lack of coordination in addressing their needs.

Nor is an income-dependent rental subsidy the correct policy approach and best use of resources for all the situations in which HUD imposes it. Voucher recipients are split 51–49 between the disabled and elderly versus other adults and 56–44 between childless households and those with children.[28] Those recipients live across the diverse housing markets of the United States, where rent–buy calculations, availability and quality of housing stock, and even the fundamental nature of the economic challenges facing the poor can vary dramatically. Yet they're all enrolled in the same program.

Housing authorities operate the program, get blamed for its poor performance, and face pressure to reform a system over which they have no real control. HUD issues rules that it doesn't itself have to implement and that cannot possibly address each locality's varied needs. It does all this in a vacuum, disconnected from the myriad other federal agencies with antipoverty programs that face comparable challenges.

The federal government's ineptitude in providing aid is far from limited to housing. Medicaid, the largest, best-known, and worst-performing of the major federal antipoverty programs, places control and much of the funding in Washington—in this case, with HHS—while leaving actual execution up to state and local agencies. But Medicaid is a mandatory entitlement, which means that it has no predetermined annual budget and no waiting list. If an eligible recipient receives an eligible medical service, the federal government automatically pays. From the states' perspective, therefore, having more uninsured, low-income residents equates to more federal dollars flowing in—hardly the recipe for committed efforts at poverty reduction, private insurance adoption, or spending restraint.

To counter this, states must provide a share of Medicaid funding themselves—anywhere from one-quarter to one-half of the total, with the federal funds arriving as a "match." In practice, though, states have subverted this restraint by tilting more of their budgets toward Medicaid so as to keep the federal funds coming. Medicaid's Disproportionate Share Hospital (DSH) payments, which compensate hospitals for the financial burden of caring for Medicaid patients at low reimbursement rates, illustrate the perverse incentives. Because the federal government matched the DSH payments that states made to hospitals, states began collecting taxes or other payments from eligible hospitals and recycling them back to those hospitals as DSH payments. The hospitals were made whole, the state budgets were unaffected, and federal money came pouring in. DSH spending exploded, rocketing from $400 million in 1988 to $17 billion in 1992.[29]

From 2000 to 2012, despite the increasingly dire situation facing state budgets, total Medicaid spending grew faster than overall health care spending and increased from 12 percent to 16 percent of overall state budgets.[30] By 2015, with no strong local incentive to restrain costs, federal and state governments were spending a staggering $568 billion on Medicaid—a tenfold increase (in constant dollars) since 1975 that accounted for almost 90 percent of the increase in safety-net spending per person in poverty.[31]

That allocation of resources might make sense if health care were the top priority for low-income households, if it were the keystone of economic opportunity, and if Medicaid delivered it well. None of those things is true. Obviously, low-income households without access to Medicaid would not allocate 90 percent of their own resources to health care, or even 50 percent. In fact, households that consumed $10,000 to $20,000 in 2012 and were ineligible for Medicaid or chose not to enroll allocated only 8 percent of their spending to health care. Housing accounted for 42 percent, food for 24 percent, and transportation for 10 percent.[32]

Nor did households that consumed slightly more prioritize health care when allocating their additional resources. Households with $20,000 to $30,000 of annual consumption spent only 9 percent of their additional funds on health care. This low priority for health care continues further up the income ladder, where it frustrated early implementation of the Affordable Care Act: even among middle-class households eligible for subsidies to buy their own health insurance, the majority chose to remain uninsured.[33]

But might it be that government knows best, wisely allocating funds to health care that low-income households lack the foresight or discipline to allocate well themselves? It would seem not. Studies repeatedly find that Medicaid recipients achieve worse outcomes than not only people with private insurance but also the uninsured.[34] In a randomized controlled study in Oregon in 2008, uninsured residents were assigned to receive Medicaid or not; the study concluded that "Medicaid coverage generated no significant improvements in measured physical health outcomes in the first 2 years."[35] A subsequent analysis found that each dollar of Medicaid spending generated only 20 to 40 cents of value for the recipients based on what they showed a willingness to pay for and how their health was affected.[36]

Critics of the Oregon study complain that it was "underpowered," meaning that it followed too few individuals for too short a time. (Such concerns were few and far between when the study's preliminary results hinted at a rosier outcome.) But longer-term studies have corroborated the finding. For instance, Stanford professor Raj Chetty and his colleagues published a study in the *Journal of the American Medical Association* that found no significant relationship between health care access and life expectancy for the poor in a given area.[37]

More worrisome than Medicaid's absolute effects is its opportunity cost. The real flaw of the Oregon study, and of enthusiasm for Medicaid generally, is that Medicaid gets compared only with no Medicaid. A study that better reflected the trade-off facing policy makers would assign Medicaid to half the participants while giving the other half housing vouchers and wage subsidies of comparable cost, which might promote not only better health but greater economic opportunity as well. Would Medicaid, then, look like an effective strategy, even for health outcomes alone? Researchers from the Yale School of Public Health attempted to answer that question by comparing health outcomes in each state to that state's ratio of health care spending to other social spending. Sure enough, the states allocating a smaller proportion of their social spending to health care achieved better health outcomes on measures from obesity to mental health to mortality.[38]

None of which suggests that Medicaid should be eliminated. Health care obviously has value and belongs in the suite of government services for the poor. But it is only one support among many, with no special claim to improving health—let alone delivering the economic opportunity that should form the core of an effective antipoverty strategy. Within Medicaid, and throughout the safety net, we have the resources available to construct a safety net that works, if we are willing to redeploy them.

* * *

Replacing the safety net's resource-transfer model with one that promotes self-sufficient families requires three major reforms: first, shift a substantial share of the safety net from a goal of maintaining people in poverty to a goal of moving them out; second, reestablish an income gap by boosting the returns to entry-level work and constraining the benefits available without work; third, increase the flexibility of safety-net programs and assign control of their resource to people at the local level who can tell the difference between different people's capacity to work and make a difference in their lives.

The wage subsidy described in the prior chapter is an ideal mechanism for achieving the first goal. Perhaps its biggest drawback as a stand-alone policy is its exorbitant cost—roughly $200 billion annually. But it can be funded by reallocating existing safety-net resources. A large share of safety-net spending already goes toward people who are working; they would benefit greatly from receiving that support in their paycheck instead of through a maze of government programs. Other benefit recipients might start to work if a wage subsidy were offered—for them too, shifting money in that direction is a clear benefit. And then some benefit recipients may see their support decline so that more can go toward supporting work. This is a trade-off, and a good one if the goal of fighting poverty is actually to reduce the number of people in poverty. The safety net's overwhelming focus on poverty maintenance has always been a mistake; there is no reason to continue it indefinitely.

Any proposal to reduce spending on any antipoverty program is invariably criticized as cruel to the poor, *even when that money would be reallocated to other programs with the same goal.* This default creates a bizarre political frame in which the more "generous," liberal position is to spend new money on new programs, while the "miserly," conservative position is to reallocate money toward more effective programs. But allocating money effectively is not a proposal about spending at all, and proposals to reallocate are not stingy or antipoor. Safety-net reforms could proceed much further if the spending debate between those wanting to increase or decrease overall budget levels were put to one side and people across the political spectrum were to focus on the question of how best to spend the money already slated to go out the door. Anyone who believes that the random agglomeration of programs over fifty years of unfocused legislation has produced precisely the ideal is, of course, welcome to defend the status quo. Most people of good faith would, one hopes, agree that some recalibration might be in order.

Shifting the safety net toward a wage subsidy would also help to accomplish the second goal, of reestablishing the income gap. Directly, it would boost wages and thus the reward to work while reducing other forms of support and thus the benefits available while not working. It also helps by creating a distinction among benefit *types*, which offers a mechanism for increasing the relative attractiveness of work without slashing benefits or increasing spending. Two families—one whose head of household works, one whose head of household does not—may both need $3,000 worth of nutritional support. But if the nonworking household receives the $3,000 in food stamps while the working household receives it as cash via a wage subsidy, the latter may feel substantially better off.

This same approach could be applied to a program, such as SSI, that still provides substantial cash support. Converting a substantial share of disability payments to in-kind benefits would continue to meet the objectives of ensuring that every American's basic needs are met while also making a job the much more attractive option. Constraints on what food stamps can purchase, as another example, are often condemned as punitive or paternalistic. But such a policy could preserve their nutritional value while reducing their notional value compared to what a subsidized wage offers.

Work requirements can also help to maintain the income gap, but here policy makers should be careful. In-kind programs like Medicaid and food stamps, to which many Republicans now want to attach work requirements, are an awkward fit for that strategy. Unlike TANF, which offered a cash benefit, the safety net should provide access to food and medical care regardless of whether one has any intention of working. Furthermore, work requirements give too much credit to the government's ability to design rules that will distinguish effectively between those who can and cannot work. And when those work requirements are *mandated* nationwide, they end up constraining the very discretion needed at the local level to make such determinations well.

This challenge highlights the importance of the third area of reform. If we want the safety net to sidestep the antipoverty paradox, we need the federal government to relinquish control over how local providers deploy resources. Washington should retain the role at which it excels: collecting and distributing funds. This brings benefits like the redistribution of resources from wealthier to poorer states and the use of federal borrowing power to smooth budgets across booms and recessions. But rather than have numerous federal agencies each administer numerous programs, the federal government would ideally have a single agency apply a formula to allocate the year's (non-wage-subsidy) safety-net spending across the states and then transfer each state's share as a lump sum. Call it the Flex Fund.

The Flex Fund sounds like a block grant, but it is not the type of program-by-program block grant typically proposed as a pretext for capping the growth of costs. To the contrary, the funding formula would be allocated based on each state's total population and would grow at the same rate as the poverty threshold itself—a figure that already factors in growth in cost of living for the relevant household. A per capita payment ensures that states will not face conditions for receiving their funds and that they won't lose funding by virtue of successful policies that make their populations less needy. Have you moved residents out of poverty so that they no longer need housing vouchers? Use the money for something else. Unlike a restructuring of taxation, this model need not reduce the progressivity of the federal funding system because there is no correlation today between state income levels and per capita federal spending. Mississippi and West Virginia are among the top ten recipients of federal dollars per resident—but so are Massachusetts and New York.[39]

With the dividing lines between programs erased, states would have genuine and complete flexibility over resource allocation as opposed to the faux flexibility of applying for waiver after waiver or delivering the federal Section 8 housing-voucher program "however you want." States happy with the existing funding allocations and program structures could continue to apply the funding as they do today. But states with better ideas—even radically different ones—would be free to pursue them. They could further subdivide funding to local governments, channel funds to private charities, or both. Only by pushing control down to the level where locally accountable entities are working directly with those in need can the safety net support those who cannot work, move those who can work toward self-sufficiency, and maintain an income gap between the two.

* * *

If centralized policy control offered functional benefits, these might at least be weighed against the benefits of relinquishing that control. It does not. The federal government is incapable of administering its programs in any area of the safety net, which is why it already forces implementation down to states and cities. Scale might in theory provide efficiency, like greater negotiating power, or less reinventing of the wheel in each jurisdiction; but in practice, the federal–state interaction tends to increase bureaucratic burdens. A significant portion of HUD's regulations aims at dictating the contents that each housing authority must put into its particular administrative plan.

Nor is the federal government elevating effective programs from around the country to ensure the adoption of best practices—as the appalling performance of existing national programs indicates. Besides, best practices are traditionally shared, not imposed. States are capable of observing the results of policies and borrowing from what works. Each can translate proven principles into the form most appropriate for its own challenges and political preferences. If a policy is so obviously a good idea that every state would benefit, why would a federal law be needed to ensure its spread?

With reestablished state and local policy autonomy, state capitals and city halls might once again become places where ambitious people work to achieve things. No doubt, some will fail, but others—working on a scale where action is possible, with control over the necessary resources and accountability for the outcome—will make progress. Over time, individual states' useful innovations would benefit their residents more directly and provide an example for others to adopt.

A Flex Fund proposal would be politically potent. It would entail no budget cuts. No state would be forced to change its programs. Indeed, states that support today's housing vouchers or Medicaid structure could band together and continue operating multistate programs. But they could not command that all other states contribute their resources to the same efforts.

States, via their federal Flex Fund dollars, their own programs, and their public–private partnerships, would be responsible for crafting a safety net to provide basic support for those outside the labor force. The federal government, via direct wage subsidies held apart from the Flex Fund, would ensure that anyone entering the labor force found significant advantages in doing so. The income gap would be easily quantifiable, and if necessary, it could be expanded by shifting additional resources out of the Flex Fund and into the wage subsidy—not a reduction in support for the poor, only a shift in who receives what share. On this foundation, efforts to attack the causes of poverty and to improve the effectiveness of antipoverty programs and encourage labor force participation might actually succeed.

CHAPTER 11

THE SOCIAL WAGES OF WORK

Finally, we need to address American culture. Because the decision to work is one made in the marketplace, purportedly in rational response to external incentives, it is especially susceptible to cultural as well as economic influences. This may seem counterintuitive: isn't the labor market the dollar's domain, while culture concerns itself with more intimate and ethical considerations? Not necessarily. Culture can refer to many things, from a society's concept of art to its religious traditions and moral values to its favorite foods. One important component, and the one most relevant here, is the norms and expectations against which a society's members understand themselves to be measured.

In this sense, culture describes the nonmonetary rewards and penalties —in terms of status and respect, pride and shame—that people earn through their behavior. Where decisions are motivated by internal passions or irrational impulses, culture in these terms is no more likely to regulate behavior than would the economy or the criminal justice system. Only to the extent that people *are* calculating the external response to their choices can they take account of social implications. In few places are people more calculating than in their decisions about work.

The social wages of work derive from cultural recognition of the obligation to provide for a self-sufficient family and make positive contributions to the larger community. If that obligation—and the enormous value of its fulfillment—is widely recognized, then work can bring with it affirmation and the pride of success. Those rewards should not hinge on the type of work, its glamour, or its salary. If anything, people who do harder jobs for lower wages deserve the greatest admiration. Idleness, meanwhile, should bring a sense of failure and some measure of shame—that is, one reason to work might be to avoid the social cost of not working.

These positive and negative components are linked but distinct. Many things in life come with substantial social consequences on only one side or the other—stealing is bad, but not stealing earns little praise; becoming a foster parent is good, but not doing so is hardly cause for condemnation. Much like with the "income gap" described in the prior chapter, if we want people to work, then we should want to maintain a large "respect gap" between idleness and work by lowering one's value while raising the other's: reprobation for the failure to engage in productive activity as an active drain on society that harms families and communities, coupled with approbation for productive activity as not just the absence of idleness but rather a major positive contribution to the wider world.

Instead, we have done the opposite.

* * *

Among the latest fashions in bourgeois self-criticism is the lament that Americans start conversations with "so, what do you do?" In some tellings, the question's offense lies in its implication that what you *do* defines who you *are*. In others, it represents a thinly veiled attempt to determine how much someone earns or where he ranks in society. But while one's vocation conveys a lot of personal information and thus invites judgment, the nature of the judgment—the way the information is evaluated—depends on culture.

Waiters, truck drivers, retail clerks, plumbers, secretaries, and others all spend their days helping the people around them and filling roles crucial to the community. They do hard, unglamorous work for limited pay to support themselves and their families. Why shouldn't they be eager to share this information with their conversation partners? Surely their replies would compare favorably with those of the derivatives trader, white-collar defense lawyer, premium-alcohol social media manager, or professor of comparative literature. If blue-collar replies instead are cause for embarrassment, or an invitation to the listener to feel superior, then something is amiss.

Yet regardless of whether a vocation's skill or income level *should* determine the respect it commands, the etiquette police have a point that for many in American society, it *does*. Plenty of people do want to know what someone does so that they can place the person in their mental hierarchy and, they hope, establish their own superiority. And plenty of people being asked feel that their answers diminish them in the eyes of many others. As the arrogant Harvard graduate student retorts when Matt Damon embarrasses him in *Good Will Hunting*'s famous bar scene, "Yeah, but I will have a degree. And you'll be servin' my kids fries at a drive-thru on our way to a skiing trip."[1] While the audience may find the guy repulsive, it's hard to avoid admitting that he landed a square blow. Indeed, the movie's central plot arc concerns whether the Damon character can stop sabotaging himself long enough to make the leap from his blue-collar roots to a more rarified, intellectual milieu—from MIT janitor to MIT researcher.

The obvious explanation for this linkage between income and status is that it reflects a superiority born of choice. We suspect that both people regard the same job as better and that only one would gladly switch places. These are, quite literally, the haves and have-nots. "I have," the white-collar conversant would seem unavoidably to say, "something you cannot."

This can't be the whole story, though, because plenty of accessible jobs do retain substantial status. Members of the armed services provide an obvious example, along with police officers and firefighters. Teachers and nurses usually have at least some postsecondary education, but their fields are hardly prestigious in terms of either academic requirements or compensation. We are perfectly capable of awarding respect and status on the basis of sacrifice and social contribution, of admiring those who do jobs that most people do not want. What we lack is recognition that just about any job fits these criteria, that work is inherently deserving of respect.

How has that happened? The broader societal trend toward an emphasis on consumption rather than production, discussed in chapter 1, provides a partial explanation. The culture's increasing individualism and the priority it places on fulfilling desires have lessened the degree to which people identify as workers and the value assigned to fulfilling obligations and serving others. It is no longer enough for a job to meet a family's needs; it also should offer a path to self-actualization—pursuing your passion, doing what you love, changing the world.

Steve Jobs encapsulated the attitude well in his iconic commencement address at Stanford University in 2005, since viewed nearly 30 million times on YouTube. "You've got to find what you love," he told the graduates. "And that is as true for your work as it is for your lovers. . . . As with all matters of the heart, you'll know when you find it. And, like any great relationship, it just gets better and better as the years roll on. So keep looking until you find it. Don't settle."[2] In this framework, most work is inadequate.

Simultaneously, as these new criteria for "good" work have been added, the old criteria that most jobs could meet have been stripped away. Taking pride in providing for a family becomes much harder when the government's package of safety-net benefits offers to do so almost as well. For men, especially, the idea that they provide a critical function by working to support their families can be hard to square with lived experience in a community of broken families where single-mother-headed households are the norm.

More direct than inferences drawn from broader social trends are the specific messages about work that rain down from the cultural heights. The noxious concept of the "dead-end job," for instance, emerged suddenly in the 1960s and surged in prevalence for several decades.[3] The message that everyone needed college came accompanied by one that other tracks were for losers. A venture capitalist can now observe unashamedly to the *New York Times* that "I think it's a bad use of a human to spend 20 years of their life driving a truck back and forth across the United States. That's not what we aspired to do as humans—it's a bad use of a human brain." (*Times* columnist Farhad Manjoo felt that such comments revealed "sincerity and sophistication.")[4]

Look at the stories told by the popular culture. In the 1970s and 1980s, the Emmy Award for Outstanding Comedy Series went routinely to shows with blue-collar characters, such as *All in the Family*, *Taxi*, *Cheers*, and *The Wonder Years*. An especially famous *Wonder Years* episode, "My Father's Office," told the story of Kevin learning about his father's career path from loading-dock worker to distribution manager and that he had dreamed of being a ship's captain. "You can't do every silly thing you want in life," Mr. Arnold told his son. "You have to make your choices. You have to try to be happy with them. I think we've done pretty well, don't you?"[5]

Since 1992, the Emmy has gone almost every year to a show about white-collar adults working in Los Angeles, Seattle, Boston, New York, or Washington, few of whom are raising children. One might make an exception for *Everybody Loves Raymond*, but the protagonist was a New York sportswriter. The one actual exception is *The Office*, about paper salesmen in Scranton, but its primary vein of humor was the miserable lives of its provincial subjects (none of whom seemed to have a family, either). In 2017, the seven nominations went to shows about an ad executive and his family in Los Angeles, professionals and their families in Los Angeles, an actor in New York, a young woman restarting her life as a nanny in New York, political operatives in New York and Washington, nerds in Silicon Valley, and rappers in Atlanta. Has a lineup starring characters male and female; gay and straight; black, white, and Hispanic, ever looked so little "like America"?

This does not just reflect market demand for what people want to see. In the drama category, for instance, alongside the usual fare about crime, politics, dystopian science fiction, fantasy, and the British aristocracy, a show called *This Is Us* appeared in 2017. It follows a blue-collar family in Pennsylvania; the dad works construction and struggles with alcoholism. That story is told through flashbacks to the 1970s and 1980s; in the modern-day segments, the now-grown-up kids are a singer, an actor, and a businessman, all working in New York City or Los Angeles. Likewise, *The Goldbergs*, starting its sixth season in 2018, is about a suburban Pennsylvania family where the father is a furniture salesman, the mom is a homemaker, and the kids learn to value their father's commitment to working every day in a job he doesn't like to provide for them. It too is set in the 1980s. Why does Hollywood think these things happened only thirty years ago?

The news media does little better, heaping constant criticism on employers for the quality and conditions of entry-level and physically strenuous jobs, delivering the unmistakable message that the jobs are not good for the people who work in them. *The Atlantic*, for instance, suggested that small cities would be better off without the full-time-with-benefits jobs offered by Amazon warehouses.[6] Or take the *Bloomberg*

Businessweek cover story, accompanied by a picture of a man missing a limb, "Inside Alabama's Auto Jobs Boom: Cheap Wages, Little Training, Crushed Limbs." Reading the actual article, one learns that Alabama's twenty-six thousand auto parts workers earned $1.3 billion in wages in 2016, implying annual salaries of roughly $50,000. The industry's OSHA records "read like Upton Sinclair, or even Dickens," the article intones, despite also noting that the traumatic-injury rate in Alabama plants is less than 10 percent above counterparts in Michigan and Ohio.[7] From 2006 to 2016, the rate of nonfatal occupational injuries and illnesses in the Alabama auto parts industry fell from 6.6 per 100 workers per year to 4.6; in Michigan, the decline was from 9.8 to 4.9. For severe incidents that caused days away from work, the Alabama rate fell from 1.5 to 0.9; Michigan saw a comparable decline from 1.4 to 0.9.[8]

Demanding compliance with safety rules and abhorring the tragedy of individual accidents is one thing; equating modern manufacturing jobs with the slaughterhouses of Sinclair's *The Jungle* is quite another. These are not jobs that people need to be rescued from taking or that employers should be attacked for offering.

Indeed, much like the wage subsidy, raising the social wages of work should influence employers as well. Businesses take account of how their actions are perceived by customers and employees. The more seriously we take the consequences of long-term unemployment and the value of work, the more seriously we will also take the consequences of laying people off and the value of creating new jobs. Culture can also influence what kinds of businesses get built in the first place. Each year, new Masters of the Universe (or at least of business administration) graduate from schools that preach "corporate social responsibility" and an obligation to better the world. Yet by all appearances, students understand this to mean either saving the climate or launching a new app rather than creating meaningful work for fellow citizens in the mold of the industrialists like Sloan, Wharton, and Stanford, for whom their schools are named.

*　*　*

Obviously, culture does change. Sometimes it drifts, sometimes demographic and technological trends alter its shape, but sometimes it responds to actual ideas. These can be big ideas, about liberty or civil rights, for instance. They can be smaller ones, like don't drive drunk. Ideas can reverse countervailing trends, alter fundamental beliefs, and instill new obligations. Societies, communities, and even individuals can achieve strong and intentional changes in culture if they grapple effectively with why and how to do so.

Teen pregnancy provides an instructive example. From 1991 to 2014, a period in which neither data nor perception would support a claim that the sexual revolution was reversed, the nation's teen birthrate fell more than 60 percent, from sixty-two to twenty-four births per thousand females.[9] Abortion rates fell just as precipitously over the same period.[10] In the midst of a growing social and economic crisis, teenagers displayed a remarkable capacity to refrain from sexual behavior that would lead to pregnancy.

This achievement has perplexed researchers. Structural factors like demographic and economic trends cannot explain it. Rather, a variety of smaller changes—in education, attitudes and norms, media messages, and medical practice—may all have played a role in discouraging the undesirable behavior.[11] An eye-opening 2014 working paper by economists at the University of Maryland and Wellesley College found a statistically significant correlation between an increase in viewership for the MTV shows *16 and Pregnant* and *Teen Mom* and a decrease in the teen birthrate, sufficient to explain a 4.3 percent decline in teen births during 2009 and 2010.[12]

But the teen pregnancy example also underscores the uncomfortable truth that a strong culture requires social consequences for bad decisions, at the very moment when the targets are at their most vulnerable. We can work to raise the social value of making good decisions, but there is no substitute for raising the cost of bad ones. That is not a pleasant task. Few people like shaming others, especially in the personal interactions within families and communities that carry the greatest weight, but also through the communication of messages across society. At our hypothetical party, a possibility always exists that the person asked "what do you do?" in fact does nothing at all. The moment might be quite awkward for him—maybe for the questioner too. But that only strengthens the cultural case for asking it.

The reluctance to make idleness an issue is especially strong among American liberals, who have expended so much energy affirming virtually all life choices and at least excusing even the worst ones. The message of "you do you" is not easily reconciled with the message of "get a job." Accountability of any sort sits uncomfortably beside the Massachusetts

Medical Society's argument to its state's Supreme Judicial Court that remaining drug free must not be made a condition of a drug addict's parole.[13] In February 2018, the *New York Times* pondered "Who's Able-Bodied Anyway?," lamenting the moral judgment implicit in describing "so-called able-bodied" recipients of government benefits in terms that imply they should work.[14]

But this is the critical point: if individuals, their families, and their communities benefit from their engagement in work, lessening the social distinction between idleness and productive activities is not an enhancement of freedom but rather a form of deprivation. Work may have large benefits, but it's also often hard, and we need to maximize the reward for pursuing it. A well-meaning effort to elevate the status of people who fail to provide for themselves, or at least insulate them from reproach, has the unavoidable consequence of reducing or erasing any "respect gap" between idleness and work. People have no problem appreciating this dynamic in their own lives and applying it in the expectations they establish for their own children. The challenge is to make those beliefs public.

Our society knows how to convey strong messages when its influential members believe strongly in them: reality shows and prime-time dramas, commencement addresses and Oscar acceptances, sports broadcasts and late-night monologues, school assemblies and corporate memos. Whatever one's politics, it is impossible to deny the great effect to which these tools have been deployed on topics ranging from immigration to climate change to gay rights to sexual harassment. If society wanted to send a strong message about work, it could. But that momentum will not build organically; influencers do not spend their days searching for issues to adopt and champion. An issue must be forced, with activists making the moral argument in public and taking initiative in their own lives.

Nor should we let public policy off the hook. In many ways, both better laws and the messages conveyed by their pursuit can help to boost the social wages of work as well.

Policy makers can help to elevate the issue and to deliver messages of their own. A choice of agenda is itself a major cultural statement about what matters and what trade-offs we intend to make. While Republicans have been right to emphasize cultural issues, their refusal to contemplate an accompanying set of economic reforms has rather undermined their argument. Promising that economic growth will take care of everything seems a little too convenient—if a culture of work is critical, where are the policies that make work more available and attractive?

Consider the variety of policies, presented in economic terms in earlier chapters, through this cultural lens. Genuine education reform that made vocational and college tracks equally attractive would substantively improve graduates' job prospects, but it would also elevate the status of jobs on that track. A commitment to using the domestic workforce to meet more of the domestic economy's needs would show that "Made in America" is not a jingoistic slogan or a marketing tactic but an actual societal priority for which we are prepared to pay. Revitalizing organized labor would boost solidarity among workers and help them to establish for themselves a more prominent place in local communities. The wage subsidy would be direct evidence for someone, in every paycheck, that society is prepared to help pay him for his work.

Alongside those changes, all of which have the potential to enhance the positive value of work, policy makers also must remain cognizant of how their policies influence the negative consequences of idleness. Here safety-net programs are the standard example. As we saw in the prior chapter, a more generous safety net has the inevitable side effect of making work relatively less (economically) attractive than not working. It has a cultural effect as well: where not working becomes economically viable and its prevalence increases, seemingly with direct societal support, norms favoring work erode.

Policy makers need to become better at taking these considerations into account. The trend toward "evidence-based policy making" has yielded an increasing expectation that policies be evaluated on the basis of empirical data from rigorous economic studies. Unsurprisingly, this leads toward assessments grounded primarily in the policy's predictable, immediate, economic effects. Those are not the only, or even necessarily the most important, effects that policies have.

Policies cannot dictate family cohesion or community health, the depth of entrepreneurial spirit or the rate of scientific progress, the faith in our institutions or the quality of our politics. But they influence all those things. And as policies steer the allocation of society's resources and the evolution of its norms, they slowly but surely shift its course—an effect more consequential than the splashes they create upon entry. As we have already seen in the overreliance on GDP and the imbalanced cost–benefit analyses of environmental regulation, valuing only the most easily measurable effects does not lead to an accurate policy assessment; it errs badly by assigning a value of zero to other factors that we know matter too.

The result: we select the policies predicted to generate the highest growth or redistribute resources most efficiently, not those best for society. An overreliance on empirical economics represents an abdication of responsibility and signals a loss of will and courage to defend ideas. To be sure, good data are crucial to making well-informed policy choices. But deferring to them blindly becomes a crutch, transforming public statesmen into the satirical corporate lackeys who declare at every meeting, "I'm for what works."

In *The Closing of the American Mind*, Allan Bloom observed,

> When the liberal, or what came to be called the utilitarian, teaching became dominant, as is the case with most victorious causes, good arguments became less necessary; and the original good arguments, which were difficult, were replaced by plausible simplifications—or by nothing. The history of liberal thought since Locke and Smith has been one of almost unbroken decline in philosophic substance.[15]

An insistence on basing policy only on that which has been empirically proven represents another misstep in that direction.

* * *

The ultimate example of a policy that may appear attractive economically but would be disastrous for society is the universal basic income (UBI). Under proposals for a UBI, the federal government would send each American (including children, in some plans) a monthly check of, say, $800 or $1,000 to cover basic needs. A couple would receive $20,000 per year, regardless of other income earned; a family with children would get more. The bloated welfare state? Streamlined! Poverty? Solved! In some proposals, funding comes from eliminating safety-net programs that would no longer be necessary. In others, massive new taxes are required too.

The UBI has lurked in the background throughout this book; before concluding, it deserves a more direct discussion. The concept is emerging quickly as the next frontier, or perhaps the logical end point, of economic piety: unconstrained growth paired with unconstrained redistribution, maximizing consumption without reference to work. Whether one's motivation is the (misguided) fear that automation spells doom for those left behind in the modern economy or just a preference among the economy's winners for maintaining the status quo, paying people regardless of whether they work appears a convenient solution.

In her campaign memoir, *What Happened*, Hillary Clinton revealed that her policy team spent weeks trying to develop a basic-income proposal for her.[16] In February 2018, the *New York Times* profiled venture capitalist Andrew Yang, who has already declared his candidacy for the Democratic Party's 2020 presidential nomination on a basic-income platform, calling it "necessary for capitalism to continue."[17] Also in February, the California Democratic Party adopted the idea in its formal platform.[18]

To prove the effectiveness of this approach, basic-income proponents are operating experiments from the Bay Area and Finland to Kenya and India in which they give a group of people free money, give another group no money, and see what happens. No doubt many well-credentialed social scientists will be doing complex regression analyses for years, but in this case, we can safely skip to the last page: people like free money better than no free money. If maximizing consumption is the goal, the plan seems sensible.

But if the Working Hypothesis is correct, we should be concerned primarily that the UBI threatens to corrupt the role of work at society's foundation. It would redefine the relationship between individuals, families, communities, and the state by giving government the role of provider. It would make work optional and render self-reliance moot; consumption would become an entitlement officially disconnected from production. Stripped of its essential role as the way to earn a living, work would instead be an activity in which to engage by choice, for enjoyment, or to afford nicer things. An underclass dependent on government handouts would no longer be one of society's greatest challenges but instead would be recast as one of its proudest achievements.

As the Working Hypothesis makes clear, the effects would not stop with work. Clearly defined responsibilities, from educating children to caring for the elderly to fighting in wars, are fundamental to a society's character. They establish the terms of relationships, the scope and role of civil society, and the expectations against which people judge one another.

Without the bedrock obligation to provide for oneself and one's family, forming and maintaining a stable family ceases to be a necessity. A community in which people capable of making positive contributions are not expected to do so is unlikely to be one that thrives on any dimension in which productive contributions are needed.

Many UBI proponents themselves recognize, and embrace, the radical nature of their idea. Writing for the leftist magazine *Jacobin*, Shannon Ikebe observed that "a UBI has been embraced in particular by the post-productivist left, which carries a strong feminist and ecological bent and rejects the traditional left's valorization of labor and the working class." Ikebe quoted other scholars describing universal basic income as a "capitalist road to communism" and a "postwork political project."[19] *Times* columnist Manjoo wrote,

> One key factor in the push for U.B.I., I think, is the idea that it could help reorder social expectations. At the moment we are all defined by work; Western society generally, but especially American society, keeps social score according to what people do and how much they make for it. The dreamiest proponents of U.B.I. see that changing as work goes away.[20]

Fair enough, destroying the social value of work is *one way* to change expectations. Indeed, just making the argument that such an outcome might be desirable is itself a cultural blow to work's value.

Others make the opposite argument, that UBI is in fact *pro-work*, because while it may reduce the cultural upside of a job, it also reduces the economic downside: a recipient does not lose the UBI when he starts to work. This contrasts with a conventional safety net, in which benefits are phased out as a recipient's earnings increase. On average, in the United States, the phase-out reduces benefits by around 30 cents for every dollar earned. But over some income ranges and for some recipients, a dollar of wages can cost the earner nearly a full dollar of benefits.[21] Some programs, such as disability insurance, can also force recipients into a binary choice: either work or receive the benefit. So, other things being equal, someone who could keep her UBI would be more likely to seek work than someone who would lose some or all of her safety-net benefits as a result.

The problem with this argument is that providing a UBI with no phase-out to all Americans would cost several times more than the existing safety net. But of course, the safety net could also do a better job if given that extra money. For example, it could circumvent the phase-out challenge simply by offering food stamps and Medicaid eligibility for all. That would cost the same as a no-phase-out UBI while avoiding the unconditional cash handouts that most badly damage the respect accorded to work. If work is a social good rather than a social ill, then— for any given spending level—safety-net reforms that respect, promote, and even subsidize employment will yield better results than a UBI that seeks to supplant it.

The best way to understand the UBI's far-reaching economic and cultural consequences is from a simpler, more personal perspective. Imagine promising your child a basic income beginning at age eighteen. This is not just providing support—most parents already do that. Within the constraints of their own resources, they may give their young-adult children assistance with educational costs and even the down payment on a first home; other government programs already seek to offer such support to those with lower incomes. But the UBI goes well beyond that, to an unconditional, irrevocable right to receive the cash for meeting basic needs: the ultimate handout, not a hand up. A child would not receive payments himself, but he would grow up expecting them in a culture that endorsed them.

So if a parent wants the UBI experience for his children, he should not only promise the payments but also envision having "the UBI talk" with each one at least once a year, beginning no later than age ten. It could go something like this:

> *Son, it is important to me that you not feel obligated to support yourself. That's my job. Nor should you feel a duty to be a productive member of society. It is a central principle of this family, rather, that you feel entitled to everything you need.*
>
> *I hope you will get a job, because I think you will find it fulfilling, and it will allow you to buy nicer things. I also hope my support will encourage you to take some extra risks and pursue a challenging career, or become an entrepreneur, or dedicate yourself to helping those less fortunate. But none of that is a condition of my support. You can also backpack through Europe*

indefinitely or just sit in the basement smoking pot. In fact, as soon as we are
done with this talk, let's go watch one of the many movies Hollywood has
produced recently in which they show the enormous benefits of those choices
and viciously mock anyone who frowns on them.

If you find a girlfriend, I'll be happy to double your payment. If you have
kids, the payment will increase further. But lest you feel tied down, rest
assured that you can break up, abandon the kids, and I'll continue mak-
ing payments anyway. And we'll start those payments as soon as you turn
eighteen, at a critical inflection point in your future.

Of course, some parents do provide their children with a system of automatic support. We call the result a "trust fund baby." The term is not synonymous with "kind, well-adjusted, productive member of society." The day when parents embrace trust-fundism as a child-rearing ideal is the day when the UBI will gain mainstream traction as a public policy.

If the UBI's advocates really believe in the policy, they should start with their own children. After all, they are not just claiming that the UBI is necessary for society; they say that entitlement to an unconditional cash stipend is beneficial to the individual recipients.[22] Freed from the imperative to earn a wage, individuals can take more risks, pursue chosen careers, and commit more time to family. The advocate's self-implementation should work especially well because his children will still live in a society that expects self-sufficiency; he gets to free ride on community norms even as he undermines them from within.

A UBI advocate planning such payments and delivering "the talk" to his children is one to take seriously. He may not be right, but at least he seems genuinely to believe that his policy is a good one. Conversely, an advocate who adopts a more traditional philosophy at home would seem to want something different for his family than he suggests imposing on everyone else. And an imposition it is, because the UBI promise (and its culture) would await every child, no matter his parents' wishes. How would parents feel about a distant but wealthy uncle named Sam creating a trust fund against their wishes and then calling their child regularly to give him "the talk"? That is the society toward which we are headed, unless we change course now.

THE LOST GENERATION

Neither economic growth nor economic redistribution will rescue America from its current predicament. If the Working Hypothesis is correct and productive pluralism—rather than boosting consumption—is our objective, then we will need to create the social and economic conditions for a robust labor market in which all Americans can be contributors, achieve self-sufficiency, and support strong families and communities.

A genuine commitment to that kind of inclusive society requires a willingness to shape institutions to that end, even when doing so is for the benefit of others or when it creates tension with other values. Such concessions are of a different character from the taxes and spending that are often confused for compassion in American politics. "Don't tell me what you value," former vice president Joe Biden liked to say. "Show me your budget and I'll tell you what you value."[1] But taxes are easy, and deficit spending is even easier, compared with reordering social priorities—reconsidering whether to tolerate more pollutants in the air we breathe, determining whose children our schools are oriented toward, deciding what constraints our national borders should impose, and, ultimately, defining what we expect of and owe one another.

The people needing to accept a departure from some of their preferences under productive pluralism would be, generally speaking, the highly skilled, college-educated "winners" of the modern economy, who command the nation's economic, political, and social heights. Perhaps it should be no surprise, then, that such an agenda has received little attention from anywhere on the political spectrum. The problem is not one of bad faith. To the contrary, people who argue that growth leads inevitably to widely shared prosperity expect that strategy to work; people who argue that sufficient public spending can substitute for what people cannot provide for themselves believe passionately that this is the case. People know how they want society ordered and wish desperately for that same thing to be good for everyone else.

So they have sought approaches in which "everybody wins." This is precisely the premise of economic piety and especially of the "open" agenda—characterized by the priority given to globalization and GDP growth above other policy goals; the hope that intensive training and education can transform those left behind into those getting ahead; and the backstop of economic redistribution, or even a basic income, if all else fails. That so many Americans feel left behind by this agenda, even as it allows their consumption to rise, is a source of honest confusion.

The irony is that openers are themselves making just the kinds of choices that they struggle to recognize when made by others. They are happy to accept higher taxes and advocate for expansive government programs if it buys peace and quiet. But they will not contemplate any deviation from the borderless, green, multicultural, college-educated, individualistic, consumption-oriented society that they prefer. They regard *their* willingness to part with money (and thus consumption) to preserve their way of life as benevolent. Yet when the targets of their largess display a comparable hierarchy of priorities, the openers assume the explanation to be ignorance, or worse.

Part of the challenge is that the objects of social redistribution are not only things about which people tend to care deeply but also ones that present more direct conflicts. Economic growth really does create a larger pie from which everyone can, at least in theory, have a larger slice—or, more crassly, the winners really can buy off the losers. But the rules governing unions or school systems or polluters or employers or immigrants or trading partners or safety-net participants must be written, one way or another. Insofar as people differently situated within society will have different preferences, someone's must prevail. Stipulate that the optimal balance between air quality and heavy domestic industry for the median American is different than for one with a degree from a prestigious law school. Who should get his way? That such issues are more nearly zero-sum in the short run, and often intensely values based as well, may explain in part why our politics has become so hostile and tribal as people have become increasingly aware that economic piety does not, in fact, make winners of everyone. Trade and immigration have generated the strongest tremors thus far, but the fault lines extend far and wide.

The key qualifier, however, is *in the short run*. In terms of immediate interests, the commitment of the typical opener to his preferred agenda makes sense. Designing society's parameters around his preferences is to his benefit. The government programs that he funds address the needs of others and assuage his lingering concerns about inequality. But proceeding on this course is a mistake.

The open agenda is not sustainable in a democracy where the majority finds itself left behind; its arguments are losing force. The rapid expansion of international trade has clearly not been good for everyone, nor can the winners compensate the losers. The benefits of aggressive environmental regulation do not outweigh the costs for those who bear them. Not everyone should go to college, nor does everyone benefit from a public school system oriented toward that goal. Neither tax cuts, on one hand, nor tax increases coupled to more generous safety-net programs, on the other, invariably expand economic opportunity in distressed communities. Again, the accusation here is not one of bad faith but rather of failure to consider issues from multiple perspectives. One suspects that an affluent, high-minded opponent of high school tracking would quickly change her view if "no tracking" meant a system designed around the needs of the median student (who will not be completing college), with enrichment classes available in the evenings for children who don't think working-class careers are for them.

Facing the collapse of the open argument, its proponents have started down the path of blaming "progress" for their failure. The story goes that "automation" or the "knowledge economy," not bad public policy, is to blame. Historically, economists and policy makers have led the effort to explain that technological innovation is good for workers throughout the economy, even as its "creative destruction" causes dislocation for some. So why, suddenly, are they so eager to throw robots and programmers under the bus? Do they really think that Americans will accept Paul Krugman's view that any given small city "effectively loses any reason to exist,"[2] and so pack up their bags and move to the outskirts of Palo Alto to walk dogs? If openers keep insisting that technology and economic progress are responsible for the nation's distress, the result will not be widespread acceptance; it will be intensifying attacks on technology and economic progress. That would be an immense tragedy, because those things are *not* in fact the cause of our problems; indeed, they must be part of any solution.

The question is not whether the open agenda will lose but rather to what. Openers can work toward a compelling and coherent vision like productive pluralism or watch irresponsible populism and ever-harsher identity politics continue their ascent on both the Left and the Right. The underlying folly of the "open" versus "closed" framing is its assumption that one side actually wants a "closed" society. Few people are inherently against international trade or legal immigration, for instance. But they rightly expect to see priority given to building and maintaining economic and social structures within which they can sustain themselves, their families, and their communities. They rightly expect that to be the nonnegotiable foundation for whatever economic and social progress comes atop it. Sharing that goal, and helping to fulfill it, is a prerequisite for advancing an open agenda *that can have broad support if pursued responsibly.*

Implicit in the open agenda is a commitment to helping those left behind by the modern economy, typically through some combination of education and economic redistribution. But we now have decades upon decades of overwhelming evidence that neither of those mechanisms provides the help promised—to the contrary, massive influxes of resources toward both have coincided precisely with the economic and social maladies that have brought the nation to its present predicament. For some, the commitment may be mere virtue signaling. But many, perhaps most, people really do care about the fate of their fellow citizens and the quality of their society and are prepared to make sacrifices on behalf of others. For them, the time has come to grapple with the real trade-offs that money can no longer obscure.

* * *

We have seen that children born in 1980 reached this decade earning no more than their parents had at the same age. But how will America look a generation hence, when those born in this decade reach their own prime working years? Will they think back sadly to their parents' experience as that of America's Lost Generation, or will they be living that same experience themselves—one by then taken for granted as just the way things are?

This book has argued that the outcome remains within our control, a function of our political commitments rather than of irresistible social or technological trends. We decide whether today's children grow up in a country where they are expected to contribute productively to society and be rewarded for doing so. We decide whether to take money out of low-wage paychecks or put extra money in. We decide how self-reliance compares with reliance on the safety net, both economically and socially, and how to help get people back on their feet when they fall.

Our children can, if we want, have the real choice of a pathway that for many will be *more* attractive than pursuing college degrees—one that leaves them, by age twenty, with real work experience and on sound financial footing. Labor organizations can stand ready to guide them in skill development, provide social insurance, and facilitate their collaboration with employers. Employers can stand eager to hire and invest in them, having built the kinds of businesses that rely on the kinds of workers America has. Everyone will compete in a global economy—no question about that—but it can be an economy in which the world's consumers are as keen on buying from us as its producers are on selling to us.

Some products might become more expensive than if we had continued buying them on the national credit card or from people who had stolen our IP. But our households will have more savings, and our innovators will have greater incentive to make larger investments in the next round of technological breakthroughs. Our environmental quality may not progress as quickly as it did over the past generation, but it will be every bit as good as today's—and probably much better. A twenty-something choosing to spend his days smoking marijuana while immersed in the latest virtual-reality experience may feel more shame because of a shift in social norms, but his classmates who work for a living will feel greater pride, form stronger families and communities, and raise children prepared to do so themselves.

First and foremost, this future requires that people from all walks of life commit to building a broader socioeconomic coalition behind the commitment to an America that works. Rather than dismissing those calling attention to the nation's very real problems because they lack answers, supporters of an open agenda can concur and contribute toward developing a solution.

Personal choices sometimes count too. Work has cultural as well as economic dimensions, but we can't legislate social change. The value that our culture assigns to work and the respect afforded to participants will depend on people's beliefs and actions—the stories they tell, the language they use, and the triggers for their outrage all matter. Whether or not productive pluralism's future viability, and, with it, the nation's long-term prosperity, is *more* important than climate change and transgender rights and a ban on semiautomatic rifles, surely it rises at least to that level. People should treat it as such.

Furthermore, insofar as social issues provide a basis for economic decision-making, the health of the domestic labor market should be a priority. Buying American should be worth the same premium as buying organic. "Corporate social responsibility" should mean, first and foremost, a responsibility to American workers, who can only find meaningful work and achieve increasing productivity in cooperation with employers who consider those outcomes to be in their best interest as well. "Social impact investing" should try to have *that* social impact.

J. D. Vance, who wrote *Hillbilly Elegy* while working in Silicon Valley, relocated to Columbus, Ohio, to help run a venture-capital fund focused on the Midwest. "There are a lot of entrepreneurs [in Silicon Valley] developing the next app for clothes shopping who say, not ironically, that 'we are changing the world,'" he told the *Financial Times*. "You're not changing the world. The guy that's developing a new therapy that's non-opioid analgesic pain relief? That guy's changing the world."[3] The message needs to reach our innovators, who proclaim frequently their passion for solving society's most pressing and challenging problems yet seem almost allergic to building enterprises that would actually do so.

No law of economics promises that the labor market will allow workers of varying skills and aptitudes to support strong families and communities. If productive pluralism is our goal, we must make the political choice to foster it. Implicit in that choice, indeed, the premise of any major political choice, is a reordering of social priorities and an acceptance of associated trade-offs—including by those whose own immediate preferences must yield. The renewal of work represents an investment in strengthening America's foundation, and like all good investments, it will repay many times over the effort and resources that it demands at first. Only with that foundation can we have confidence in the integrity of whatever we build next, in our families and communities and as a nation.

ACKNOWLEDGMENTS

Several people share heaviest responsibility for my good fortune to think and write about public policy for a living. Lanhee Chen, policy director for Mitt Romney's presidential campaign, gave me the extraordinary opportunity to lead the campaign's domestic policy shop, often learning as I went. Reihan Salam, executive editor of *National Review*, encouraged me to publish a blog post, then a print article, then a cover story, and many of the ideas in this book appeared first in the magazine's pages. Vanessa Mendoza and Howard Husock helped me to create a career doing this kind of work at the Manhattan Institute for Policy Research.

I have been especially fortunate over the past three years to have the support of the Institute, under president Larry Mone's leadership, to pursue whatever topics I thought important in whatever directions they led. Troy Senik has championed this project since my first scattershot email on the subject. And the Institute's unparalleled book program shepherded it from vague idea to glossy paperweight—Bernadette Serton transformed the proposal from something I found interesting to something that a potential publisher or reader might; Michele Jacob made sure potential readers would become actual ones; Preston Turner and A. J. Cortese provided invaluable assistance with fact-checking and preparation of the notes.

City Journal's Brian Anderson and Paul Beston edited every page, and every page is better for it. Those parts that read clearly and persuasively do so thanks to their enormous effort. Those that do not are invariably the result of my stubborn refusal to accept their advice on some point. My agent, Andrew Stuart, was instrumental in guiding me through the publishing process—a process made remarkably smooth by Roger Kimball and his team at Encounter Books.

Some of this book's chapters began as essays elsewhere, and I thank those publications for helping to strengthen my arguments then and for allowing me to repurpose the writing now. Along with *National Review* and *City Journal*, *National Affairs* has provided a frequent home for my work. Its editor, Yuval Levin, has been a role model for me in attempting to make constructive contributions to our national debates, and he offered invaluable guidance and encouragement as the book took shape. He and several others—Jacob Reses, David Azerrad, Brad Wilcox, Ted Lee, and Alex Armlovich—were especially generous with their time and intellect in reviewing and commenting on substantial portions of the manuscript. More people than I could possibly acknowledge have influenced my thinking with their own ideas and their critiques of mine, including Rob Atkinson, Sean Clifford, Max Eden, Ed Glaeser, Tamar Jacoby, Mike Needham, Henry Olsen, Caleb Orr, Ramesh Ponnuru, Bruce Reed, Isabel Sawhill, J. D. Vance, and Adam White, as well as all the members of the Working Class Group convened by Opportunity America, the American Enterprise Institute, and the Brookings Institution.

Finally, and most importantly, I am grateful to my family. My parents, Linda and David, taught me the importance of work, family, and community long before I knew anything about public policy. My wife, Kristine, is the hero of our own little family and my daily reminder of what matters in life. The burden of this project fell heavily on her—it consumed too much of my time and left me irritable for too much of the rest—yet she remained unfailingly supportive even when my only progress for the day was rewriting a paragraph three times and then deciding just to delete it.

My preschool-age daughters Eliza and Rosalie did their best to offer their own support for a process they could not fathom, faithfully and hopefully inquiring each night at dinner, "Is your book done yet?" Whether that is, in fact, a helpful thing to ask repeatedly of a writer is beside the point. Much of the book is written to them and for them, about the country I hope they inherit. And yes, girls, the book is done.

NOTES

INTRODUCTION: THE WORKING HYPOTHESIS

1 Hillary Clinton's speech accepting the Democratic Party's nomination for president in 2016 provides a good illustration. "Democrats, we are the party of working people," she declared. "My primary mission as president will be to create more opportunity and more good jobs with rising wages right here in the United States."

But her ideas for achieving this mission would obstruct it. Some bullet points were non sequiturs (campaign finance reform, voting rights, expanding Social Security, establishing a "right to affordable health care," protecting "a woman's right to make her own health care decisions"). Most were counterproductive efforts to raise the cost of employing workers while doing nothing to increase their value, either directly (taxing layoffs, raising the minimum wage, mandating "equal pay"; see chapters 8 and 9) or by increasing regulatory burdens and operational costs (stricter financial regulation, fighting climate change; see chapter 5). The obligatory inclusion of "comprehensive immigration reform" was a promise to worsen an existing imbalance by expanding the supply of unskilled workers faster than demand for their work (see chapter 7).

Her only idea bearing a rational relationship to her goal was to "stand up to China" (also see chapter 7), but her track record—as, among other things, the nation's top diplomat—entailed "standing up to China" on women's rights and climate change, not on behalf of American workers. The item's inclusion owed more to her opponent's emphasis on it than to her own party's ideology or agenda. Hillary Rodham Clinton, remarks at the Democratic National Convention, Philadelphia, July 28, 2016, https://www.washingtonpost.com/news/the-fix/wp/2016/07/28/here-is-hillary-clintons-presidential-nomination-acceptance-speech/.

2 Joshua Hawley, the Republican candidate for the U.S. Senate in Missouri as this book went to press, emphasized this dimension of conservatism in a 2012 essay for *National Affairs*: "Conservatives' aim must be not merely to cut spending, but to reform the American economy to include more citizens in meaningful work. Getting to that more inclusive economy will require conservatives to think beyond austerity, and also to think beyond mere economic growth. . . . Getting disadvantaged workers into the labor force will require structural renovation. This need not make conservatives blanch. America's capitalist economy is constantly evolving. Conservatives should not try to control it, but simply to use wise policy to nudge it toward greater inclusion of disadvantaged workers." Hawley, "Rediscovering Justice," *National Affairs*, Winter 2012, https://www.nationalaffairs.com/publications/detail/rediscovering-justice.

3 James Surowiecki, "Exporting I.P.," *New Yorker*, May 14, 2007, http://www.newyorker.com/magazine/2007/05/14/exporting i p; Orly Lobel, "Filing for a Patent versus Keeping Your Invention a Trade Secret," *Harvard Business Review*, November 21, 2013, https://hbr.org/2013/11/filing-for-a-patent-versus-keeping-your-invention-a-trade-secret.

CHAPTER 1: AS AMERICAN AS ECONOMIC PIE

1 "GDP: One of the Great Inventions of the 20th Century," *Survey of Current Business* 80, no. 1 (2000): 7, https://fraser.stlouisfed.org/files/docs/publications/SCB/2000-09 /SCB_012000.pdf.

2 Simon Kuznets, "National Income, 1929–1932," S. Doc. No. 124, 73rd Cong., 2nd sess. (1934), 7, https://fraser.stlouisfed.org/files/docs/publications/natincome_1934/19340104 _nationalinc.pdf.

3 Adam Smith (1723–90), *An Inquiry into the Nature and Causes of the Wealth of Nations*, edited by R. H. Campbell and A. S. Skinner (Oxford: Oxford University Press, 1976), vol. 2, bk. 4, ch. 8, para. 49.

4 Clifford Cobb, Ted Halstead, and Jonathan Rowe, "If the GDP Is Up, Why Is America Down?," *The Atlantic*, October 1995, https://www.theatlantic.com/past/docs/politics /ecbig/gdp.htm.

5 Ben Sasse, *The Vanishing American Adult: Our Coming-of-Age Crisis—and How to Rebuild a Culture of Self-Reliance* (New York: St. Martin's Press, 2017), 122.

6 Emma Green, "The Disappearance of Virtue from American Politics," *The Atlantic*, May 29, 2017, https://www.theatlantic.com/politics/archive/2017/05/ben-sasse-virtue-politics /528015/.

7 This list may not be exhaustive. Remarks including the phrase by all of these presidents are available via the American Presidency Project, University of California, Santa Barbara, http://www.presidency.ucsb.edu/.

8 "Current-Dollar and 'Real' GDP," U.S. Bureau of Economic Analysis, https://bea.gov /national/xls/gdplev.xlsx.

9 Data cited throughout this book on the size of the social safety net are drawn from the author's prior work compiling a database of federal- and state-level social spending. Detailed data and accompanying methodology can be found in Oren Cass, *Over-Medicaid-ed: How Medicaid Distorts and Dilutes America's Safety Net* (New York: Manhattan Institute for Policy Research, May 2016), appendix, https://www.manhattan -institute.org/html/over-medicaid-ed-how-medicaid-distorts-and-dilutes-americas-safety-net-8890.html.

10 Susan Dudley and Melinda Warren, *Regulators' Budget Reflects President Trump's Priorities: An Analysis of the U.S. Budget for Fiscal Years 1960 through 2018* (Washington, D.C.: George Washington University Regulatory Studies Center, July 2017), table A-5, http://regulatorystudies.columbian.gwu.edu/files/downloads/Final Regulators%27 Budget.pdf

11 Rachel Sheffield and Robert Rector, "Air Conditioning, Cable TV, and an Xbox: What Is Poverty in the United States Today?" (Backgrounder 2575, Heritage Foundation, Washington, D.C., July 2011), https://www.heritage.org/poverty-and-inequality/report /air-conditioning-cable-tv-and-xbox-what-poverty-the-united-states.

12 The poll question's exact wording is "In general, are you satisfied or dissatisfied with the way things are going in the United States at this time?" "Satisfaction with the United States," Gallup, http://news.gallup.com/poll/1669/general-mood-country.aspx.

13 These figures compare the tops of two business cycles, from 1979 (prior to the start of a recession in 1980) to 2007 (the Great Recession began in December of that year), converted from nominal to constant dollars using the Consumer Price Index (CPI). All figures are median weekly earnings for full-time wage and salary workers. "Labor Force Statistics from the Current Population Survey," U.S. Bureau of Labor Statistics, https:// www.bls.gov/cps/earnings.htm. Many economists argue that the CPI is an inappropriate measure of inflation and show that wages look less stagnant using alternative measures. This issue is discussed further in note 22.

14 "Historical Income Tables: People," U.S. Census Bureau, tables P-16 and P-17, https://

www.census.gov/data/tables/time-series/demo/income-poverty/historical-income
-people.html; "Poverty Thresholds," U.S. Census Bureau, https://www.census.gov/data
/tables/time-series/demo/income-poverty/historical-poverty-thresholds.html.

15 "Labor Force Statistics from the Current Population Survey," U.S. Bureau of Labor
Statistics, https://www.bls.gov/cps/.

16 Nicholas Eberstadt, "Our Miserable 21st Century," *Commentary*, March 2017, https://
www.commentarymagazine.com/articles/our-miserable-21st-century/.

17 Lawrence F. Katz and Alan B. Krueger, "The Rise and Nature of Alternative Work
Arrangements in the United States, 1995–2015" (Working Paper 22667, National Bureau
of Economic Research, Cambridge, Mass., September 2016), 8, http://www.nber.org
/papers/w22667.

18 Over that period, the share of Americans in Murray's "Fishtown" cohort declines from
64 percent of the population to 30 percent, but his analysis shows that the trends remain
similar if focused on a constant 30 percent share of the population. Charles Murray,
Coming Apart: The State of White America, 1960–2010 (New York: Crown Forum, 2012),
149–52. Murray eventually widens his analysis and shows that the story he has told for
white America is mirrored in the nation's working class across racial groups (273–81).

19 Murray, *Coming Apart*, 159, 275, 233, 252–53, 192.

20 Cass, *Over-Medicaid-ed*, appendix.

21 "Historical Poverty Tables: People and Families—1959 to 2016," U.S. Census Bureau,
table 2, https://www.census.gov/data/tables/time-series/demo/income-poverty
/historical-poverty-people.html.

22 The Bureau of Labor Statistics uses the Consumer Price Index (CPI) to measure
inflation and convert between nominal and real dollars—a convention adopted
frequently in government analyses and used, for instance, to adjust Social Security
benefits over time. Many economists argue that CPI overstates the rise in prices a typical
household faces, which leads to the understatement of real wage gains. They prefer to
use an alternative measure developed by the Bureau of Economic Analysis called the
Personal Consumption Expenditure (PCE) index, which the Federal Reserve uses to
evaluate the economy's inflation rate and which tends to report lower levels of inflation.
Using PCE, real wage growth appears somewhat higher. Other issues in measuring
long-term changes in average compensation abound, such as how to account for workers
who have exited the labor force or for the rising cost of payroll taxes and fringe benefits,
especially health care. Scott Winship, "Men's Rising Earnings," *National Review*, July 1,
2013, https://www.nationalreview.com/magazine/2013/07/01/mens-rising-earnings/. This
book uses CPI for its inflation adjustments throughout, to remain consistent with other
cited analyses that tend to use CPI themselves. Using CPE, median weekly earnings
for full-time wage and salary workers rose 18 percent rather than 1 percent from 1979 to
2007, still an anemic result. Workers with a high school degree or less still experienced
a decline. Under any methodology, the labor market has produced poor outcomes, and
wage growth remains only one line of evidence for this conclusion.

23 Steven Pinker, "The Enlightenment Is Working," *Wall Street Journal*, February 10, 2018,
https://www.wsj.com/articles/the-enlightenment-is-working-1518191343.

24 Ben Bernanke, "When Growth Is Not Enough," remarks prepared for delivery on June
26, 2017, at the European Central Bank Forum on Central Banking at Sintra, https://
www.brookings.edu/wp-content/uploads/2017/06/es_20170626
_whengrowthisnotenough.pdf.

25 Jonathan Vespa, *The Changing Economics and Demographics of Young Adulthood: 1975–2016*
(Washington, DC: US Census Bureau, April 2017), 2, https://www.census.gov/content
/dam/Census/library/publications/2017/demo/p20-579.pdf.

26 Raj Chetty, David Grusky, Maximilian Hell, Nathaniel Hendren, Robert Manduca, and

Jimmy Narang, "The Fading American Dream: Trends in Absolute Income Mobility since 1940" (Working Paper 22910, National Bureau of Economic Research, Cambridge, Mass., December 2016), http://www.nber.org/papers/w22910.

27 Bruce Stokes, *Global Publics More Upbeat about the Economy: But Many Are Pessimistic about Children's Future* (Washington, D.C.: Pew Research Center, June 2017), 15, http://www.pewglobal.org/2017/06/05/global-publics-more-upbeat-about-the-economy/.

28 Anne Case and Angus Deaton, "Rising Morbidity and Mortality in Midlife among White Non-Hispanic Americans in the 21st Century," *Proceedings of the National Academy of Sciences of the United States of America* 112, no. 49 (2015): 15078–83, https://doi.org/10.1073/pnas.1518393112.

29 "'Two Americas,' Updated," *Wall Street Journal*, November 20, 2017, https://www.wsj.com/articles/an-update-on-the-two-americas-1510784348; Anne Case and Angus Deaton, "Mortality and Morbidity in the 21st Century" (Brookings Papers on Economic Activity, Brookings Institution, Washington, D.C., Spring 2017), 406, figure 3, https://www.brookings.edu/wp-content/uploads/2017/08/casetextsp17bpea.pdf.

30 Joel Achenbach and Dan Keating, "Drug Crisis Is Pushing Up Death Rates for Almost All Groups of Americans," *Washington Post*, June 9, 2017, https://www.washingtonpost.com/national/health-science/the-drug-crisis-is-now-pushing-up-death-rates-for-almost-all-groups-of-americans/2017/06/09/971d8424-4aa1-11e7-a186-60c031eab644_story.html.

31 Lenny Bernstein and Christopher Ingraham, "Fueled by Drug Crisis, U.S. Life Expectancy Declines for a Second Straight Year," *Washington Post*, December 21, 2017, https://www.washingtonpost.com/national/health-science/fueled-by-drug-crisis-us-life-expectancy-declines-for-a-second-straight-year/2017/12/20/2e3f8dea-e596-11e7-ab50-621fe0588340_story.html.

32 Sally C. Curtin, Margaret Warner, and Holly Hedegaard, "Increase in Suicide in the United States, 1999–2014" (Data Brief 241, Centers for Disease Control and Prevention, Atlanta, Ga., April 2016), https://www.cdc.gov/nchs/products/databriefs/db241.htm.

33 "Overdose Death Rates," National Institute on Drug Abuse, September 2017, https://www.drugabuse.gov/related-topics/trends-statistics/overdose-death-rates/.

34 Christopher M. Jones, "Epidemiological Overview of the U.S. Opioid Epidemic and Past Drug Crises," presentation to the National Academy of Medicine annual meeting, October 16, 2017, https://nam.edu/wp-content/uploads/2017/11/1_CJones-NAM-Slides.pdf; for further discussion of the opioid crisis in comparison to past epidemics, see Christopher Caldwell, "American Carnage," *First Things*, April 2017, https://www.firstthings.com/article/2017/04/american-carnage.

35 Bernstein and Ingraham, "U.S. Life Expectancy Declines."

36 Dennis H. Osmond, "Epidemiology of HIV/AIDS in the United States" (HIV InSite, University of California, San Francisco, March 2003), table 3, http://hivinsite.ucsf.edu/InSite?page=kb-01-03.

37 "Real' GDP."

38 Shayndi Raice and Eric Morath, "In Cities with Low Unemployment, Wages Finally Start to Get Bigger," *Wall Street Journal*, January 1, 2018, https://www.wsj.com/articles/in-cities-with-low-unemployment-wages-finally-start-to-get-bigger-1514808001; David Lynch, "'This Is Super Tight': Companies Struggle to Find Retail Workers in a Hot Economy," *Washington Post*, January 12, 2018, https://www.washingtonpost.com/business/economy/this-is-super-tight-companies-struggle-to-find-retain-workers-in-a-hot-economy/2018/01/12/0c1ce97e-f7cf-11e7-b34a-b85626af34ef_story.html; Ben Casselman, "Jailed, Shunned, but Now Hired in Tight Market," *New York Times*, January 14, 2018, https://www.nytimes.com/2018/01/13/business/economy/labor-market-inmates.html.

39 "Labor Force Statistics from the Current Population Survey," U.S. Bureau of Labor Statistics, https://www.bls.gov/cps/.

40 "Labor Force Statistics from the Current Population Survey," https://www.bls.gov/cps
    /earnings.htm; "Wage Growth Tracker," Federal Reserve Bank of Atlanta, March 12,
    2018, https://www.frbatlanta.org/chcs/wage-growth-tracker.aspx.

41 "Labor Productivity (Output per Hour): Nonfarm Business," U.S. Bureau of Labor
    Statistics, https://www.bls.gov/lpc/.

42 Danielle Kurtzleben, "Here's How Many Bernie Sanders Supporters Ultimately Voted
    for Trump," National Public Radio, https://www.npr.org/2017/08/24/545812242/1-in-10
    -sanders-primary-voters-ended-up-supporting-trump-survey-finds/.

43 Jon Huang, Samuel Jacoby, Michael Strickland, and K. K. Rebecca Lai, "Election 2016:
    Exit Polls," *New York Times*, November 8, 2016, http://www.nytimes.com/interactive
    /2016/11/08/us/politics/election-exit-polls.html.

44 "Drawbridges Up: The New Divide in Rich Countries Is Not between Left and Right
    but between Open and Closed," *The Economist*, July 30, 2016, http://www.economist.
    com/news/briefing/21702748-new-divide-rich-countries-not-between-left-and-right
    -between-open-and.

45 Fareed Zakaria, "The Politics of the Future: Be Open and Armed," *Washington Post*, July
    7, 2016, http://www.washingtonpost.com/opinions/the-politics-of-the-future-be-open
    -and-armed/2016/07/07/fd171ce0-447b-11e6-8856-f26de2537a9d_story.html.

46 Allan Bloom, *The Closing of the American Mind: How Higher Education Has Failed
    Democracy and Impoverished the Souls of Today's Students* (New York: Simon and Schuster,
    1987), 26–27.

47 Mark Zuckerberg, remarks at Harvard University, Cambridge, Mass., May 25, 2017,
    https://news.harvard.edu/gazette/story/2017/05/mark-zuckerbergs-speech-as-written
    -for-harvards-class-of-2017/.

CHAPTER 2: PRODUCTIVE PLURALISM

1   Arthur Goldsmith and Timothy Diette, "Exploring the Link between Unemployment
    and Mental Health Outcomes" (*SES Indicator*, American Psychological Association,
    Washington, D.C., April 2012), http://www.apa.org/pi/ses/resources/indicator/2012/04
    /unemployment.aspx.

2   Steve Crabtree, "In U.S., Depression Rates Higher for Long-Term Unemployed,"
    Gallup, June 9, 2014, http://www.gallup.com/poll/171044/depression-rates-higher
    -among-long-term-unemployed.aspx. Gallup is careful to note that its survey identifies
    only a correlation and does not prove causation, but both intuition and other research
    suggest that the relationship is at least in part causal, e.g., Margaret W. Linn, R. Sandifer,
    and S. Stein, "Effects of Unemployment on Mental and Physical Health," *American
    Journal of Public Health* 75, no. 5 (1985): 502–6, https://www.ncbi.nlm.nih.gov/pmc
    /articles/PMC1646287/.

3   Andrew E. Clark and Andrew J. Oswald, "A Simple Statistical Model for Measuring
    How Life Events Affect Happiness," *International Journal of Epidemiology* 31, no. 6
    (2002): 1139–1144, https://doi.org/10.1093/ije/31.6.1139; Edward L. Glaeser, "The War on
    Work—and How to End It," *City Journal*, 2017, https://www.city-journal.org/html/war
    -work-and-how-end-it-15250.html.

4   Andrew E. Clark, Ed Diener, Yannis Georgellis, and Richard E. Lucas, "Lags and Leads
    in Life Satisfaction: A Test of the Baseline Hypothesis," *Economic Journal* 118, no. 529
    (2008): F222–43, http://www.jstor.org/stable/20108833.

5   Charles Murray, *Coming Apart: The State of White America, 1960–2010* (New York: Crown
    Forum, 2012), 262.

6   David Azerrad, "How Equal Should Opportunities Be?," *National Affairs*, Summer 2016,
    https://www.nationalaffairs.com/publications/detail/how-equal-should-opportunities-be.

7   Michael Madowitz, Alex Rowell, and Katie Hamm, *Calculating the Hidden Cost of
    Interrupting a Career for Child Care* (Washington, D.C.: Center for American

Progress, June 2016), https://www.americanprogress.org/issues/early-childhood/reports/2016/06/21/139731/calculating-the-hidden-cost-of-interrupting-a-career-for-child-care/.

8 Brigid Schulte and Alieza Durana, *The New America Care Report* (Washington, D.C.: New America, September 2016), https://www.newamerica.org/better-life-lab/policy-papers/new-america-care-report/.

9 A good example of an income-smoothing policy is the proposal to allow workers to borrow against future Social Security benefits to fund paid parental leave. Kristin A. Shapiro and Andrew G. Biggs, "A Simple Plan for Parental Leave," *Wall Street Journal*, January 25, 2018, https://www.wsj.com articles/a-simple-plan-for-parental-leave-1516836442.

10 Richard V. Reeves, "Saving Horatio Alger: Equality, Opportunity and the American Dream" (Brookings Essay, Brookings Institution, Washington, D.C., August 20, 2014), http://csweb.brookings.edu/content/research/essays/2014/saving-horatio-alger.html.

11 Raj Chetty, Nathaniel Hendren, Patrick Kline, and Emmanuel Saez, "Where Is the Land of Opportunity? The Geography of Intergenerational Mobility in the United States" (Working Paper 19843, National Bureau of Economic Research, Cambridge, Mass., January 2014), 40, http://www.nber.org/papers/w19843.

12 W. Bradford Wilcox, William J. Doherty, Helen Fisher, William A. Galston, Norval D. Glenn, John Gottman, Robert Lerman et al., *Why Marriage Matters: Twenty-Six Conclusions from the Social Sciences*, 2nd ed. (New York: Institute for American Values, 2005), http://americanvalues.org/catalog/pdfs/why_marriage_matters2.pdf.

13 Rose McDermott, James H. Fowler, and Nicholas A. Christakis, "Breaking Up Is Hard to Do, Unless Everyone Else Is Doing It Too: Social Network Effects on Divorce in a Longitudinal Sample," *Social Forces* 92, no. 2 (2013): 491–519, https://doi.org/10.1093/sf/sot096.

14 Murray, *Coming Apart*; Robert D. Putman, *Our Kids: The American Dream in Crisis* (New York: Simon and Schuster, 2015).

15 John Edwards, remarks at the Democratic National Convention, Boston, July 28, 2004, http://www.washingtonpost.com/wp-dyn/articles/A22230-2004Jul28.html.

16 American Enterprise Institute, *A Discussion with Friedrich von Hayek* (Washington, D.C.: American Enterprise Institute, April 9, 1975), 6, http://www.aei.org/wp-content/uploads/2016/03/Conversation01.pdf (emphasis original).

17 "How the Government Measures Unemployment," U.S. Bureau of Labor Statistics, June 2014, 2, https://www.bls.gov/cps/cps_htgm.pdf.

18 "Americans' Financial Security: Perception and Reality" (Issue Brief, Pew Charitable Trusts, Philadelphia, March 2015), 7, http://www.pewtrusts.org/en/research-and-analysis/issue-briefs/2015/02/americans-financial-security-perceptions-and-reality.

19 Savings rates used here are annual averages calculated from monthly data. "U.S. Bureau of Economic Analysis, Personal Saving Rate," Federal Reserve Bank of St. Louis, https://fred.stlouisfed.org/series/PSAVERT.

20 "Our Common Future" (United Nations World Commission on Environment and Development, Geneva, Switzerland, June 1987), ch. 2, http://www.un-documents.net/wced-ocf.htm.

21 John Tierney, "Betting on the Planet," *New York Times Magazine*, December 2, 1990, http://www.nytimes.com/1990/12/02/magazine/betting-on-the-planet.html.

22 Patrick J. Deneen uses a similar metaphor, writing that "the triumphant march of liberalism has succeeded in at once drawing down the social and natural resources that liberalism did not create and cannot replenish, but which sustained liberalism even as its advance eroded its own unacknowledged foundations." Deneen, *Why Liberalism Failed* (New Haven, Conn.: Yale University Press, 2018), 30.

23 "U.S. Bureau of Economic Analysis, Shares of Gross Domestic Product: Imports of

Goods and Services," Federal Reserve Bank of St. Louis, https://fred.stlouisfed.org /series/B021RE1A156NBEA.

24 Gustavo López and Jynnah Radford, "Facts on U.S. Immigrants, 2015," Pew Research Center, May 3, 2017, http://www.pewhispanic.org/2017/05/03/facts-on-u-s-immigrants/.

25 Esteban Ortiz-Ospina and Max Roser, "Trust," Our World in Data, 2017, https:// ourworldindata.org/trust.

26 César A. Hidalgo and Ricardo Hausmann, "The Building Blocks of Economic Complexity," *Proceedings of the National Academy of Sciences of the United States of America* 106, no. 26 (2009): 10570–75, https://doi.org/10.1073/pnas.0900943106; "Complexity Matters: A New Atlas Reveals the Building Blocks of Economic Growth," *The Economist* (blog), October 27, 2011, https://www.economist.com/blogs/freeexchange/2011/10/ building-blocks-economic-growth.

27 Janet Adamy and Paul Overberg, "Struggling Americans Once Sought Greener Pastures—Now They're Stuck," *Wall Street Journal*, August 2, 2017, https://www.wsj.com /articles/struggling-americans-once-sought-greener-pasturesnow-theyre-stuck -1501686801.

28 Chang-Tai Hsieh and Enrico Moretti, "Housing Constraints and Spatial Misallocation" (Working Paper 21154, National Bureau of Economic Research, Cambridge, Mass., May 2015), http://www.nber.org/papers/w21154.

29 "Population of the States and Counties of the United States: 1790 to 1990," U.S. Census Bureau, https://www.census.gov/population/www/censusdata/pop1790-1990.html; Jason Long and Henry E. Siu, "Refugees from Dust and Shrinking Land: Tracking the Dust Bowl Migrants" (Working Paper 22108, National Bureau of Economic Research, Cambridge, Mass., March 2016), https://www.nber.org/papers/w22108.

CHAPTER 3: THE LABOR MARKET

1 Peter Suderman, "Young Men Are Playing Video Games Instead of Getting Jobs. That's OK. (For Now.)," *Reason*, July 2017, http://reason.com/archives/2017/06/13/young-men -are-playing-video-ga.

2 Myron Magnet, *The Dream and the Nightmare: The Sixties' Legacy to the Underclass* (New York: William Morrow, 1993), ch. 1.

3 Magnet estimates the couple's income in the early 1990s at $31,000 to $40,000 ($53,000 to $68,000 in 2016 dollars). In 2016, median wages in the New York metropolitan area for a short-order cook and a housekeeping cleaner were $9.58 and $15.30 per hour, respectively, equivalent to $50,000 in annual income from two full-time jobs. "May 2016 Metropolitan and Nonmetropolitan Area Occupational Employment and Wage Estimates: New York–Jersey City–White Plains, NY–NJ Metropolitan Division," U.S. Bureau of Labor Statistics, https://www.bls.gov/oes/current/oes_35614.htm.

4 Josh Katz, "How Nonemployed Americans Spend Their Weekdays: Men vs. Women," *New York Times*, January 6, 2015, https://www.nytimes.com/interactive/2015/01/06 /upshot/how-nonemployed-americans-spend-their-weekdays-men-vs-women.html; Mark Aguiar, Mark Bils, Kerwin Kofi Charles, and Erik Hurst, "Leisure Luxuries and the Labor Supply of Young Men" (Working Paper 23552, National Bureau of Economic Research, Cambridge, Mass., June 2017), http://www.nber.org/papers/w23552.

5 Claudia Geist, "Marriage Formation in Context: Four Decades in Comparative Perspective," *Social Sciences* 6, no. 1 (2017): 9–24, https://doi.org/10.3390/socsci6010009; David Autor, David Dorn, and Gordon Hanson, "When Work Disappears: Manufacturing Decline and the Falling Marriage-Market Value of Young Men" (Working Paper 23173, National Bureau of Economic Research, Cambridge, Mass., February 2017), http://www.nber.org/papers/w23173.

6 Stephan Lindner and H. Elizabeth Peters, "How Does Unemployment Affect Family

Arrangements for Children?" (Low-Income Working Families Paper 29, Urban Institute, Washington, D.C., August 2014), 9, table 3, https://www.urban.org/research/publication /how-does-unemployment-affect-family-arrangements-children; Liana C. Sayer, Paula England, Paul Allison, and Nicole Kangas, "She Left, He Left: How Employment and Satisfaction Affect Men's and Women's Decisions to Leave Marriages," *American Journal of Sociology* 116, no. 6 (2011): 1982–2018, https://doi.org/10.1086/658173.

7 William Julius Wilson, *The Truly Disadvantaged: The Inner City, the Underclass, and Public Policy* (Chicago: University of Chicago Press, 1987). For a contemporary discussion of Wilson's hypothesis, see Isabel Sawhill and Joanna Venator, "Is There a Shortage of Marriageable Men?" (Center on Children and Families Brief 56, Brookings Institution, Washington, D.C., September 2015), https://www.brookings.edu/wp-content/uploads /2016/06/56-Shortage-of-Marriageable-Men.pdf.

8 Autor et al., "When Work Disappears."

9 Andrew J. Cherlin, David C. Ribar, and Suzumi Yasutake, "Nonmarital First Births, Marriage, and Income Inequality," *American Sociological Review* 81, no. 4 (2016): 749–70, 763, https://doi.org/10.1177/0003122416653112.

10 Steven Raphael and Rudolf Winter-Ebmer, "Identifying the Effect of Unemployment on Crime," *Journal of Law and Economics* 44, no. 1 (2001): 259–83, http://www.jstor.org /stable/10.1086/320275; Alex Hollingsworth, Christopher J. Ruhm, and Kosali Simon, "Macroeconomic Conditions and Opioid Abuse" (Working Paper 23192, National Bureau of Economic Research, Cambridge, Mass., February 2017), http://www.nber.org /papers/w23192.

11 Austin Nichols, Josh Mitchell, and Stephan Lindner, *Consequences of Long-Term Unemployment* (Washington, D.C.: Urban Institute, 2013), https://www.urban.org /research/publication/consequences-long-term-unemployment; Joanna Venator and Richard V. Reeves, "Parental Unemployment Hurts Kids' Futures and Social Mobility" (Social Mobility Memo, Brookings Institution, Washington, D.C., November 25, 2013), https://www.brookings.edu/blog/social-mobility-memos/2013/11/25/parental -unemployment-hurts-kids-futures-and-social-mobility/.

12 John Edwards, remarks at the Democratic National Convention, Boston, July 28, 2004, http://www.washingtonpost.com/wp-dyn/articles/A22230-2004Jul28.html.

13 Edward L. Glaeser, "The War on Work—and How to End It," *City Journal*, 2017, https:// www.city-journal.org/html/war-work-and-how-end-it-15250.html.

CHAPTER 4: A FUTURE FOR WORK

1 Christopher Matthews, "Summers: Automation Is the Middle Class' Worst Enemy," *Axios*, June 4, 2017, https://www.axios.com/summers-automation-is-the-middle-class-worst-enemy-1513302420-754facf2-aaca-4788-9a41-38f87fbodd99.html.

2 Stephen Hawking, "This Is the Most Dangerous Time for Our Planet," *The Guardian*, December 1, 2016, https://www.theguardian.com/commentisfree/2016/dec/01/stephen -hawking-dangerous-time-planet-inequality.

3 Claire Cain Miller, "The Long-Term Jobs Killer Is Not China. It's Automation," *New York Times*, December 21, 2016, https://www.nytimes.com/2016/12/21/upshot/the-long -term-jobs-killer-is-not-china-its-automation.html.

4 Editorial, "The Rage against Trade," *New York Times*, August 7, 2016, https://www .nytimes.com/2016/08/07/opinion/sunday/the-rage-against-trade.html.

5 Iain Duncan Smith, "A Conservatism That Addresses the Challenges of the 21st Century: Good for Me Good for My Neighbor," remarks prepared for delivery at the American Enterprise Institute, Washington, D.C., April 18, 2016, http://www.aei.org /press/prepared-remarks-a-conservatism-that-addresses-the-challenges-of-the-21st -century-good-for-me-good-for-my-neighbor/.

6   David Rotman, "The Relentless Pace of Automation," *MIT Technology Review*, February 13, 2017, https://www.technologyreview.com/s/603465/the-relentless-pace-of -automation/.

7   "Labor Productivity (Output per Hour): Nonfarm Business," U.S. Bureau of Labor Statistics, https://www.bls.gov/lpc/.

8   Data for employed share of the population begin in 1948 and stood at 56.6 percent that January. In 1972, the value ranged from 56.7 to 57.3 percent. "Labor Force Statistics from the Current Population Survey: Employment-Population Ratio," U.S. Bureau of Labor Statistics, https://www.bls.gov/cps/.

9   Median wage data are available beginning only in the 1970s. The figure for men is used here because the trend in overall median wage-or-salary-income data is skewed downward by an increasing share of part-time workers as women, who were three times more likely than men to be working part time in 1968, entered the labor force. Women's median income rose 53 percent during the period. Median family income doubled. "Measuring 50 Years of Economic Change Using the March Current Population Survey" (Current Population Report P60-203, U.S. Census Bureau, Washington, D.C., 1998), table C-6, table C-11, https://www.census.gov/prod/3/98pubs/p60-203.pdf; "Labor Force Statistics from the Current Population Survey."

10 Vehicle sales increased from 6.3 million in 1951 to 13.6 million in 1972. "U.S. Car and Truck Sales, 1931–2016," WardsAuto, 2017, http://wardsauto.com/datasheet/us-car-and -truck-sales-1931-2014.

11 Vehicle miles per capita increased from 3,017 in 1950 to 6,147 in 1975. *Transportation Energy Data Book: Edition 36* (Oak Ridge, Tenn.: Oak Ridge National Laboratory, 2017), ch. 8, table 8.2, http://cta.ornl.gov/data/tedb36/Edition36_Chapter08.pdf.

12 Estimates in 1972 for foreign-made light trucks imputed from 1976 figure and growth in foreign-made car sales from 1972 to 1976. "Motor Vehicle Unit Retail Sales," U.S. Bureau of Economic Analysis, https://www.bea.gov/national/xls/gap_hist.xlsx.

13 "Air Transport: Facts and Figures," Air Transport Association of America, 1948, http:// airlines.org/wp-content/uploads/2014/08/1948.pdf (passengers and miles on p. 4, fatalities on p. 2); *Annual Report of the U.S. Scheduled Airline Industry* (Washington, D.C.: Air Transport Association of America, 1973), 24, http://airlines.org/wp-content /uploads/2014/08/1973.pdf (passengers and miles on p. 24, fatalities on p. 40).

14 James Bessen, *Learning by Doing: The Real Connection between Innovation, Wages, and Wealth* (New Haven, Conn.: Yale University Press, 2015), 108, figure 7.1.

15 Claire Cain Miller, "Smarter Robots Move Deeper into Workplace," *New York Times*, December 16, 2014, https://www.nytimes.com/2014/12/16/upshot/as-robots-grow -smarter-american-workers-struggle-to-keep-up.html.

16 "Labor Productivity (Output per Hour): Nonfarm Business."

17 Manufacturing productivity data from the Bureau of Labor Statistics (BLS) begin only in the late 1980s. Data reported here reflect Bureau of Economic Analysis (BEA) figures for value added in the manufacturing sector, converted from current to real dollars using the Chain-Type Price Index provided by BEA and then divided by annual manufacturing employment totals provided by BLS. In years for which both BLS and BEA data are available, annual figures differ but tell parallel stories. "Gross -Domestic-Product-(GDP)-by-Industry Data: Value Added," U.S. Bureau of Economic Analysis, https://bea.gov/industry/gdpbyind_data.htm; "Labor Productivity (Output per Hour): Manufacturing," U.S. Bureau of Labor Statistics, https://www.bls.gov/lpc/; "Employment, Hours, and Earnings from the Current Employment Statistics Survey (National): Manufacturing," U.S. Bureau of Labor Statistics, http://www.bls.gov/ces/

18 Lawrence Mishel and Josh Bivens, *The Zombie Robot Argument Lurches On* (Washington, D.C.: Economic Policy Institute, May 2017), 9–10, figure A, http://epi.org/126750.

19 Robert D. Atkinson and John Wu, *False Alarmism: Technological Disruption and the U.S. Labor Market, 1850–2015* (Washington, D.C.: Innovation Technology and Innovation Foundation, May 2017), https://itif.org/publications/2017/05/08/false-alarmism-technological-disruption-and-us-labor-market-1850-2015.

20 "Employment, Hours, and Earnings from the Current Employment Statistics Survey (National)."

21 Georg Graetz and Guy Michaels, "Robots at Work" (CEP Discussion Paper 1335, London School of Economics and Political Science, London, March 2015), http://cep.lse.ac.uk/pubs/download/dp1335.pdf.

22 David H. Autor, David Dorn, and Gordon H. Hanson, "Untangling Trade and Technology: Evidence from Local Labour Markets," *The Economic Journal* 125 (May 2015): 644, https://economics.mit.edu/files/11564.

23 Claire Cain Miller, "Evidence That Robots Are Winning the Race for American Jobs," *New York Times*, March 29, 2017, https://www.nytimes.com/2017/03/28/upshot/evidence-that-robots-are-winning-the-race-for-american-jobs.html; Jeff Guo, "We're So Unprepared for the Robot Apocalypse," *Washington Post*, March 30, 2017, https://www.washingtonpost.com/news/wonk/wp/2017/03/30/were-so-unprepared-for-the-robot-apocalypse/.

24 Daron Acemoglu and Pascual Restrepo, "Robots and Jobs: Evidence from US Labor Markets" (Working Paper 23285, National Bureau of Economic Research, Cambridge, Mass., March 2017), http://www.nber.org/papers/w23285.

25 "Employment, Hours, and Earnings from the Current Employment Statistics Survey (National)."

26 "Gross-Domestic-Product-(GDP)-by-Industry Data"; "Employment, Hours, and Earnings from the Current Employment Statistics survey (National)."

27 Michael J. Hicks and Srikant Devaraj, *The Myth and the Reality of Manufacturing in America* (Muncie, Ind.: Ball State University, June 2015), https://projects.cberdata.org/reports/MfgReality.pdf.

28 Barack Obama, remarks by the president in Farewell Address, Chicago, January 10, 2017, https://obamawhitehouse.archives.gov/the-press-office/2017/01/10/remarks-president-farewell-address.

29 Derek Thompson, "A World without Work," *The Atlantic*, July/August 2015, https://www.theatlantic.com/magazine/archive/2015/07/world-without-work/395294/.

30 Catherine Clifford, "Elon Musk: 'Robots Will Be Able to Do Everything Better Than Us,'" CNBC, July 17, 2017, https://www.cnbc.com/2017/07/17/elon-musk-robots-will-be-able-to-do-everything-better-than-us.html.

31 Robert J. Gordon, "Productivity Growth in the U.S. and Europe: Past, Present, and Future," presentation at the IMF Institute, Washington, D.C., April 25, 2011, slide 11, http://economics.weinberg.northwestern.edu/robert-gordon/files/ConfPres/ProdGrowthUSEurope.pdf.

32 Lee Gomes, "Google Self-Driving Car Will Be Ready Soon for Some, in Decades for Others," *IEEE Spectrum*, March 18, 2016, https://spectrum.ieee.org/cars-that-think/transportation/self-driving/google-selfdriving-car-will-be-ready-soon-for-some-in-decades-for-others.

33 Ania Monaco, "Edison's Pearl Street Station Recognized with Milestone," *The Institute (IEEE)*, July 2011, http://theinstitute.ieee.org/tech-history/technology-history/edisons-pearl-street-station-recognized-with-milestone810; *Agriculture 1950: A Graphic Summary* (Washington, D.C.: U.S. Census Bureau, 1952), 72, 80, https://www2.census.gov/prod2/decennial/documents/41667073v5p6ch4.pdf.

34 Walmart sales for 1998 include Sam's Club. Wal-Mart Stores, Inc., Form 10-K, Fiscal Year 1998, 22; Wal-Mart Stores, Inc., Annual Report, Fiscal Year 1980, 3.

35 Amazon.com, Inc., Form 10-K, Fiscal Year 2017, 25; Amazon.com, Inc., Form 10-K, Fiscal Year 1999, 4.

36 Allan Collard-Wexler and Jan De Loecker, "Reallocation and Technology: Evidence from the US Steel Industry," *American Economic Review* 105, no. 1 (2015): 135–36, https://doi.org/10.1257/aer.20130090.

37 Hal Sirkin, Michael Zinser, and Justin Rose, "How Robots Will Redefine Competitiveness," Boston Consulting Group, September 23, 2015, https://www.bcg.com/publications/2015/lean-manufacturing-innovation-robots-redefine-competitiveness.aspx.

38 Rodney Brooks, "The Seven Deadly Sins of AI Predictions," *MIT Technology Review*, October 6, 2017, https://www.technologyreview.com/s/609048/the-seven-deadly-sins-of-ai-predictions/.

39 Mike Ramsey, "Tesla Sells More Cars; Loses Two Executives," *Wall Street Journal*, May 5, 2016, https://www.wsj.com/articles/tesla-loses-two-manufacturing-executives-1462382198; Tim Higgins, "Tesla Misses Goal for Model 3," *Wall Street Journal*, October 3, 2017, https://www.wsj.com/articles/tesla-misses-model-3-production-goals-1506976496; Tim Higgins, "Tesla Signals Better Model 3 Output," *Wall Street Journal*, February 8, 2018, https://www.wsj.com/articles/tesla-posts-smaller-than-expected-loss-1518039313.

40 Katie Burke and Sharon Silke Carty, "Tesla's Real Capacity Problem? Too Many Employees," *Autoweek*, June 14, 2017, http://autoweek.com/article/green-cars/teslas-fremont-plant-doesnt-have-enough-parking-employees-because-plant-so.

41 Carl Benedikt Frey and Michael A. Osborne, "The Future of Employment: How Susceptible Are Jobs to Computerisation?," Oxford University, September 17, 2013, https://www.oxfordmartin.ox.ac.uk/downloads/academic/The_Future_of_Employment.pdf.

42 Melanie Arntz, Terry Gregoryi, and Ulrich Zierahni, "The Risk of Automation for Jobs in OECD Countries: A Comparative Analysis" (Social, Employment, and Migration Working Paper 189, Organisation for Economic Co-operation and Development, Paris, May 2016), https://doi.org/10.1787/5jlz9h56dvq7-en.

43 James Manyika, Michael Chui, Mehdi Miremadi, Jacques Bughin, Katy George, Paul Willmott, and Martin Dewhurst, *A Future That Works: Automation, Employment, and Productivity* (McKinsey Global Institute, January 2017), 5, 12, https://www.mckinsey.com/global-themes/digital-disruption/harnessing-automation-for-a-future-that-works.

44 Elon Musk (@elonmusk), "Yes, excessive automation at Tesla was a mistake. To be precise, my mistake. Humans are underrated," Twitter, April 13, 2018, 2:54 p.m., https://twitter.com/elonmusk/status/984882630947753984.

45 Michael Mandel, *The Creation of a New Middle Class? A Historical Perspective on Job and Wage Growth in the Digital Sector* (Washington, D.C.: Progressive Policy Institute, March 2017), 5–6, http://www.progressivepolicy.org/wp-content/uploads/2017/03/Tech-middle-class-3-9-17b.pdf.

46 "Employment, Hours, and Earnings from the Current Employment Statistics Survey (National)."

47 Christina D. Romer, "Do Manufacturers Need Special Treatment?," *New York Times*, February 5, 2012, http://www.nytimes.com/2012/02/05/business/do-manufacturers-need-special-treatment-economic-view.html.

48 Author's analysis of BLS data. "May 2016 National Industry-Specific Occupational Employment and Wage Estimates," U.S. Bureau of Labor Statistics, https://www.bls.gov/oes/.

49 "State and Area Employment, Hours, and Earnings: Pittsburgh, PA—'Manufacturing' and 'Health Care and Social Assistance,'" U.S. Bureau of Labor Statistics, https://www.bls.gov/sae/; "May 2016 Metropolitan and Nonmetropolitan Area Occupational

Employment and Wage Estimates: Pittsburgh, PA," U.S. Bureau of Labor Statistics, https://www.bls.gov/oes/current/oes_38300.htm.

50 Income change is for 1989–2016. "Historical Income Tables: Metropolitan Statistical Areas (MAs): Table MSA1, Median Household Income by Metropolitan Statistical Area (MSA): 1969, 1979, and 1989," U.S. Census Bureau, https://www.census.gov /data/tables/time-series/dec/historical-income-metro.html; "American FactFinder: Median Income in the Past 12 Months (in 2016 Inflation-Adjusted Dollars)," U.S. Census Bureau, https://factfinder.census.gov/faces/tableservices/jsf/pages/productview. xhtml?pid=ACS_16_1YR_S1903.

51 U.S. Department of Agriculture, "SNAP Questions and Suggested Answers," Supplemental Nutrition Assistance Program (SNAP) Community Outreach Partner Toolkit, https://www.fns.usda.gov/sites/default/files/SNAP_Basics_Q%26As.pdf.

52 Chris Arnade, "'The Pill Mill of America': Where Drugs Mean There Are No Good Choices, Only Less Awful Ones," *The Guardian*, May 17, 2017, https://www.theguardian. com/society/2017/may/17/drugs-opiod-addiction-epidemic-portsmouth-ohio.

53 Spending figures exclude personal insurance and pension contributions, which are treated as savings, as well as charitable contributions. "Consumer Expenditure Survey: Table 1110, Deciles of Income before Taxes," U.S. Bureau of Labor Statistics, 2016, https:// www.bls.gov/cex/tables.htm.

54 Capital spending can go toward nonphysical assets like software, as well, but structures and equipment have traditionally been the primary categories. "2017 Capital Spending Report: U.S. Capital Spending Patterns 2006–2015," U.S. Census Bureau, chart 3, https:// www.census.gov/library/publications/2017/econ/2017-csr.html.

55 Enrico Moretti, *The New Geography of Jobs* (Boston: Mariner Books, 2012), 3–5, 74–75.

56 *Time*, September 17, 1990, https://content.time.com/time/covers/0,16641,19900917,00. html.

57 Paul Krugman, "The Gambler's Ruin of Small Cities (Wonkish)," *New York Times*, December 30, 2017, https://www.nytimes.com/2017/12/30/opinion/the-gamblers-ruin-of -small-cities-wonkish.html.

58 Derek Thompson, "Why So Many Americans Are Saying Goodbye to Cities," *The Atlantic*, April 4, 2017, https://www.theatlantic.com/business/archive/2017/04 /why-is-everyone-leaving-the-city/521844/.

59 "Population of the 100 Largest Urban Places: 1950," U.S. Census Bureau, https://www .census.gov/population/www/documentation/twps0027/tab18.txt; "Annual Estimates of the Resident Population for Incorporated Places of 50,000 or More, Ranked by July 1, 2016 Population: April 1, 2010 to July 1, 2016," U.S. Census Bureau, https://www.census .gov/data/tables/2016/demo/popest/total-cities-and-towns.html.

60 Tyler Cowen, "Why Don't Cities Grow without Limit?," *Marginal Revolution* (blog), January 1, 2018, http://marginalrevolution.com/marginalrevolution/2018/01/dont-cities -grow-without-limit.html.

61 Karen Harris, Andrew Schwedel, and Austin Kimson, "Spatial Economics: The Declining Cost of Distance," Bain and Company, February 2016, http://www.bain.com /publications/articles/spatial-economics-the-declining-cost-of-distance.aspx.

CHAPTER 5: THE ENVIRONMENT AND THE ECONOMY

1 Coral Davenport, "E.P.A. to Introduce Sweeping New Controls on Smog-Causing Ozone Emissions," *New York Times*, November 26, 2014, https://www.nytimes. com/2014/11/26/us/politics/obama-to-introduce-sweeping-new-controls-on-ozone -emissions.html.

2 "8-Hour Ozone (2008) Designated Area/State Information with Design Values," U.S. Environmental Protection Agency, https://www3.epa.gov/airquality/greenbook/hbtcw. html; "Table 1. County-Level Design Values for the 2015 8-Hour Ozone NAAQS," U.S.

Environmental Protection Agency, December 21, 2017, https://www.epa.gov
/ozone-designations/ozone-designations-guidance-and-data.

3 "Statement by the President on the Ozone National Ambient Air Quality Standards,"
Office of the Press Secretary, White House, September 2, 2011, https://obamawhitehouse.
archives.gov/the-press-office/2011/09/02/statement-president-ozone-national-ambient
-air-quality-standards.

4 Coral Davenport, "New Limit for Smog-Causing Emissions Isn't as Strict as Many Had
Expected," *New York Times*, October 1, 2015, https://www.nytimes.com/2015/10/02/us
/politics/epa-to-unveil-new-limit-for-smog-causing-ozone-emissions.html.

5 "EPA Proposes Smog Standards to Safeguard Americans from Air Pollution," U.S.
Environmental Protection Agency, November 26, 2014.

6 Kamala Harris (@KamalaHarris), "It's 2017. The ability to breathe clean air and live in a
safe and healthy environment should not be a partisan issue." Twitter, July 20, 2017, 6:00
p.m., https://twitter.com/KamalaHarris/status/888171692543152128.

7 "Table of Historical Ozone National Ambient Air Quality Standards (NAAQS)," U.S.
Environmental Protection Agency, https://www.epa.gov/ozone-pollution/table
-historical-ozone-national-ambient-air-quality-standards-naaqs.

8 "NASA: Background Ozone a Major Issue in U.S. West," Jet Propulsion Laboratory,
National Aeronautics and Space Administration, September 29, 2015, https://www.jpl
.nasa.gov/news/news.php?feature=4723.

9 "Ozone Standard Exceedances in National Parks," National Park Service, November 28,
2017, https://www.nature.nps.gov/air/Monitoring/exceed.cfm.

10 "Regulatory Impact Analysis of the Final Revisions to the National Ambient Air
Quality Standards for Ground-Level Ozone" (EPA-452/R-15–007, U.S. Environmental
Protection Agency, Research Triangle Park, N.C., September 2015), ch. 5, https://www
.epa.gov/sites/production/files/2016-02/documents/20151001ria.pdf.

11 Francis M. Bator, "The Anatomy of Market Failure," *Quarterly Journal of Economics* 72,
no. 3 (1958): 351, https://doi.org/10.2307/1882231.

12 "Integrated Science Assessment for Ozone and Related Photochemical Oxidants" (EPA
600/R-10/076F, U.S. Environmental Protection Agency, Research Triangle Park, N.C.,
February 2013), ch. 6.6, https://cfpub.epa.gov/ncea/isa/recordisplay.cfm?deid=247492;
"Quantitative Health Risk Assessment for Particulate Matter" (EPA-452/R-10-005, U.S.
Environmental Protection Agency, Research Triangle Park, N.C., June 2010), https://
www3.epa.gov/ttn/naaqs/standards/pm/data/PM_RA_FINAL_June_2010.pdf.

13 W. Kip Viscusi, "The Value of Life: Estimates with Risks by Occupation and Industry"
(Harvard John M. Olin Discussion Paper Series 422, Harvard Law School, Cambridge,
Mass., May 2003), http://www.law.harvard.edu/programs/olin_center/papers/pdf/422
.pdf.

14 "Regulatory Impact Analysis of the Proposed Revisions to the National Ambient Air
Quality Standards for Ground-Level Ozone" (EPA-452/P-14-006, U.S. Environmental
Protection Agency, Research Triangle Park, N.C., November 2014), tables 5-19, 5-20,
5C-1, 5C-3, https://www3.epa.gov/ttnecas1/regdata/RIAs/20141125ria.pdf.

15 All figures updated to 2016 dollars. EPA describes benefits in the 2011 report as
incremental to those in the 1997 report, all of which are measured against a baseline of
no pollution control. *The Benefits and Costs of the Clean Air Act, 1970 to 1990* (Research
Triangle Park, N.C.: U.S. Environmental Protection Agency, October 1997), 54, https://
www.epa.gov/clean-air-act-overview/benefits-and-costs-clean-air-act-1970-1990
-retrospective-study; *The Benefits and Costs of the Clean Air Act from 1990 to 2020*
(Research Triangle Park, N.C.: U.S. Environmental Protection Agency, April 2011),
abstract and p. 7-5, https://www.epa.gov/clean-air-act-overview/benefits-and-costs
-clean-air-act-1990–2020-second-prospective-study.

16 Carmen DeNavas, Bernadette D. Proctor, and Jessica C. Smith, "Income, Poverty, and Health Insurance Coverage in the United States: 2010" (Current Population Report P60-239, U.S. Census Bureau, Washington, D.C., September 2011), 33, https://www .census.gov/prod/2011pubs/p60-239.pdf.

17 "Individual Complete Report (Publication 1304), Table 1.1: All Returns: Selected Income and Tax Items, by Size and Accumulated Size of Adjusted Gross Income, Tax Year 2010," Internal Revenue Service, https://www.irs.gov/statistics/soi-tax-stats-individual -statistical-tables-by-size-of-adjusted-gross-income.

18 "Regulatory Impact Analysis for the Final Mercury and Air Toxics Standard" (EPA -452/R-11-011, U.S. Environmental Protection Agency, Research Triangle Park, N.C., December 2011), table ES-4, https://www3.epa.gov/ttnecas1/regdata/RIAs/matsriafinal .pdf.

19 "Benefits and Costs of Cleaning Up Toxic Air Pollution from Power Plants," EPA Fact Sheet, U.S. Environmental Protection Agency, December 2011, https://www.epa.gov /sites/production/files/2015-11/documents/20111221matsimpactsfs.pdf.

20 "2016 Draft Report to Congress on the Benefits and Costs of Federal Regulations and Agency Compliance with the Unfunded Mandates," Office of Management and Budget, 2016, 11-12, https://obamawhitehouse.archives.gov/sites/default/files/omb/assets /legislative_reports/draft_2016_cost_benefit_report_12_14_2016_2.pdf; Susan E. Dudley, "OMB's Reported Benefits of Regulation: Too Good to Be True?," *Regulation*, Summer 2013, 27–29, https://regulatorystudies.columbian.gwu.edu/files/downloads/Dudley _OMB_BC_Regulation-v36n2-4.pdf.

21 Oren Cass, "Will EPA Cuts Harm America's Air Quality?," Manhattan Institute for Policy Research, April 2017, https://www.manhattan-institute.org/html/will-epa-cuts -harm-americas-air-quality-10228.html.

22 Emily Underwood, "The Polluted Brain: Evidence Builds That Dirty Air Causes Alzheimer's, Dementia," *Science*, January 26, 2017, http://doi.org/10.1126/science.aal0656.

23 Daniel Chaitin, "EPA Chief: Light Pollution 'in Our Portfolio,'" *Washington Examiner*, December 30, 2015, http://www.washingtonexaminer.com/epa-chief-light-pollution -in-our-portfolio/article/2579307.

24 Elena Kagan, "Presidential Administration," *Harvard Law Review* 114 (2001): 2277, https://harvardlawreview.org/wp-content/uploads/pdfs/vol114_kagan.pdf.

25 Executive Order 12291 of February 17, 1981, "Federal Regulation," *Code of Federal Regulations* (1981): 127, https://www.archives.gov/federal-register/codification/executive -order/12291.html.

26 "Safety Recommendation A-95-051," National Transportation Safety Board, May 16, 1995, 10–11, https://www.ntsb.gov/_layouts/ntsb.recsearch/Recommendation. aspx?Rec=A-95-051.

27 FAA reply to NTSB, "Safety Recommendation A-95-051," June 7, 1995; Thomas B. Newman, Brian D. Johnston, and David C. Grossman, "Effects and Costs of Requiring Child-Restraint Systems for Young Children Traveling on Commercial Airplanes," *Archives of Pediatric and Adolescent Medicine* 157, no. 10 (2003): 969–74, https://doi .org/10.1001/archpedi.157.10.969.

28 NTSB reply to FAA, "Safety Recommendation A-95-051," December 13, 2006.

29 Michael A. Livermore, "Cost–Benefit Analysis and Agency Independence," *University of Chicago Law Review* 81 (2014): 629–32, https://lawreview.uchicago.edu/publication /cost-benefit-analysis-and-agency-independence.

30 Nathaniel O. Keohane and Sheila M. Olmstead, *Markets and the Environment* (Washington, D.C.: Island Press, 2007), 31.

31 *Regulatory Impact Analysis for Ground-Level Ozone (2014)*, table 5-10.

32 *Regulatory Impact Analysis for Ground-Level Ozone (2014)*, 1–10, tables 7-2 and 7-8.

33 Randy Becker and Vernon Henderson, "Effects of Air Quality Regulations on Polluting

Industries," *Journal of Political Economy* 108, no. 2 (2000): 379–421, https://doi
.org/10.1086/262123.

34 Michael Greenstone, "The Impacts of Environmental Regulations on Industrial Activity:
Evidence from the 1970 and 1977 Clean Air Act Amendments and the Census of
Manufactures," *Journal of Political Economy* 110, no. 6 (2002): 1175–219, https://doi
.org/10.1086/342808.

35 W. Reed Walker, "The Transitional Costs of Sectoral Reallocation: Evidence from the
Clean Air Act and the Workforce," *Quarterly Journal of Economics* 128, no. 4 (2013):
1787–835, https://doi.org/10.1093/qje/qjt022.

36 Austin Nichols, Josh Mitchell, and Stephan Lindner, *Consequences of Long-Term
Unemployment* (Washington, D.C.: Urban Institute, 2013), https://www.urban.org
/research/publication/consequences-long-term-unemployment.

37 Anne Case and Angus Deaton, "Rising Morbidity and Mortality in Midlife among
White Non-Hispanic Americans in the 21st Century," *Proceedings of the National
Academy of Sciences of the United States of America* 112, no. 49 (2015): 15078–83, https://doi
.org/10.1073/pnas.1518393112.

38 Emphasis original. Anne Case and Angus Deaton, "Mortality and Morbidity in the 21st
Century," *Brookings Papers on Economic Activity*, Spring 2017, 397, https://www.brookings
.edu/wp-content/uploads/2017/08/casetextsp17bpea.pdf.

39 "RegData: A QuantGov Product," Mercatus Center at George Mason University, http://
quantgov.org/regdata/.

40 Antony Davies, *Regulation and Productivity* (Arlington, Va.: Mercatus Center, 2014),
https://www.mercatus.org/publication/regulation-and-productivity.

41 Darren Goode, "Obama's Smog Plan Splits Black Leaders," *Politico*, September 10,
2015, https://www.politico.com/story/2015/09/epa-smog-rule-battle-lines-drawn-in
-poor-communities-213481.

42 "Our Nation's Air: Status and Trends through 2010" (EPA-454/R-12-001, U.S.
Environmental Protection Agency, Research Triangle Park, N.C., February 2012), figure
3, https://www.epa.gov/sites/production/files/2017–11/documents/trends_brochure_2010
.pdf; "Ozone Trends," U.S. Environmental Protection Agency, https://www.epa.gov
/air-trends/ozone-trends.

43 "Air Quality—National Summary," U.S. Environmental Protection Agency, https://
www.epa.gov/air-trends/air-quality-national-summary.

44 Robert Stavins, "Moving beyond Vintage-Differentiated Regulation," *Huffington Post*,
May 25, 2011, https://www.huffingtonpost.com/robert-stavins/moving-beyond-vintage
-dif_b_184199.html.

45 Whitman v. American Trucking Assns., Inc., 531 U.S. 457 (2001), https://supreme.justia
.com/cases/federal/us/531/457/.

46 "National Environmental Policy Act: Little Information Exists on NEPA Analyses"
(GAO-14–369, U.S. Government Accountability Office, Washington, D.C., April 2014),
13, https://www.gao.gov/assets/670/662543.pdf.

47 *Causes and Extent of Environmental Delays in Transportation Projects* (Washington, D.C.:
TransTech Management, Inc., December 2003), 6, https://trid.trb.org/view/750944.

48 Joe Biden, "What You Might Not Know about the Recovery," *New York Times*, July 26,
2009, http://www.nytimes.com/2009/07/26/opinion/26biden.html; Michael Grabell,
"How Not to Revive an Economy," *New York Times*, February 12, 2012, http://www
.nytimes.com/2012/02/12/opinion/sunday/how-the-stimulus-fell-short.html.

49 Barack Obama, "Remarks in Chicago Announcing Energy and Environment Team,"
Chicago, December 15, 2008, http://www.presidency.ucsb.edu/ws/index.php?pid-85080.

50 Peter Baker, "What Does He Do Now?," *New York Times Magazine*, October 17, 2010,
http://www.nytimes.com/2010/10/17/magazine/17obama-t.html.

51 Kristen Lombardi and John Solomon, "Obama Administration Gives Billions in Stimulus Money without Environmental Safeguards," *Washington Post*, November 28, 2010, http://www.washingtonpost.com/wp-dyn/content/article/2010/11/28/AR2010112804379.html.

52 Philip K. Howard, *Two Years Not Ten Years: Redesigning Infrastructure Approvals* (Brooklyn, N.Y.: Common Good, September 2015), 16–18, http://commongood.3cdn.net/c613b4cfda258a5fcb_e8m6b5t3x.pdf.

53 Oren Cass, "Step on the Gas! How to Extend America's Energy Advantage" (Issue Brief 35, Manhattan Institute for Policy Research, New York, July 2015), 7–10, https://www.manhattan-institute.org/html/step-gas-how-extend-americas-energy-advantage-6355.html.

54 Kenneth J. Arrow, Maureen L. Cropper, George C. Eads, Robert W. Hahn, Lester B. Lave, Roger G. Noll, Paul R. Portney et al., "Is There a Role for Benefit-Cost Analysis in Environmental, Health, and Safety Regulation?," *Science* 272, no. 5259 (1996): 221–22, http://doi.org/10.1126/science.272.5259.221.

55 Jeff Rosen, "Putting Regulators on a Budget," *National Affairs*, Spring 2016, https://www.nationalaffairs.com/publications/detail/putting-regulators-on-a-budget.

CHAPTER 6: HOW THE OTHER HALF LEARNS

1 *Digest of Education Statistics, 2016*, February 2018, table 104.20, https://nces.ed.gov/programs/digest/d16/tables/dt16_104.20.asp.

2 Author's analysis of *Digest of Education Statistics*, tables 219.10, 302.10, and 326.40; "The Labor Market for Recent College Graduates: Underemployment," Federal Reserve Bank of New York, January 12, 2018, https://www.newyorkfed.org/research/college-labor-market/college-labor-market_underemployment_rates.html.

3 Mickey Kaus, "The Most Important Chart," *kausfiles.com* (blog), May 17, 2017, http://www.kausfiles.com/2017/05/17/the-most-important-chart/.

4 These figures compare the tops of two business cycles, from 1979 (prior to the start of a recession in 1980) to 2007 (the Great Recession began in December of that year), converted from nominal to constant dollars using either the Consumer Price Index or the Personal Consumption Expenditures Index. All figures are median weekly earnings for full-time wage and salary workers. "Labor Force Statistics from the Current Population Survey," U.S. Bureau of Labor Statistics, https://www.bls.gov/cps/earnings.htm.

5 *Digest of Education Statistics*, table 236.55.

6 *Digest of Education Statistics*, tables 221.85 and 222.85.

7 David H. Freedman, "The War on Stupid People," *The Atlantic*, July/August 2016, https://www.theatlantic.com/magazine/archive/2016/07/the-war-on-stupid-people/485618/.

8 *Digest of Education Statistics*, table 226.20.

9 *Digest of Education Statistics*, table 219.10.

10 "Fact Sheet: President Obama Announces High School Graduation Rate Has Reached New High," Office of the Press Secretary, White House, October 17, 2016, https://obamawhitehouse.archives.gov/the-press-office/2016/10/17/fact-sheet-president-obama-announces-high-school-graduation-rate-has.

11 Lance Izumi, "Fake Achievement: The Rising High School Graduation Rate," Heritage Foundation, July 20, 2017, https://www.heritage.org/2017-index-culture-and-opportunity/fake-achievement-the-rising-high-school-graduation-rate.

12 *Digest of Education Statistics*, table 219.35.

13 Joy Resmovits, "Federal Audit Finds Problems with California's Graduation Rate Calculations," *Los Angeles Times*, January 17, 2018, http://www.latimes.com/local/education/la-me-edu-california-graduation-audit-20180117-story.html.

14 Alejandra Matos, "Entire Senior Class at D.C.'s Ballou High School Applies to College," *Washington Post*, March 27, 2017, https://www.washingtonpost.com/local /education/entire-senior-class-at-dcs-ballou-high-school-applies-to-college/2017/03/27 /c15a275c-0f36-11e7-9b0d-d27c98455440_story.html.

15 Kate McGee, "What Really Happened at the School Where Every Graduate Got into College," National Public Radio, November 28, 2017, https://www.npr.org/sections /ed/2017/11/28/564054556/what-really-happened-at-the-school-where-every-senior-got -into-college; Max Eden and Alice B. Lloyd, "Unearned Diplomas," *Weekly Standard*, January 1, 2018, http://www.weeklystandard.com/unearned-diplomas/article/2010947.

16 James S. Coleman et al., *Equality of Educational Opportunity* (Washington, D.C.: U.S. Department of Health, Education, and Welfare, 1966), 21–22, https://files.eric.ed.gov /fulltext/ED012275.pdf.

17 Stephen L. Morgan and Sol Bee Jung, "Still No Effect of Resources, Even in the New Gilded Age?," *Russell Sage Foundation Journal of the Social Sciences* 2, no. 5 (2016): 83, 110, https://doi.org/10.7758/RSF.2016.2.5.05.

18 Bruno V. Manno and Chester E. Finn Jr., "A Progress Report on Charter Schools," *National Affairs*, Summer 2015, https://www.nationalaffairs.com/publications/detail/a -progress-report-on-charter-schools.

19 Jay P. Greene, "Evidence for the Disconnect between Changing Test Scores and Changing Later Life Outcomes," *EducationNext*, November 7, 2016, http:// educationnext.org/evidence-for-the-disconnect-between-changing-test-scores-and -changing-later-life-outcomes/.

20 *Digest of Education Statistics*, tables 326.10, 326.20, and 326.40.

21 David J. Deming, "Increasing College Completion with a Federal Higher Education Matching Grant" (Hamilton Project 2017-03, Brookings Institution, Washington, D.C., April 2017), 2 and figure 1, http://www.hamiltonproject.org/papers/increasing_college _completion_with_a_federal_higher_education_matching_gran.

22 *Digest of Education Statistics*, table 104.20.

23 Camille L. Ryan and Kurt Bauman, *Educational Attainment in the United States: 2015* (Report P20-578, U.S. Census Bureau, Washington, D.C., March 2016), 9, https://www .census.gov/content/dam/Census/library/publications/2016/demo/p20-578.pdf.

24 Thomas D. Snyder, *120 Years of American Education: A Statistical Portrait* (Washington, D.C.: U.S. Department of Education, January 1993), table 24, https://nces.ed.gov /pubs93/93442.pdf.

25 Scott Jaschik and Doug Lederman, *2017 Survey of College and University Presidents* (Washington, D.C.: Inside Higher Ed, 2017), 23, https://www.insidehighered.com /booklet/2017-inside-higher-ed-survey-college-and-university-presidents.

26 Doug Lederman and Scott Jaschik, "Political Turmoil, Public Misunderstanding: A Survey of Presidents," *Inside Higher Ed*, March 10, 2017, https://www.insidehighered. com/news/survey/political-turmoil-public-misunderstanding-survey-presidents.

27 Rachel Fishman, "College Decisions Survey: Deciding to Go to College," New America, May 28, 2015, https://www.newamerica.org/education-policy/edcentral/collegedecisions/.

28 Lucia Anderson Weathers, "Gallup–Lumina Foundation Poll Finds Overwhelming Majority of Americans Support Increasing Attainment," Lumina Foundation, April 16, 2015, https://www.luminafoundation.org/news-and-views/gallup-2015.

29 *Learning for Jobs* (Paris: OECD, 2010), 13, http://www.oecd.org/education/skills-beyond -school/Learning%20for%20Jobs%20book.pdf.

30 Sandra Salmans, "The Tracking Controversy," *New York Times*, April 10, 1988, https:// www.nytimes.com/1988/04/10/education/the-tracking-controversy.html.

31 Paul Beston, "When High Schools Shaped America's Destiny," *City Journal*, 2017, https:// www.city-journal.org/html/when-high-schools-shaped-americas-destiny-15254.html.

32　Tom Loveless, *How Well Are American Students Learning?* (Washington, D.C.: Brookings Institution, March 2013), 13–14, https://www.brookings.edu/research /the-resurgence-of-ability-grouping-and-persistence-of-tracking/.

33　Jeffrey J. Selingo, "Blue Collar Redefined," *New York Times*, February 5, 2017, https:// www.nytimes.com/2017/01/30/education/edlife/factory-workers-college-degree -apprenticeships.html.

34　David Azerrad, "How Equal Should Opportunities Be?," *National Affairs*, Summer 2016, https://www.nationalaffairs.com/publications/detail/how-equal-should-opportunities-be.

35　Selingo, "Blue Collar Redefined."

36　William C. Symonds, Robert Schwartz, and Ronald F. Ferguson, *Pathways to Prosperity: Meeting the Challenge of Preparing Young Americans for the 21st Century* (Cambridge, Mass.: Harvard University, February 2011), 15, 20, https://dash.harvard.edu /handle/1/4740480.

37　Steven Malanga, "Vocational Ed, Reborn," *City Journal*, 2017, https://www.city-journal .org/html/vocational-ed-reborn-15253.html.

38　"Multiple Employment and Training Programs" (Report GAO-11-92, U.S. Government Accountability Office, Washington, D.C., January 2011), 5, 11, https://www.gao.gov/new .items/d1192.pdf.

39　Sheena McConnell, Kenneth Fortson, Dana Rotz, Peter Schochet, Paul Burkander, Linda Rosenberg, Annalisa Mastri, and Ronald D'Amico, *Providing Public Workforce Services to Job Seekers: 15-Month Impact Findings on the WIA Adult and Dislocated Worker Programs* (Washington, D.C.: Mathematica Policy Research, May 2016), xxii, https:// www.mathematica-mpr.com/our-publications-and-findings/publications/providing-public-workforce-services-to-job-seekers-15-month-impact-findings-on-the-wia-adult.

40　Amy Goldstein, *Janesville: An American Story* (New York: Simon and Schuster, 2017), 169–70.

41　Author's visit to Jefferson Community and Technical College.

42　Sophie Quinton, "How Did These Kids Score Good Jobs Right Out of High School?," *National Journal*, March 5, 2013, https://www.theatlantic.com/business /archive/2013/03/how-did-these-kids-score-good-jobs-right-out-of-high-school/425715/; "About Alamo Academies," Alamo Academies, http://www.alamoacademies.com /about-alamo-academies/.

43　Sven Böll, "Skills Gap Bumps Up against Vocational Taboo," *Wall Street Journal*, September 12, 2014, https://www.wsj.com/articles/skills-gap-bumps-up-against-vocational-taboo-1410473392.

CHAPTER 7: OF BORDERS AND BALANCE

1　Theodore Levitt, "The Globalization of Markets," *Harvard Business Review*, May 1983, https://hbr.org/1983/05/the-globalization-of-markets.

2　Antonio Olivo, "After Decades in America, the Newly Deported Return to a Mexico They Barely Recognize," *Washington Post*, March 3, 2017, https://www.washingtonpost. com/world/the_americas/mexico-prepares-to-absorb-a-wave-of-deportees-in-the -trump-era/2017/03/03/a7bd624a-f86c-11e6-aa1e-5f735ee31334_story.html.

3　Ben Casselman and Michelle Cheng, "Trump's Plan to Cut Legal Immigration Could Hurt the Economy," *FiveThirtyEight*, August 4, 2017, https://fivethirtyeight .com/features/trumps-plan-to-cut-legal-immigration-could-hurt-the-economy/; Timothy Noah and Marianne Levine, "Will the Immigration Bill Boost Economic Growth?," *Politico*, August 2, 2017, https://www.politico.com/story/2017/08/02 /immigration-bill-economic-growth-241267.

4　Jared Bernstein, "A Quick, Simple Way to See How Restricting Legal Immigration Is Anti-growth," *Washington Post*, August 3, 2017, https://www.washingtonpost.com

/news/posteverything/wp/2017/08/03/a-quick-simple-way-to-see-how-restricting-legal
-immigration-is-anti-growth/.

5 Bob Davis, "The Thorny Economics of Illegal Immigration," *Wall Street Journal*,
February 9, 2016, https://www.wsj.com/articles/the-thorny-economics-of-illegal
-immigration-1454984443.

6 Ethan Lewis, "How Immigration Affects Workers: Two Wrong Models and a Right
One," *Cato Journal* 37, no 3. (2017): 461–472, https://object.cato.org/sites/cato.org/files
/serials/files/cato-journal/2017/9/cato-journal-v37n3.pdf. An important question remains
of how best to define the labor market's segments. Some economists, including Lewis,
argue that immigrants occupy unique niches within the labor market and thus compete
primarily with each other rather than affecting native workers. But in their absence,
demand for the goods and services that they help to provide would still exist, and
employers would seek to provide it with native workers—even if the jobs themselves
take on a somewhat different character. Manual laborers picking vegetables by hand and
machine operators driving combines differ in many ways, but they indeed compete for
employment on farms.

7 Giovanni Peri, "The Impact of Immigration on Wages of Unskilled Workers," *Cato
Journal* 37, no. 3 (2017): 449–460, https://object.cato.org/sites/cato.org/files/serials/files
/cato-journal/2017/9/cato-journal-v37n3.pdf.

8 Gustavo López and Jynnah Radford, "Facts on U.S. Immigrants, 2015," Pew Research
Center, May 3, 2017, http://www.pewhispanic.org/2017/05/03/facts-on-u-s-immigrants/.

9 *2016 Yearbook of Immigration Statistics* (Washington, D.C.: U.S. Department of
Homeland Security, November 2017), table 1, https://www.dhs.gov/immigration
-statistics/yearbook/2016.

10 López and Radford, "Facts on U.S. Immigrants"; Richard Fry, "Today's Newly Arrived
Immigrants Are the Best-Educated Ever," Pew Research Center, October 5, 2015,
http://www.pewresearch.org/fact-tank/2015/10/05/todays-newly-arrived-immigrants
-are-the-best-educated-ever/.

11 "Foreign-Born Workers: Labor Force Characteristics—2016," U.S. Bureau of Labor
Statistics, May 18, 2017, table 1, https://www.bls.gov/news.release/pdf/forbrn.pdf.

12 "Foreign-Born Workers: Labor Force Characteristics—2016," table 4.

13 Immigrants account for a majority of "Misc. personal appearance workers" (63 percent),
"Graders, sorters of agricultural products" (60 percent), "Plasterers and stucco masons"
(59 percent), "Sewing machine operators" (55 percent), and "Misc. agricultural workers"
(52 percent). Drew DeSilver, "Immigrants Don't Make Up a Majority of Workers in
Any U.S. Industry," Pew Research Center, March 16, 2017, http://www.pewresearch.org
/fact-tank/2017/03/16/immigrants-dont-make-up-a-majority-of-workers-in-any-u-s
-industry/.

14 Dylan Matthews, "North Carolina Needed 6,500 Farm Workers. Only 7 Americans
Stuck It Out," *Washington Post*, May 15, 2013, https://www.washingtonpost.com
/news/wonk/wp/2013/05/15/north-carolina-needed-6500-farm-workers-only-7
-americans-stuck-it-out/.

15 Natalie Kitroeff and Geoffrey Mohan, "Wages Rise on California Farms. Americans
Still Don't Want the Job," *Los Angeles Times*, March 17, 2017, http://www.latimes.com
/projects/la-fi-farms-immigration/.

16 DeSilver, "Immigrants Don't Make Up a Majority."

17 Paul Davison, "Home Depot to Donate $50M to Train Construction Workers, Address
Severe Shortage," *USA Today*, March 8, 2018, https://www.usatoday.com/story
/money/2018/03/08/exclusive-home-depot-donate-50-m-train-construction-workers
-address-severe-shortage/403659002/.

18 "Points-Based Immigration Systems," Law Library of Congress, March 2013, https://
www.loc.gov/law/help/points-based-immigration/index.php.

19 Jens Manuel Krogstad, Jeffrey S. Passel, and D'Vera Cohn, "5 Facts about Illegal Immigration in the U.S.," Pew Research Center, April 27, 2017, http://www.pewresearch.org/fact-tank/2017/04/27/5-facts-about-illegal-immigration-in-the-u-s/.

20 "Trade (% of GDP)," World Bank, https://data.worldbank.org/indicator/NE.TRD.GNFS.ZS.

21 Irwin M. Stelzer, "Trump and Trade," *Weekly Standard*, December 9, 2016, http://www.weeklystandard.com/trump-and-trade/article/2005750.

22 Analysis based on author's provisional sorting of product classifications in "Exports and Imports, Total 3-Digit SITC, 2015–Present," U.S. Census Bureau, https://www.census.gov/foreign-trade/statistics/country/sitc/index.html; "U.S. International Trade in Goods and Services," U.S. Census Bureau, https://www.census.gov/foreign-trade/statistics/historical/index.html. Category subtotals do not sum to overall totals due to unclassified transactions.

23 "U.S. Trade with World (Total) in Advanced Technology Products: Monthly and Cumulative Data," U.S. Census Bureau, https://www.census.gov/foreign-trade/statistics/product/atp/2017/12/ctryatp/atp0001.html.

24 Robert D. Atkinson, "How Trump Can Stop China from Eating Our Lunch," *Washington Post*, April 5, 2017, https://www.washingtonpost.com/opinions/global-opinions/how-trump-can-stop-china-from-eating-our-lunch/2017/04/05/b83e4460-1953-11e7-bcc2-7d1a0973e7b2_story.html.

25 "China: Effects of Intellectual Property Infringement and Indigenous Innovation Policies on the U.S. Economy" (Publication 4226, Investigation 332-519, U.S. International Trade Commission, Washington, D.C., May 2011), https://www.usitc.gov/publications/332/pub4226.pdf.

26 James MacGregor, "China's Drive for 'Indigenous Innovation': A Web of Industrial Policies," U.S. Chamber of Commerce, July 2010, https://www.uschamber.com/report/china%E2%80%99s-drive-indigenous-innovation-web-industrial-policies.

27 Michael Riley and John Walcott, "China-Based Hacking of 760 Companies Shows Cyber Cold War," *Bloomberg Businessweek*, December 14, 2011, https://www.bloomberg.com/news/articles/2011-12-13/china-based-hacking-of-760-companies-reflects-undeclared-global-cyber-war; "Cyber Attacks Blamed on China," *BBC News*, January 31, 2013, http://www.bbc.com/news/world-asia-china-21272613.

28 Siobhan Gorman and Danny Yadron, "U.S. Presses Beijing on Corporate Espionage," *Wall Street Journal*, June 7, 2013, https://www.wsj.com/articles/SB10001424127887324069104578527323576340846.

29 Dennis C. Blair and Keith Alexander, "China's Intellectual Property Theft Must Stop," *New York Times*, August 15, 2017, https://www.nytimes.com/2017/08/15/opinion/china-us-intellectual-property-trump.html.

30 Keith Bradsher and Paul Mozur, "China's Plan to Build Its Own High-Tech Industries Worries Western Businesses," *New York Times*, March 7, 2017, https://www.nytimes.com/2017/03/07/business/china-trade-manufacturing-europe.html.

31 Andrea Rothman, "China's Homemade C919 Jet Posed for First Flight by End-April," *Bloomberg News*, March 17, 2017, https://www.bloomberg.com/news/articles/2017-03-17/china-s-homemade-c919-jet-poised-for-first-flight-by-end-april.

32 Dong Lyu, "China's COMAC Expects Mass Production of C919 Plane after 2021," *Bloomberg News*, February 5, 2018, https://www.bloomberg.com/news/articles/2018-02-06/china-s-comac-expects-mass-production-of-c919-plane-after-2021.

33 "Tesla Eyes Shanghai as Front-Runner for China Production," *Bloomberg News*, June 20, 2016, https://www.bloomberg.com/news/articles/2016-06-20/shanghai-said-to-be-front-runner-for-tesla-china-production-site.

34 Simon Constable, "Mr. Trump, Here's Why Trade Deficits Are Good," *Forbes*, February

27, 2017, https://www.forbes.com/sites/simonconstable/2017/02/27/mr-trump-heres -why-trade-deficits-are-good/.

35   Christina D. Romer, "Do Manufacturers Need Special Treatment?," *New York Times*, February 5, 2012, http://www.nytimes.com/2012/02/05/business/do-manufacturers-need -special-treatment-economic-view.html; Clyde V. Prestowitz Jr., "Beyond Laissez Faire," *Foreign Policy*, Summer 1992, https://doi.org/10.2307/1149161.

36   "Complexity Matters: A New Atlas Reveals the Building Blocks of Economic Growth," *The Economist* (blog), October 27, 2011, https://www.economist.com/blogs/ freeexchange/2011/10 /building-blocks-economic-growth.

37   Erica E. Phillips, "Oh, Scrap: China, the Biggest Buyer of America's Trash, Wants No More," *Wall Street Journal*, October 8, 2017, https://www.wsj.com/articles/america-is -no-1-in-exporting-trashwhat-if-no-one-wants-it-anymore-1507483011.

38   N. Gregory Mankiw, "Retesting Congress in Free Trade 101," *New York Times*, April 26, 2015, https://www.nytimes.com/2015/04/26/upshot/economists-actually-agree-on-this -point-the-wisdom-of-free-trade.html.

39   David Autor, David Dorn, and Gordon H. Hanson, "The China Shock: Learning from Labor-Market Adjustment to Large Changes in Trade," *Annual Review of Economics* 8 (October 2016): 205–40, https://doi.org/10.1146/annurev-economics-080315-015041.

40   Gauti B. Eggertsson, Neil R. Mehrotra, and Lawrence H. Summers, "Secular Stagnation in the Open Economy," *American Economic Review* 106, no. 5 (2016): 503–7, https://doi .org/10.1257/aer.p20161106.

41   Vivek Wadhwa, "Trump's Demand That Apple Must Make iPhones in the U.S. Actually Isn't That Crazy," *Washington Post*, May 17, 2016, https://www.washingtonpost.com /news/innovations/wp/2016/05/17/trumps-demand-that-apple-must-make-iphones -in-the-u-s-actually-isnt-that-crazy/.

42   Justin Rose and Martin Reeves, "Rethinking Your Supply Chain in an Era of Protectionism," *Harvard Business Review*, March 22, 2017, https://hbr.org/2017/03 /rethinking-your-supply-chain-in-an-era-of-protectionism.

43   "Shale Gas Lures Global Manufacturers to US Industrial Revival," Reuters, March 26, 2013, https://www.reuters.com/article/idUSL6N0CE57M20130326; "Steelmaker Voestalpine Establishes Trump-Monitoring Taskforce," Reuters, February 16, 2017, https://in.reuters.com/article/voestalpine-usa/steelmaker-voestalpine-establishes- trump-monitoring-taskforce-idINL8N1G16RH.

44   James K. Jackson, "U.S. Trade with Free Trade Agreement (FTA) Partners," Congressional Research Service, November 9, 2016, table 3, https://fas.org/sgp/crs/misc /R44044.pdf.

45   William Mauldin, "TPP Exit Marks Sharp Shift on Trade," *Wall Street Journal*, January 24, 2017, https://www.wsj.com/articles/trump-withdraws-u-s-from-trans-pacific -partnership-1485191020. The partnership's eleven other countries moved forward without the United States and reached an agreement in early 2018. The Trump administration subsequently expressed interest in rejoining. Alan Rappeport, "Mnuchin Floats Rejoining Trans-Pacific Partnership, Trade Deal Trump Shelved," *New York Times*, February 27, 2018, https://www.nytimes.com/2018/02/27/us/politics/mnuchin-tpp -trans-pacific-partnership-trump.html.

46   "Mr. Trump Meets Mr. Xi," *Wall Street Journal*, April 5, 2017, https://www.wsj.com /articles/mr-trump-meets-mr-xi-1491348290.

47   Robert D. Atkinson and Stephen J. Ezell, *Innovation Economics: The Race for Global Advantage* (New Haven, Conn.: Yale University Press, 2012).

48   Gary P. Pisano and Willy C. Shih, "Does America Really Need Manufacturing?," *Harvard Business Review*, March 2012, https://hbr.org/2012/03/does-america-really -need-manufacturing.

49 *The Wassenaar Arrangement on Export Controls for Conventional Arms and Dual-Use Goods and Technologies* (The Hague, December 1995), http://www.wassenaar.org/public -documents/; Brian Spegele, "China Wants U.S. to Drop Tech Export Limits, or It Will Shop Elsewhere," *Wall Street Journal*, April 14, 2015, https://www.wsj.com/articles /china-wants-u-s-to-drop-tech-export-limits-or-it-will-shop-elsewhere-1429014924.

50 Janosch Delcker, "Sigmar Gabriel's Mission to Halt China's Investment Spree," *Politico Europe*, November 1, 2016, https://www.politico.eu/article/sigmar-gabriels-mission -to-halt-chinas-investment-spree/; Janosch Delcker, "Germany's Chinese Investment Problem," *Politico Europe*, November 25, 2016, https://www.politico.eu/article /germanys-chinese-investment-problem-sigmar-gabriel-eu/.

51 Nicolas E. Magud, Carmen M. Reinhart, and Kenneth S. Rogoff, "Capital Controls: Myth and Reality—a Portfolio Balance Approach" (Working Paper 16805, National Bureau of Economic Research, Cambridge, Mass., February 2011), http://www.nber.org /papers/w16805.

52 Jagdish N. Bhagwati, "The Capital Myth: The Difference between Trade in Widgets and Dollars," *Foreign Affairs*, May/June 1998, https://www.foreignaffairs.com/articles /asia/1998-05-01/capital-myth-difference-between-trade-widgets-and-dollars.

53 "Capital Controversies: Is the Case for Free Financial Flows as Strong as That for Free Trade?," *The Economist*, May 21, 1998, http://www.economist.com/node/372519.

CHAPTER 8: MORE PERFECT UNIONS

1 "The One with George Stephanopoulos," *Friends*, season 1, episode 4, dir. James Burrows, aired October 13, 1994, on NBC.

2 Wages adjusted to remove employee-side payroll taxes but to include overtime and bonuses otherwise classified as benefits. "Employer Costs for Employee Compensation—September 2017," U.S. Bureau of Labor Statistics, December 15, 2017, table 5, https://www.bls.gov/news.release/pdf/ecec.pdf.

3 "Safety and Health Regulations for Construction," 29 CFR 1926.1052(c)(7), https://www .law.cornell.edu/cfr/text/29/1926.1052.

4 Katie Loehrke, "Phobias Can Be Frightening for HR," *Workforce*, August 26, 2015, http:// www.workforce.com/2015/08/26/phobias-can-be-frightening-for-hr/.

5 Lawrence F. Katz and Alan B. Krueger, "The Rise and Nature of Alternative Work Arrangements in the United States, 1995–2015" (Working Paper 22667, National Bureau of Economic Research, Cambridge, Mass., September 2016), 8, http://www.nber.org /papers/w22667.

6 Barry T. Hirsch, "Sluggish Institutions in a Dynamic World: Can Unions and Industrial Competition Coexist?," *Journal of Economic Perspectives* 22, no. 1 (2008): 156, figure 1, http://doi.org/10.1257/jep.22.1.153.

7 "Top Organization Contributors," Center for Responsive Politics, https://www .opensecrets.org/orgs/list.php.

8 Anne Kim and Stefan Hankin, *Union Voters and Democrats* (Washington, D.C.: Progressive Policy Institute, May 2011), 5, http://progressivefix.com/wp-content/uploads/ 2011/05/05.2011-Kim_Hankin_Union-Vote-and-Democrats.pdf.

9 Excludes depreciation and rental income. Greg Ip, "In Labor vs. Capital, Labor Is Now Winning," *Wall Street Journal*, August 8, 2016, https://blogs.wsj.com/economics/2016/08 /08/in-labor-vs-capital-labor-is-now-winning/.

10 Richard B. Freeman and Joel Rogers, "Worker Representation and Participation Survey (WRPS)," data for the book *What Workers Want* (Ithaca, N.Y.: Cornell University Press, 1999), http://users.nber.org/~freeman/wrps.html; Richard B. Freeman, "Do Workers Still Want Unions? More Than Ever" (Briefing Paper 182, Economic Policy Institute, Washington, D.C., February 22, 2007), 5, http://www.sharedprosperity.org/bp182/bp182 .pdf.

11 "January 2017 Political Survey, Final Topline," Pew Research Center, http://assets.
pewresearch.org/wp-content/uploads/sites/12/2017/01/27152758
/Business-labor-topline-for-release.pdf.

12 "Litigation Regarding State Amendments," National Labor Relations Board, January 14,
2011, https://www.nlrb.gov/news-outreach/fact-sheets/fact-sheet-archives/litigation
-regarding-state-amendments.

13 "Right to Work States Timeline," National Right to Work Committee, https://nrtwc
.org/facts/state-right-to-work-timeline-2016/.

14 Rich Yeselson, "Fortress Unionism," *Democracy*, Summer 2013, https://democracyjournal
.org/magazine/29/fortress-unionism/.

15 Thomas Geoghegan, *Only One Thing Can Save Us: Why America Needs a New Kind of
Labor Movement* (New York: New Press, 2014), 9, 81.

16 Neal E. Boudette, "Union Suffers Big Loss at Tennessee VW Plant," *Wall Street Journal*,
February 15, 2014, https://www.wsj.com/articles/union-vote-at-volkswagen-tennessee
-plant-heading-to-close-1392379887; Steven Greenhouse, "VW Workers in Tennessee to
Vote on Union," *New York Times*, February 3, 2014, https://www.nytimes
.com/2014/02/04/business/volkswagen-workers-in-tennessee-to-vote-on-union
-membership.html.

17 Richard B. Freeman and Joel Rogers, *What Workers Want*, updated ed. (Ithaca, N.Y.:
Cornell University Press, 2006), 84–85, exhibit 3.8.

18 79 Cong. Rec. 2371 (February 21, 1935) (statement of Sen. Wagner), https://www.gpo.gov
/fdsys/pkg/GPO-CRECB-1935-pt3-v79/pdf/GPO-CRECB-1935-pt3-v79-1-1.pdf.

19 Ertan Tuncer and Ellen Terrell, "The Flint, Michigan, Sit-Down Strike (1936–37),"
Library of Congress, July 2012, https://www.loc.gov/rr/business/businesshistory
/February/flint.html; "The Historic 1936–37 Flint Auto Plant Strikes," *Detroit News*, June
22, 1997, http://blogs.detroitnews.com/history/1997/06/22/the-historic-1936–37-flint
-auto-plant-strikes/.

20 Jeffrey McCracken, "Detroit's Symbol of Dysfunction: Paying Employees Not to Work,"
Wall Street Journal, March 1, 2006, https://www.wsj.com/articles/SB114118143005186163.

21 John Herr, "What Should Unions Do?," *Harvard Business Review*, May–June 1991,
https://hbr.org/1991/05/what-should-unions-do.

22 Cynthia L. Estlund, "Economic Rationality and Union Avoidance: Misunderstanding
the National Labor Relations Act," *Texas Law Review* 71 (1993): 931–32, http://
heinonline.org/HOL/LandingPage?handle=hein.journals/tlr71&div=39; Benjamin I.
Sachs, "The Unbundled Union: Politics without Collective Bargaining," *Yale Law Journal*
123, no. 1 (2013): 179, https://www.yalelawjournal.org/essay/the-unbundled-union.

23 Totals differ from those reported by the U.S. Bureau of Labor Statistics in its Current
Employment Statistics because they are derived instead from its Current Population
Survey. Barry Hirsch and David Macpherson, "Union Membership, Coverage, Density,
and Employment among Private Sector Manufacturing Workers, 1973–2017," Union
Membership and Coverage Database from the CPS, 2018, http://unionstats.com/.

24 Matthew Dimick, "Labor Law, New Governance, and the Ghent System," *North
Carolina Law Review* 90, no. 2 (2012): 323–24, 333, http://scholarship.law.unc.edu/cgi
/viewcontent.cgi?article=4539&context=nclr.

25 Dimick, "Labor Law," 364.

26 Yuval Levin, *The Fractured Republic: Renewing America's Social Contract in the Age of
Individualism* (New York: Basic Books, 2016), 140.

27 Gary S. Becker, "Investment in Human Capital: A Theoretical Analysis," *Journal of
Political Economy* 70, no. 5 (1962): 9–49, http://www.jstor.org/stable/1829103.

28 "Training Capacity Talking Points," North America's Building Trades' Unions,
November 23, 2016, https://nabtu.org/wp-content/uploads/2017/03/Building-Trades
-Training-Capacity-Talking-Points-11-23-16.pdf.

29 "Our Partners," Culinary Academy of Las Vegas, 2018, http://www.theculinaryacademy
   .org/our-history/.

30 Jon Ralston, "Much at Stake Economically, Politically in Station, Culinary Fight,"
   Las Vegas Sun, January 22, 2012, https://lasvegassun.com/news/2012/jan/22/much-stake
   -economically-politically-station-culina/.

31 "100 Best Companies to Work For," *Fortune*, February 4, 2008, http://archive.fortune
   .com/magazines/fortune/bestcompanies/2008/full_list/index.html.

32 *Ocean's Eleven*, dir. Steven Soderbergh (2001), http://www.imdb.com/title/tt0240772
   /quotes.

33 Jillian Kay Melchior, "The Fight for Mixed Martial Arts in New York," *National Review*,
   November 18, 2013, https://www.nationalreview.com/2013/11/fight-mixed-martial-arts
   -new-york-jillian-kay-melchior/.

34 David Lapp and Amber Lapp, "Alone in the New America," *First Things* (blog), February
   2014, https://www.firstthings.com/article/2014/02/alone-in-the-new-america.

35 L. Fulton, "Workplace Representation in Europe," European Trade Union Institute,
   2016, http://www.worker-participation.eu/National-Industrial-Relations/Countries
   /Germany/Workplace-Representation; Daniel J. Gifford, "Labor Policy in Late
   Twentieth Century Capitalism: New Paradoxes for the Democratic State," *Hofstra Law
   Review* 26, no. 1 (1997): 129, https://scholarlycommons.law.hofstra.edu/cgi/viewcontent
   .cgi?article=1987&context=hlr.

36 Mark Barenberg, "Democracy and Domination in the Law of Workplace Cooperation:
   From Bureaucratic to Flexible Production," *Columbia Law Review* 94, no. 3 (1994):
   753–983, http://www.jstor.org/stable/1123248.

37 Barenberg, "Democracy and Domination," 761.

38 Tyler Cowen, "How Will the Sharing Economy Alter Job Training?,"
   Marginal Revolution (blog), June 15, 2015, http://marginalrevolution.com/
   marginalrevolution/2015/06/the
   -sharing-economy-and-the-future-of-job-training.html.

39 Ross Douthat and Reihan Salam, *Grand New Party: How Republicans Can Win the
   Working Class and Save the American Dream* (New York: Doubleday, 2008), 228.

40 Sachs, "The Unbundled Union," 154.

CHAPTER 9: THE WAGE SUBSIDY

1 "Foxconn in Wisconsin: Wisconn Valley Facts and Figures," Wisconsin Economic
   Development Corporation, 2017, http://legis.wisconsin.gov/assembly/25/tittl/media/1136
   /wisconn-valley-press-kit.pdf; Jason Stein and Patrick Marley, "Wisconsin Assembly
   Panel Advances $3 Billion in Incentives for Foxconn," *Milwaukee Journal Sentinel*,
   August 14, 2017, https://www.jsonline.com/story/news/politics/2017/08/14/3-billion
   -wisconsin-foxconn-incentives-up-first-vote-monday/564455001/.

2 Jason Stein and Patrick Marley, "Foxconn Could Get up to $200 Million in Cash a Year
   from State Residents for up to 15 Years," *Milwaukee Journal Sentinel*, July 28, 2017,
   https://www.jsonline.com/story/news/politics/2017/07/28/foxconn-could-get-up-200
   -million-cash-year-state-residents-up-15-years/519687001/.

3 Stein and Marley, "Foxconn Could Get up to $200 Million."

4 Julie Bosman, "In Wisconsin, Second Thoughts on Foxconn," *New York Times*, August 11,
   2017, https://www.nytimes.com/2017/08/10/us/foxconn-jobs-wisconsin-walker-tax
   -incentives.html.

5 Chris Hayes (@chrislhayes), "Wut," Twitter, July 28, 2017, 1:01 p.m., https://twitter.com
   /chrislhayes/status/890995518788292609.

6 *Urban Dictionary*, s.v. "wut," http://www.urbandictionary.com/define.php?term=wut.

7 Stein and Marley, "Foxconn Could Get up to $200 Million."

8   "Average Supplemental Nutrition Assistance Program (SNAP) Benefits Per Person, FY2015," Kaiser Family Foundation, https://www.kff.org/other/state-indicator /avg-monthly-snap-benefits/; "Medicaid Spending Per Full-Benefit Enrollee, FY2014," Kaiser Family Foundation, https://www.kff.org/medicaid/state-indicator/medicaid -spending-per-full-benefit-enrollee/.

9   "Benefits of Supplemental Security Income," Wisconsin Department of Health Services, October 28, 2016, https://www.dhs.wisconsin.gov/ssi/benefits.htm.

10 "Overview of the Federal Tax System as in Effect for 2017" (Report JCX-17-17, Joint Committee on Taxation, U.S. Cong., March 2017), table A-6, https://www.jct.gov /publications.html?id=4989.

11 Payroll taxes are assessed on earnings only up to a cap, which in 2017 was $127,200. Thus, while low- to moderate-income earners pay the tax on every dollar, high-income earners pay no payroll tax on each dollar they earn above the cap. "Payroll Tax Rates," Tax Policy Center, February 13, 2017, http://www.taxpolicycenter.org/statistics/payroll-tax-rates.

12 The share paid by all these forms of income taxation rose from 77 percent to 91 percent as excise taxes fell from 19 percent to 5 percent. As a share of income taxation, individual income taxes remained at roughly 50 percent, while corporate taxes fell from 34 to 10 percent and payroll taxes rose from 14 to 40 percent. "Table 2.2. Percentage Composition of Receipts by Source: 1934–2023," Historical Tables, Office of Management and Budget, https://www.whitehouse.gov/omb/historical-tables/.

13 "WOTC Tax Credit Amounts," Employment and Training Administration, U.S. Department of Labor, January 17, 2017, https://www.doleta.gov/business/incentives /opptax/benefits.cfm.

14 Laura Meckler, "Hillary Clinton Proposes Tax Credit for Businesses to Train Apprentices," *Wall Street Journal*, June 17, 2015, https://www.wsj.com/articles/hillary -clinton-to-propose-tax-credit-for-businesses-to-train-apprentices-1434535202.

15 "Statistics for Tax Returns with EITC," Internal Revenue Service, January 17, 2018, https://www.eitc.irs.gov/eitc-central/statistics-for-tax-returns-with-eitc/statistics-for -tax-returns-with-eitc.

16 "Earned Income Credit (EIC): For Use in Preparing 2017 Returns" (Publication 596, Internal Revenue Service, Washington, D.C., January 2018), 35, https://www.irs.gov/pub /irs-pdf/p596.pdf.

17 Working two thousand hours at $7.25 per hour would generate $14,500 of earnings, which yields for a single or married parent with two children an EITC payment of $5,616. Total income would therefore equal $20,116, or $10.06 per hour. "Earned Income Credit (EIC)."

18 Robert I. Lerman, "JOIN: A Jobs and Income Program for American Families," in *Public Employment and Wage Subsidies*, Studies in Public Welfare 19 (Washington, D.C.: Joint Economic Committee, December 1974).

19 Edmund S. Phelps, *Rewarding Work: How to Restore Participation and Self-Support to Free Enterprise* (Cambridge, Mass.: Harvard University Press, 1997).

20 EMPLEO Act, S. 38, 115th Cong. (2017), https://www.congress.gov/bill/115th-congress /senate-bill/38.

21 *The President's Proposal to Expand the Earned Income Tax Credit* (Washington, D.C.: Executive Office of the President, March 2014), https://obamawhitehouse.archives. gov/sites/default/files/docs/eitc_report_0.pdf; *Expanding Opportunity in America* (Washington, D.C.: House Budget Committee, July 2014), http://budget.house.gov /uploadedfiles/expanding_opportunity_in_america.pdf; Joanna Venator and Richard V. Reeves, *Are Obama and Ryan Proposals for an EITC Expansion Pro- or Anti-Mobility?* (Washington, D.C.: Brookings Institution, August 14, 2014), https://www.brookings.edu /research/are-obama-and-ryan-proposals-for-an-eitc-expansion-pro-or-anti-mobility/.

22 The bill does provide for a one-time, $500 advance against the end-of-year credit. Grow American Incomes Now Act of 2017, H.R. 3757, 115th Cong. (2017), https://www .congress.gov/bill/115th-congress/house-bill/3757/all-info; Greg Ferenstein, "Wages Are Stagnating, Robots Are Taking Our Jobs. This Democrat Has a $1.4 Trillion Solution," *Vox*, September 16, 2017, https://www.vox.com/the-big-idea/2017/9/13/16301644 /ro-khanna-eitc-wages-democratic-agenda-working-class.

23 Tax Cuts and Jobs Act, H.R. 1, 115th Cong. (2017), https://www.congress.gov/bill/115th -congress/house-bill/1; Michael D. Shear and Michael Tackett, "With Tax Overhaul, Trump Fulfills a Campaign Promise and Flexes Republican Muscle," *New York Times*, December 20, 2017, https://www.nytimes.com/2017/12/20/us/politics/with-tax-overhaul -trump-fulfills-a-campaign-promise-and-flexes-republican-muscle.html.

24 Jesse Rothstein, "Is the EITC as Good as an NIT? Conditional Cash Transfers and Tax Incidence," *American Economic Journal: Economic Policy* 2, no. 1 (2010): 177–208, https:// doi.org/10.1257/pol.2.1.177; "Credit Where Taxes Are Due," *The Economist*, July 2, 2015, http://www.economist.com/news/finance-andeconomics/21656710-reducing-wage -subsidies-would-hurt-workers-more-their-employers-credit-where.

25 Ken Jacobs, Ian Perry, and Jenifer MacGillvary, "The High Public Cost of Low Wages," UC Berkeley Labor Center, April 2015, http://laborcenter.berkeley.edu/pdf/2015/the -high-public-cost-of-low-wages.pdf.

26 Patricia Cohen, "Counting Up Hidden Costs of Low Pay," *New York Times*, April 13, 2015, https://www.nytimes.com/2015/04/13/business/economy/working-but-needing -public-assistance-anyway.html.

27 Corporate Responsibility and Taxpayer Protection Act of 2017, H.R. 2814, 115th Cong. (2017), https://www.congress.gov/bill/115th-congress/house-bill/2814/all-info; "Rep. Khanna Introduces the Corporate Responsibility and Taxpayer Protection Act," press release, Office of Rep. Ro Khanna, June 7, 2017, https://khanna.house.gov/media /pressreleases/release-rep-khanna-introduces-corporate-responsibility-and-taxpayer -protection.

28 A more optimistic story suggests that better-paid workers will become more productive and stay in their jobs longer, retroactively justifying their raises—though if this were true, employers might have discovered it already. Most likely, it is true in some cases and, generally, those cases are ones in which employers pay higher wages. A related, confounding issue is that higher wages will tend to attract more highly skilled workers. If a $10-per-hour job becomes a $15-per-hour job, and the employer then hires a $15-per-hour worker to do it, the minimum-raise hike is "free" to the economy. But that conclusion does not hold for the no-longer-employed $10-per-hour worker. For a discussion of potential productivity gains from wage increases, see Justin Wolfers and Jan Zilinsky, "Higher Wages for Low-Income Workers Lead to Higher Productivity," *Realtime Economic Issues Watch* (blog), January 13, 2015, https://piie.com/blogs /realtime-economic-issues-watch/higher-wages-low-income-workers-lead-higher -productivity.

29 "City Council Approves $15/Hour Minimum Wage in Seattle," Council News Release, June 2, 2014, http://www.seattle.gov/news/newsdetail_council.asp?ID=14430.

30 Seattle Minimum Wage Study Team, *Report on the Impact of Seattle's Minimum Wage Ordinance on Wages, Workers, Jobs, and Establishments through 2015* (Seattle: University of Washington, 2016), 21–23, https://evans.uw.edu/sites/default/files/MinWageReport -July2016_Final.pdf.

31 Seattle Minimum Wage Study Team, "Minimum Wage Increases, Wages, and Low -Wage Employment: Evidence from Seattle" (Working Paper 23532, National Bureau of Economic Research, Cambridge, Mass., May 2018), http://www.nber.org/papers/w23532.

CHAPTER 10: FOR THOSE WHO CANNOT WORK

1 Heather Reynolds, remarks at "New Thinking about Poverty and Economic Mobility," The Capitol, Washington, D.C., January 18, 2017.

2 Michael Alison Chandler, "D.C. among First in Nation to Require Child-Care Workers to Get College Degrees," *Washington Post*, March 31, 2017, https://www.washingtonpost.com/local/social-issues/district-among-the-first-in-nation-to-require-child-care-workers-to-get-college-degrees/2017/03/30/d7d59e18-0fe9-11e7-9d5a-a83e627dc120_story.html.

3 Oren Cass, *Over-Medicaid-ed: How Medicaid Distorts and Dilutes America's Safety Net* (New York: Manhattan Institute for Policy Research, May 2016), appendix, https://www.manhattan-institute.org/html/over-medicaid-ed-how-medicaid-distorts-and-dilutes-americas-safety-net-8890.html.

4 "Income and Poverty in the United States: 2016," U.S. Census Bureau, September 2017, table 3, https://www.census.gov/data/tables/2017/demo/income-poverty/p60-259.html.

5 "Historical Poverty Tables: People and Families—1959 to 2016," U.S. Census Bureau, table 2, https://www.census.gov/data/tables/time-series/demo/income-poverty/historical-poverty-people.html.

6 "Supplemental Nutrition Assistance Program (SNAP): State Level Participation and Benefits," U.S. Department of Agriculture, March 2018, https://www.fns.usda.gov/pd/supplemental-nutrition-assistance-program-snap.

7 Households with income up to 400 percent of the federal poverty level qualify for insurance-premium tax credits. "Subsidized Coverage," HealthCare.gov, https://www.healthcare.gov/glossary/subsidized-coverage/.

8 Arloc Sherman, *Official Poverty Measure Masks Gains Made over Last 50 Years* (Washington, D.C.: Center on Budget and Policy Priorities, September 2013), https://www.cbpp.org/research/official-poverty-measure-masks-gains-made-over-last-50-years.

9 Erica L. Reaves and MaryBeth Musumeci, *Medicaid and Long-Term Services and Supports: A Primer* (Menlo Park, Calif.: Kaiser Family Foundation, December 2015), https://www.kff.org/medicaid/report/medicaid-and-long-term-services-and-supports-a-primer/.

10 Michael Tanner and Charles Hughes, *The Work versus Welfare Trade-Off: An Analysis of the Total Level of Welfare Benefits by State* (Washington, D.C.: Cato Institute, 2013), 3 and table 4, https://www.cato.org/publications/white-paper/work-versus-welfare-trade.

11 *Effective Marginal Tax Rates for Low- and Moderate-Income Workers* (Washington, D.C.: Congressional Budget Office, November 2015), figure 1, https://www.cbo.gov/publication/50923.

12 Gary D. Alexander, "Welfare's Failure and the Solution," presentation at the American Enterprise Institute, Washington, D.C., July 2012, slide 8, http://www.aei.org/wp-content/uploads/2012/07/-alexander-presentation_10063532278.pdf.

13 Caitlin Dewey, "The Surprising Argument for Extending Food Stamps to Pets," *Washington Post*, January 23, 2018, https://www.washingtonpost.com/news/wonk/wp/2018/01/23/the-surprising-argument-for-extending-food-stamps-to-pets/.

14 "Historical Income Tables: People," U.S. Census Bureau, tables P-16 and P-17, https://www.census.gov/data/tables/time-series/demo/income-poverty/historical-income-people.html; "Poverty Thresholds," U.S. Census Bureau, https://www.census.gov/data/tables/time-series/demo/income-poverty/historical-poverty-thresholds.html.

15 *Federal Spending for Means-Tested Programs, 2007 to 2027* (Washington, D.C.: Congressional Budget Office, February 2017), table 1, https://www.cbo.gov/publication/52405; "TANF Financial Data—FY 2016," U.S. Department of Health and Human Services, February 1, 2018, https://www.acf.hhs.gov/ofa/resource/tanf-financial

-data-fy-2016; "TANF Caseload Data 2016," U.S. Department of Health and Human Services, January 12, 2017, https://www.acf.hhs.gov/ofa/resource/tanf-caseload-data-2016.

16 "Overlap and Duplication in Food and Nutrition Service's Nutrition Programs" (Audit Report 27001-0001-10, U.S. Department of Agriculture, Washington, D.C., June 2013), https://www.usda.gov/oig/webdocs/27001–0001–10.pdf.

17 *Cato Handbook for Policymakers*, 8th ed. (Washington, D.C.: Cato Institute, 2017), 437, https://www.cato.org/cato-handbook-policymakers/cato-handbook-policy-makers -8th-edition-2017.

18 *Federal Housing Assistance for Low-Income Households* (Washington, D.C.: Congressional Budget Office, September 2015), https://www.cbo.gov/publication/50782.

19 "Other Federal Requirements," 24 CFR 5.105(a)(2), https://www.law.cornell.edu/cfr /text/24/5.105; "Discretionary Pet Rules," 24 CFR 5.318(b)(1)(ii), https://www.law.cornell. edu/cfr/text/24/5.318.

20 "NYCHA 2017 Fact Sheet," New York City Housing Authority, April 13, 2017, http:// www1.nyc.gov/assets/nycha/downloads/pdf/factsheet.pdf.

21 "Workers Asking to Cut Their Hours Because of Bump in Seattle's Minimum Wage," KIRO 7, June 8, 2015, http://www.kiro7.com/video?videoId=35129473&videoVersion=1.0.

22 *Federal Housing Assistance for Low-Income Households*; Aaron Shrank, "It's a Long Wait for Section 8 Housing in U.S. Cities," *Marketplace*, January 3, 2018, https://www. marketplace.org/2018/01/03/wealth-poverty/its-long-wait-section-8-housing-us-cities.

23 "Section 8—Applicants," New York City Housing Authority, March 13, 2018, http:// www1.nyc.gov/site/nycha/section-8/applicants.page.

24 Christopher Swope, "Section 8 Is Broken," *Governing*, May 2002, https://shelterforce. org/2003/01/01/section-8-is-broken/.

25 Alana Semuels, "How Housing Policy Is Failing America's Poor," *The Atlantic*, June 24, 2015, https://www.theatlantic.com/business/archive/2015/06/section-8-is-failing/396650/.

26 "Section 8 Income Limits—FY 2015," U.S. Department of Housing and Urban Development, https://www.huduser.gov/datasets/il/il15/Section8_IncomeLimits_Rev .pdf.

27 "Supplemental Nutrition Assistance Program (SNAP)," New York State Office of Temporary and Disability Assistance, https://otda.ny.gov/programs/snap/.

28 "Policy Basics: The Housing Choice Voucher Program," Center on Budget and Policy Priorities, May 3, 2017, https://www.cbpp.org/research/housing/policy-basics-the -housing-choice-voucher-program.

29 John Holahan and David Liska, *Where Is Medicaid Spending Headed?* (Washington, D.C.: Kaiser Family Foundation, November 1996), https://www.kff.org/medicaid/report /where-is-medicaid-spending-headed-report/.

30 *State Health Care Spending on Medicaid: A 50-State Study of Trends and Drivers of Cost* (Philadelphia: Pew Charitable Trusts and MacArthur Foundation, July 2014), figures 3 and 11, http://www.pewtrusts.org/en/multimedia/data-visualizations/2014 /medicaid-spending-growth.

31 Cass, *Over-Medicaid-ed*, appendix.

32 Cass, *Over-Medicaid-ed*, 10–12.

33 Yevgeniy Feyman, "Issues 2016: Will Obamacare Lead to Universal Coverage?," Manhattan Institute for Policy Research, April 2016, https://www.manhattan-institute. org/html/issues-2016-will-obamacare-lead-universal-coverage-8773.html.

34 Avik Roy, *How Medicaid Fails the Poor* (New York: Encounter, 2013), 19–23.

35 Katherine Baicker, Sarah L. Taubman, Heidi L. Allen, Mira Bernstein, Jonathan H. Gruber, Joseph P. Newhouse, Eric C. Schneider et al., "The Oregon Experiment— Effects of Medicaid on Clinical Outcomes," *New England Journal of Medicine* 368 (2013): 1713–22, http://doi.org/10.1056/NEJMsa1212321.

36 Amy Finkelstein, Nathaniel Hendren, and Erzo F. P. Luttmer, "The Value of Medicaid: Interpreting Results from the Oregon Health Insurance Experiment" (Working Paper 21308, National Bureau of Economic Research, Cambridge, Mass., June 2015), http://www.nber.org/papers/w21308.

37 Raj Chetty, Michael Stepner, Sarah Abraham et al., "The Association between Income and Life Expectancy in the United States, 2001–2014," *Journal of the American Medical Association* 315, no. 16 (2016): 1750–66, http://doi.org/10.1001/jama.2016.4226.

38 Elizabeth H. Bradley, Maureen Canavan, Erika Rogan, Kristina Talbert-Slagle, Chima Ndumele, Lauren Taylor, and Leslie A. Curry, "Variation in Health Outcomes: The Role of Spending on Social Services, Public Health, and Health Care, 2000–09," *Health Affairs* 35, no. 5 (2016): 760–68, http://doi.org/10.1377/hlthaff.2015.0814.

39 Includes only nonretirement benefits, as presented in the related materials available for download. "Federal Spending in the States: 2004 to 2013" (Issue Brief, Pew Charitable Trusts, Philadelphia, December 2014), table 3, http://www.pewtrusts.org/en/research-and-analysis/issue-briefs/2014/12/federal-spending-in-the-states.

CHAPTER II: THE SOCIAL WAGES OF WORK

1 *Good Will Hunting*, dir. Gus Van Sant (1997), http://www.imdb.com/title/tt0119217/quotes.

2 Steve Jobs, remarks at Stanford University, Palo Alto, Calif., June 12, 2005, https://news.stanford.edu/2005/06/14/jobs-061505/; Stanford, "Steve Jobs' 2005 Commencement Address," YouTube, 15:04, March 7, 2008, https://www.youtube.com/watch?v=UF8uR6Z6KLc.

3 "Ngram Viewer: Dead-End Jobs," Google Books, https://books.google.com/ngrams/graph?content=dead-end+jobs.

4 Farhad Manjoo, "A Plan in Case Robots Take the Jobs: Give Everyone a Basic Income," *New York Times*, March 3, 2016, https://www.nytimes.com/2016/03/03/technology/plan-to-fight-robot-invasion-at-work-give-everyone-a-paycheck.html.

5 "My Father's Office," *The Wonder Years*, season 1, episode 3, dir. Jeffrey D. Brown, aired March 29, 1988, http://www.imdb.com/title/tt0750338/.

6 Alana Semuels, "What Amazon Does to Poor Cities," *The Atlantic*, February 1, 2018, https://www.theatlantic.com/business/archive/2018/02/amazon-warehouses-poor-cities/552020/.

7 Peter Waldman, "Inside Alabama's Auto Jobs Boom: Cheap Wages, Little Training, Crushed Limbs," *Bloomberg Businessweek*, March 27, 2017, https://www.bloomberg.com/news/features/2017-03-23/inside-alabama-s-auto-jobs-boom-cheap-wages-little-training-crushed-limbs.

8 "Nonfatal Occupational Injuries and Illnesses Data by Industry (SOII)," U.S. Bureau of Labor Statistics, February 13, 2018, https://www.bls.gov/iif/oshstate.htm.

9 Brady E. Hamilton, Joyce A. Martin, Michelle J. K. Osterman, Sally C. Curtin, and T. J. Mathews, "Births: Final Data for 2014," in "Trends in Teen Pregnancy and Childbearing," *National Vital Statistics Reports* 64, no. 12 (2015), table A (15–19 years old), https://www.cdc.gov/nchs/data/nvsr/nvsr64/nvsr64_12.pdf.

10 Kathryn Kost, Isaac Maddow-Zimet, and Alex Arpaia, *Pregnancies, Births, and Abortions among Adolescents and Young Women in the United States, 2013: National and State Trends by Age, Race and Ethnicity* (New York: Guttmacher Institute, August 2017), figure 1, https://www.guttmacher.org/report/us-adolescent-pregnancy-trends-2013.

11 Heather D. Boonstra, "What Is Behind the Declines in Teen Pregnancy Rates?," *Guttmacher Policy Review* 17, no. 3 (2014), https://www.guttmacher.org/gpr/2014/09/what-behind-declines-teen-pregnancy-rates.

12 Melissa S. Kearney and Phillip B. Levine, "Media Influences on Social Outcomes: The Impact of MTV's '16 and Pregnant' on Teen Childbearing" (Working Paper 19795, National Bureau of Economic Research, Cambridge, Mass., January 2014), http://www.nber.org/papers/w19795.

13 Brief for the Massachusetts Medical Society, *Commonwealth v. Eldred*, Supreme Judicial Court of Massachusetts no. 12279, September 2017, http://www.massmed.org/Advocacy/Eldred-Amicus-Brief-Final/.

14 Emily Badger and Margot Sanger-Katz, "Who's Able-Bodied Anyway?," *New York Times*, February 3, 2018, https://www.nytimes.com/2018/02/03/upshot/medicaid-able-bodied-poor-politics.html.

15 Allan Bloom, *The Closing of the American Mind: How Higher Education Has Failed Democracy and Impoverished the Souls of Today's Students* (New York: Simon and Schuster, 1987), 210.

16 Hillary Rodham Clinton, *What Happened* (New York: Simon and Schuster, 2017), 239.

17 Kevin Roose, "His 2020 Slogan: Beware of Robots," *New York Times*, February 11, 2018, https://www.nytimes.com/2018/02/10/technology/his-2020-campaign-message-the-robots-are-coming.html.

18 Catherine Clifford, "Free Cash Handouts Take a Step Closer to Mainstream Thanks to California Democrats," CNBC, March 12, 2018, https://www.cnbc.com/2018/03/12/california-democratic-party-platform-supports-universal-basic-income.html; "2018 Platform," adopted at the 2018 California Democrats State Convention, February 25, 2018, https://www.cadem.org/our-party/standing-committees/body/CDP-Platform-2018.pdf.

19 Shannon Ikebe, "The Wrong Kind of UBI," *Jacobin*, January 21, 2016, https://www.jacobinmag.com/2016/01/universal-basic-income-switzerland-finland-milton-friedman-kathi-weeks/.

20 Eduardo Porter and Farhad Manjoo, "Competing Visions for a Post-work Future," *New York Times*, March 9, 2016, https://www.nytimes.com/2016/03/09/business/economy/a-future-without-jobs-two-views-of-the-changing-work-force.html.

21 *Effective Marginal Tax Rates for Low- and Moderate-Income Workers* (Washington, D.C.: Congressional Budget Office, November 2015), figures 1 and 4, https://www.cbo.gov/publication/50923.

22 The "what about your own kids?" argument is usually a cheap rhetorical ploy. Advocates of foreign military interventions don't eagerly send their children into battle, nor do advocates of higher taxes voluntarily pay higher taxes themselves, because they never claim that fighting wars or paying taxes benefits the individual. Their argument is that society as a whole would benefit. By contrast, UBI proponents do not argue that their proposal is an imposition worth asking everyone to make for society's benefit; they position it as preferable for the individual recipients.

CONCLUSION: THE LOST GENERATION

1 Joe Biden (@VP44), "I often say: Don't tell me what you value. Show me your budget & I'll tell you what you value. #POTUSBudget makes our values crystal clear," Twitter, February 9, 2016, 12:57 p.m., https://twitter.com/vp44/status/697132255752261632.

2 Paul Krugman, "The Gambler's Ruin of Small Cities (Wonkish)," *New York Times*, December 30, 2017, https://www.nytimes.com/2017/12/30/opinion/the-gamblers-ruin-of-small-cities-wonkish.html.

3 Shawn Donnan, "Hillbilly Elegist JD Vance: 'The People Calling the Shots Really Screwed Up,'" *Financial Times*, February 2, 2018, https://www.ft.com/content/bd801c3c-fab7-11e7-9b32-d7d59aace167.

INDEX